49.95

MAKING SOMETHING HAPPEN

making

AMERICAN POLITICAL POETRY

something

BETWEEN THE WORLD WARS

happen

MICHAEL THURSTON

THE UNIVERSITY OF NORTH CAROLINA PRESS Chapel Hill & London

© 2001
The University of North Carolina Press
All rights reserved
Manufactured in the United States of America
Set in Monotype Bembo and Publicity Gothic types
by Tseng Information Systems, Inc.
The paper in this book meets the guidelines for
permanence and durability of the Committee on
Production Guidelines for Book Longevity of the
Council on Library Resources.

Selections from Edwin Rolfe, *Collected Poems,*
edited by Cary Nelson and Jefferson Hendricks
(Urbana: University of Illinois Press, 1993),
© Board of Trustees of the University of Illinois,
and Muriel Rukeyser, *U.S. 1* (New York: Covici
and Friede, 1938), © Muriel Rukeyser, have been
reprinted with permission.

Library of Congress Cataloging-in-Publication Data
Thurston, Michael, 1965–
Making something happen : American political poetry
between the world wars / Michael Thurston.
    p. cm. — (Cultural studies of the United States)
Includes bibliographical references and index.
ISBN 0-8078-2654-5 (alk. paper) —
ISBN 0-8078-4979-0 (pbk. : alk. paper)
1. American poetry—20th century—History and
criticism.   2. Politics and literature—United States—
History—20th century.   3. Political poetry, American
—History and criticism.   4. World War, 1914–1918—
Influence.   5. World War, 1939–1945—Causes.
I. Title.   II. Series.
PS310.P6 T48   2001
811′.5209358—dc21   2001023771

05   04   03   02   01   5   4   3   2   1

CONTENTS

ILLUSTRATIONS

ACKNOWLEDGMENTS

Sections of this book were presented in 1993 at the Twentieth Century Literature Conference, the Midwest Modern Language Association Conference, and the Modern Language Association Convention. Part of Chapter 2 was first published as "'All Together, Black and White': Langston Hughes on Scottsboro," *College Literature* 22 (October 1995): 30–49. A section of Chapter 4 appeared as "Documentary Modernism as Popular Front Poetic: Muriel Rukeyser's *Book of the Dead,*" *Modern Language Quarterly* 60 (March 1999): 59–84.

I have been fortunate to work at two institutions that provided money and time without which I could not have finished this project. The University of Illinois granted me a Pauline Gragg Fellowship and a University Fellowship. Yale University awarded me a Morse Fellowship. The Whitney Humanities Center funded my research with two A. Whitney Griswold Junior Faculty Research Grants. In addition, the Veterans of the Abraham Lincoln Brigade awarded a version of Chapter 1 the George Watt Prize, which helped me in the research and revision of that chapter. For all of this assistance, I am grateful. I also thank Patricia C. Willis, curator of the American Literature Collection at the Beinecke Rare Book and Manuscript Library, Yale University, and the staffs of the Beinecke Rare Book and Manuscript Library, the University of Illinois Rare Book Room, the Mortimer Rare Book Room at Smith College, and the Manuscript Collection at the Library of Congress.

I would like to thank Cary Nelson, Michael Bérubé, Janet Lyon, and Emily Watts for their guidance and advice on my doctoral thesis at the University of Illinois. Cary Nelson has continued to be a valued mentor, adviser, example, resource, and reader, and I remain indebted to him. Elizabeth Davies, John D'Errico, Amy Farmer, Eric Gardner, Robert McRuer, and Robert Nowatzki read early drafts of individual chapters and provided helpful suggestions as well as great dinners. For their challenging and productive discussions of all or part of the manuscript, I thank Nigel Alderman, Langdon Hammer, Tyrus Miller, Jim Smethurst, James Sullivan, the members of Yale's Americanist Colloquium, and my students in courses on modern American poetry at Illinois and Yale. Among the latter group, I am especially indebted to Sonya Posmentier and Stephen Weiss for their insights and tough questions. For as long as I have known him, Barry Faulk has been an indefatigable reader and sounding board, as well as a friend whose example illustrates all the good things Aristotle wrote about friendship. Thanks, Barry. For their very useful recommendations for revisions, I am indebted to Alan Trachtenberg, Walter Kalaidjian, Carla Kaplan, and an anonymous reader for the University of North Carolina Press. And I thank Sian Hunter and Paula Wald for shepherding this book through the publication process.

For aid and comfort, distraction and almost infinite patience with my distractedness, I thank my families (immediate, extended, and in-law), especially Lisa, Abby, Katie, and Megan, to whom I dedicate this book with all my love.

Making Something Happen

Introduction

MAKING SOMETHING HAPPEN

Not so very long ago, there lived a poet whom we'll call E. Brought up in a city in the eastern United States, E. decided early on that he would be a poet. He wrote poems while in high school, studied literature and languages, set out to learn from "the tradition" and then supersede it. After experiencing difficulties both in his work life and in his poetic career, E. enjoyed some success with books published by small presses his friends operated. Renowned in the limited circles in which he moved, E. became something of an arbiter of literary quality. He published criticism and, indeed, tried to define the terms by which new poetry should be judged. But his effort to devote wholehearted attention to matters literary was made difficult by events in the extraliterary world. The worldwide financial depression of the 1930s deepened his already intense interest in politics, and E. spent much of his energy working for political causes, both as a writer and in other capacities. When hostilities broke out between Fascists and leftists in several European countries, E. dedicated himself to the defense of a European country to which he had grown intensely attached. He wrote poems about the country and its troubles, he wrote journalistic articles about it, he wrote letters to officials expressing his concern over events and their significance, he wrote and delivered radio speeches. He opposed the United States, his native country, in his devotion to something he saw as larger than national loyalties. These activities, once the war was over, got him into trouble at home, trouble with the law and trouble with parts of the literary establishment, in which his poems were no longer welcome.

E., of course, is Ezra Pound (1885–1971).[1] Brought up in Philadelphia, educated in languages at Hamilton College and the University of Pennsylvania, fired from his first teaching job at Wabash College, Pound published his first book himself and through the 1920s depended on the presses of his friends and acquaintances. A forceful critical intellect and a shrewd judge of new poetry, Pound made himself the center of poetic modernism (a term he did not use himself) and helped construct the framework through which we still read the poets for whom he proselytized. Interested since the early 1910s in economics and history, Pound devoted himself to these and to political efforts during the 1930s, and when war grew increasingly imminent in Europe and he saw his beloved Italy threatened, he took up verbal arms in poetry, in prose, and on the radio. The difficulties these activities brought him are famous: an outdoor prison cell in Pisa, a controversial Bollingen Prize in 1949, and thirteen years in St. Elizabeth's Hospital.

But E. is also Edwin Rolfe, the Communist writer and unofficial poet laureate of the Spanish Civil War's Abraham Lincoln Brigade. Born in Philadelphia in 1909, briefly educated at the University of Wisconsin's Experimental College, Rolfe was called to poetry early on. Indeed, he took the pseudonym Edwin Rolfe only after being forbidden to publish any more poems in his high school newspaper. Rolfe spent most of his life in New York, moving in 1943 to California, where he lived until his death in 1954.[2] Throughout the 1930s and for scattered periods later in his life, Rolfe worked as a writer, taking jobs with the *Daily Worker, Sport and Play,* the Furniture Workers Industrial Union's *Furniture Worker,* the *New Masses, Action: Magazine for Jewish Masses,* and the *Partisan Review,* on whose editorial board Rolfe served in the magazine's early years. More important, he also wrote poems, publishing some in the publications he worked for and some in *Poetry, Pagany,* and the *New York Times.* His first book, *To My Contemporaries,* inaugurated his friend, Sol Funaroff's, Dynamo Press poetry series.

A member of the Young Communist League even in high school, Rolfe throughout his life was interested in Marxist economics and politics. He participated in union and party activities in various roles. When the Spanish army, led by General Francisco Franco, rebelled against the Popular Front coalition government, Rolfe answered the party's call for soldiers in the International Brigades. In Spain, he edited *Volunteer for Liberty,* the brigades' English-language magazine; gave talks on Radio Madrid; and coordinated troop movements. He fought in the Ebro offensive, the International Brigades' last in the war. Upon his return from Spain, Rolfe—a "premature antifascist"— was barred from combat service in the U.S. Army during World War II, denied screenwriting employment in Hollywood, and called to testify before the House Un-American Activities Committee (HUAC). Rolfe worked for Tass, the Soviet news agency; wrote a history of the Lincoln Brigade; and collaborated on documentary film projects and a novel, *The Glass Room.* It became so difficult for him to publish his poems that he brought out his second book, *First Love and Other Poems* (1951), in an edition of just 375 copies at his own expense.[3] In fact, Rolfe's last two books of poetry, *First Love and Other Poems* and *Permit Me Refuge,* were published during the early 1950s, at the height of the postwar anti-Communist inquisition, the last posthumously. The books, as Allen Guttmann has remarked, suffered under the inquisition, coming out at a moment when the political commitments registered in the poems were cause for public humiliation and criminal prosecution (264). Rolfe died of a heart attack on May 24, 1954.

Similar stories, Pound's and Rolfe's, but one of them we have heard before, whereas the other has all but disappeared from literary history.[4] There are many reasons for this. Pound wrote a great deal more than Rolfe did; his cantos alone triple Rolfe's entire poetic output. Pound was a central agent in literary movements at the heart of most histories of twentieth-century poetry, while Rolfe was a peripheral figure, writing in and for an audience that, though not much smaller than Pound's intended audience, was much less influential and culturally central. And Pound was, by most standards of literary judgment, a much more gifted and accomplished poet. But these standards of centrality and quality are themselves bound up with an assumption, or a set of assumptions, about poetry captured in W. H. Auden's famous shorthand: "[P]oetry makes nothing happen."

Auden's assertion is one of the most famous in modern poetry, as familiar and oft-repeated as "April is the cruelest month" or "Death is the mother of beauty." Like those lines, it has become a shibboleth. Through its repetition, it has engraved itself as an inscription or an epitaph. The latter, of course, is the most appropriate association, for the line occurs midway through what might be the most famous elegy in modern English poetry, "In Memory of W. B. Yeats." More than this, the pronouncement effectively inters the view shared by many poets throughout the 1930s that poetry could, quite directly and concretely, make something happen.

Though this instrumental view of poetry's political possibilities shaped the work of some poets close to him (especially Stephen Spender and C. Day Lewis), Auden never really held it himself; he frequently expressed in his verse the pressures exerted on private life by the inexorable forces of history but continually resisted the temptation to yoke poetry to any specific political program.[5] Faced with the ascent of Hitler in Germany and the gains of Fascists across Europe, Auden registered a palpable dread that certainly seems anti-Fascist, but he asserted in essays and practiced in verse the argument that poetry must remain separate from politics. Even when deciding to travel to Spain during the Spanish Civil War and join the International Brigades against Franco, Auden kept his writing and his political commitments rigidly compartmentalized. To E. R. Dodds, he wrote on the eve of his departure for Spain: "I am not one of those who believe that poetry need or even should be directly political, but in a critical period such as ours, I do believe that the poet must have direct knowledge of the major political events" (quoted in Carpenter, *W. H. Auden,* 207). And Auden's experience of politics in Spain seems to have soured him even on "direct knowledge of the major political events." Auden recorded little about his travels in Spain in 1937, published only a few paragraphs describing Valencia, and refused to comment on his experiences when he returned to England (211–15). When asked by Nancy Cunard to contribute to a collection of writers' position statements on the Spanish government, Auden's response was lukewarm though clearly opposed to Franco and fascism (220). And Auden's most sustained writing about the Civil War, "Spain," continues his practice of working through a pressing historical situation without taking a firm political position, of fending off agendas with polished and powerful ambiguity.[6]

By 1939, Auden had become even more dubious about poetry's capacity to intervene in the political. He had become more distrustful of the realm of politics, had even come to feel compromised by speaking out on politics outside of his poems. In March of that year, he wrote to Dodds again about his relationship to politics: "The real decision came after making a speech at a dinner in New York to get money for Spanish Refugees when I suddenly found I could do it, that I could make a fighting demagogic speech and have the audience roaring. I felt just covered with dirt afterwards. . . . Never, *never* again will I speak at a political meeting" (quoted in Carpenter, *W. H. Auden,* 256; emphasis in original). It was in this frame of mind, in the midst of this more extreme turn away from politics, that Auden wrote the section of "In Memory of W. B. Yeats" in which the famous line occurs, a section not included in the poem's initial publication (257). That passage is worth quoting now in full:

> You were silly like us: your gift survived it all;
> The parish of rich women, physical decay,
> Yourself; mad Ireland hurt you into poetry.
> Now Ireland has her madness and her weather still,
> For poetry makes nothing happen: it survives
> In the valley of its saying where executives
> Would never want to tamper; it flows south
> From ranches of isolation and the busy griefs,
> Raw towns that we believe and die in; it survives,
> A way of happening, a mouth. (Auden 248)

On one hand, this passage forcefully dissociates poetry from praxis. And as Samuel Hynes shows in his study of "the Auden generation," this is not what Carpenter calls a categorical rejection of "all Auden's attempts during the previous ten years to involve his poetry in politics" (*W. H. Auden,* 256) but a continuation and distillation of what Auden, throughout the preceding decade, had thought about poetry as it relates to politics. On the other hand, in the poem's context, Auden's pronouncement is more nuanced, more equivocal than the oft-cited short form would have us think. The line, after all, includes not only "poetry makes nothing happen" but also the words that link this thought in a syntax of continuity and make it part of something larger and more complex. History, the force that through society drives politics, drives poetry as well; "mad Ireland," with its class divisions, sectarian strife, and nationalist struggles, provoked the great poet's great poems. But history will continue to happen in spite of the poems' power. Human drives and divisions are as constant, and as constantly shifting, as the weather, and poetry cannot change this fact. But this is not to say that poetry is powerless or dead. "It survives," Auden assures us not once but twice: "it survives, / A way of happening, a mouth." Far removed from the direct action of "executives," poetry remains, an agency if not an act. At the very least, then, it makes itself happen, and as Auden's own poem demonstrates by its influence, poetry makes other poems (and critical judgments) happen. At his elegy's conclusion, Auden specifies a broader potential for poetry:

> With the farming of a verse
> Make a vineyard of the curse,
> Sing of human unsuccess
> In a rapture of distress;
>
> In the deserts of the heart
> Let the healing fountain start,
> In the prison of his days
> Teach the free man how to praise. (249)

Even now, at the end of the 1930s and in the midst of a European war, after his skeptical experiments with instrumental verse and political commitment, after proclaiming poetry's inability to affect the machinations of history, Auden holds out a vital role for poetry: the transformation of lived experience into fruitful freedom through the cultivation of imagination. So while "poetry makes nothing happen" in that it cannot directly effect change in history, it makes quite a lot happen in the indirect and mediated ways Auden leaves open for it.

Auden's, of course, is the road most often taken in modern poetry as poet after poet resolves to fashion from his or her subjective responses and linguistic resources a set of interventions not in politics but in imagination. These poets' best efforts have resulted in poems we rightly value. But while Auden's poetic pronouncement is limited in specific ways by his poem's occasion, by its historical moment, and by the rest of the text, the line has come to summarize a set of institutional assumptions about poetry as a special kind of discourse, removed from the world of action and consequence and thus prevented from acting, prevented from having consequences. When, for example, Wayne Booth sets out to summarize his and his colleagues' initial opposition to ethical criticism, he turns to Auden: "We knew that sophisticated critics never judge a fiction by any effect it might have on readers. 'Poetry,' we were fond of quoting to each other, 'makes nothing happen'" (4). Denied the power to catalyze, poetry, in this view, ascends to the inert nobility reserved for elements that cannot combine. A poem, after all, is usually written by an individual and read by individuals. Poems seem the worst possible avenues for political action. They are personal, interior, walled off by form and function from the world of practical politics. And those assumptions set in place a seductive corollary: poems that try to make something happen in the direct way that Auden rules out in his elegy are bad. So poetry cannot do political work, and when it tries to, it is doomed to (poetic and political) failure.

This set of assumptions dominated American literary institutions for a generation, from the late 1930s until the rise of a newly politicized literary criticism in the 1960s. During this time, writers' and readers' expectations changed in fundamental ways. Things widely thought possible for poetry just a few years earlier were now almost universally judged impossible. Poetry could no longer successfully address the political, and poets who tried found that they could not publish, that there were no readers for their work. This decoupling of poetry and politics was brought about by the confluence of national politics, especially the anti-Communist inquisition (beginning before World War II with the Dies Committee and continuing in the activities of Senator Joseph McCarthy and the HUAC in the late 1940s and 1950s), and literary politics, where new, formalist methodologies wrought deep changes in the institutions that publish, recirculate, evaluate, and preserve literary works. The terms for literary study in the United States were largely set by this confluence. When Cleanth Brooks, founding father of the New Criticism and coauthor (with Robert Penn Warren) of *Understanding Poetry,* the textbook that would make it the dominant model of poetic pedagogy in the postwar United States, discusses the 1935 anthology *Proletarian Literature of the United States* in his 1939 volume *Modern Poetry and the Tradition,* he easily dismisses political poetry on the basis of these assumptions. "The characteristic fault of [this] type of poetry," Brooks writes, "is *sentimentality,*" the appeal to readers' emotions in an attempt to "move" them (50; emphasis in original).[7] Instead of the intellectualism, the allusive texture and abstruse difficulty of the modern poetry Brooks values (poetry consonant with the tradition of poetry that requires New Critical exegesis), the poems in *Proletarian Literature* speak in a common and comprehensible language, allude to contemporary events rather than to classical literature, and seek to involve their readers emotionally. These poems, if not transparent, are at least legible to an untrained reader. But these are precisely the qualities that allow Brooks to "convict poems of Genevieve Taggard, Langston Hughes, and others in the collection" (51). Political poetry mistakes its mission; it diverts from the expected and sanctioned track and refuses to remain aloof, concerned only with irony and internal coherence. It tries to make something happen.

Brooks's judgments and the assumptions that undergird them are shared by unlikely allies on the political Left. The refrain that political poetry equals bad poetry was sounded early and often by the vocal coeditors of the *Partisan Review,* William Phillips and Philip Rahv. In their assessment of "literature in a political decade" in Horace Gregory's 1937 *New Letters in America,* they tell the story of poetry's emergence from the esoteric hideout of modernist experiment in an attempt to "become the conscience of history spurring on the working class to its 'inevitable' tasks" (171). In the hands of Communist poets, though, poetry was degraded, reduced to banal evocations of the mythology of the barricades. Some poets, those "of a more sober and organic radicalism, who were aware of the responsibilities of the medium and of the realities of the period," began in the wake of sloganeering poetry to demand high aesthetic standards and to recoil from the "leftist" political dogmatism of such critics as Granville Hicks and Mike Gold (174). These writers realized that they must write not only out of a sense of political mission but also out of an aesthetic sense independent of political orthodoxies. Literature that seeks to express "truth" rather than the political program of a specific party is inherently more revolutionary than the supposedly revolutionary writing of those who toe the party line more closely. Phillips and Rahv's comments in "Literature in a Political Decade" are typical of their comments, and those of the *Partisan Review* generally, during the middle and late 1930s, when they broke off relations with the Communist Party and began to attack its cultural politics (adapting for this purpose the Leninist epithet, "leftism"). Alan Wald summarizes the *Partisan Review* position of the late 1930s: "Phillips and Rahv arrived at a new assessment of the relationship of revolutionary politics and radical literature. Above all, they concluded that writers and critics must be free of all partisan political and organizational pressure" ("Revolutionary Intellectuals," 192). By 1937, Rahv, who earlier in the decade had expressed reservations about the experimental advances of the 1920s, had come to find in the modernist retreat from overt political or social commentary the signs of a disaffection with the modern world that was, because it registered a rebellion against capitalism and commodity fetishism, more revolutionary than the "leftist" work of Communist poets.

Of course, the critical philosophies behind such judgments—whether Brooks's or Phillips and Rahv's—are implicated in political agendas of their own. The position of the *Partisan Review* intellectuals—that overtly and instrumentally political literature suffers from the constellation of weaknesses they call leftism (disregard for literary or poetic values, tendentiousness, sociological analysis masquerading as literary criticism)—has become "firmly established among American literary historians" (Murphy, 2). But as James Murphy demonstrates, this position's success was achieved partly through the self-interested and partisan interpretation of debates over cultural politics by active participants in those debates. Justifiably dismayed by Communist Party control over left-wing writers, Phillips and Rahv move to articulate a new, anti-Communist revolutionary aesthetic (something like literary modernism) that requires as its "other" a concrete manifestation (or set of manifestations) of the political writing they repudiate; the *Partisan Review* group cast in that position the explicitly and instrumentally political "proletarian movement" in literature.[8]

New Critical dismissals of political poetry are similarly motivated by political priorities. As John Fekete, Walter Kalaidjian, and others have pointed out, the New Criticism is the academic wing of a broader cultural movement, southern agrarianism, whose agenda, Kalaidjian writes, is "outspokenly political" ("Marketing Modern Poetry," 300). The New Criticism, according to Fekete, developed precisely in reaction to the Marxist criticism that had evolved and grown in sophistication throughout the 1930s. The cultural politics of the New Criticism are linked, he writes, "with the political culture of the period, and, as in the rest of the modern critical tradition, the cultural methodology reveals its politics directly" (49). These cultural politics, Kalaidjian writes, are based on a critique of the new consumer society, then rising to dominance in American culture. But this critique was itself "doubly politicized in its proactive, anti-

Communist agenda. Not just a front for cultural 'squirearchy,' agrarianism aimed to turn the tide of the emergent socialist culture that was gaining considerable momentum in America between the wars" ("Marketing Modern Poetry," 302). Theorized and elaborated in essays published in Seward Collins's *American Review,* the agrarian agenda was, in Kalaidjian's phrase, "an American version of Italian fascism" (without, it must be noted, a Duce) (302), marked not only by a reactionary nationalism but also by open affirmation of racism to the extent of supporting slavery (as John Crowe Ransom and Frank Lawrence Owsley did) and advancing rationales for lynching as a means to maintain white supremacy (as Allen Tate did).[9]

The politics behind literary judgments have been much more explicit during the repoliticizing of American literary institutions since the 1960s. New Critical assumptions are no longer universally shared; indeed, they are often explicitly opposed. And in the 1980s and 1990s, literary studies have vigorously sought and found the political in every mode of literary discourse. Indeed, the last generation or so of American literary scholarship has done much to broaden our sense of the political and to draw critical attention to the political dimensions of literary texts and cultural practices.[10] Marxist and post-Marxist theories of literary production have provided an array of techniques by which we can trace the connections between narrative designs or rhetorical figures and the structures of power in a society. Bakhtinian language theory, especially as it is laid out in V. N. Volosinov's *Marxism and the Philosophy of Language,* finds the fundamental components of literature, words themselves, political by virtue of all linguistic systems' socio-ideological character. Critical models developed around the distinctive literatures of African America have foregrounded the racial politics inherent in literary forms and traditions. Perhaps most important, feminist modes of criticism have powerfully demonstrated, again and again, the inextricability of the personal and the political.[11] Indeed, politically attuned readings have become so ubiquitous that they have enabled Michael Bérubé to map contemporary American literary studies according to critics' theoretical/political allegiances:

[E]ither you believe in the forces of containment and recuperation, in which case it becomes your job to show how the seemingly "liberatory" or "progressive" aspects of the culture ultimately serve the conservative purpose of perpetuating a political order in which "freedom" is but a name for a particularly deceptive form of self-policing, *or* you believe in hegemony and resistance, in which case it becomes your job to show how the seemingly "repressive" or "reactionary" aspects of the culture ultimately can be made to serve surprisingly (yet reassuringly) liberatory or progressive ends. (*Employment of English*, 11; emphasis in original)

Even poetry, that genre apparently unfit for political discourse, is now linked with politics in the *Princeton Encyclopedia of Poetry and Poetics'* three-page entry on "politics and poetry" (960–63).

Our readings and our understanding of textual systems have been wonderfully enriched by the broad and capacious model of cultural politics that informs much contemporary literary criticism. At the same time, though, the vast majority of this criticism still is focused on canonical writers who never hoped their work would make something political happen. We still have not turned much attention to those writers who wrote with direct political intentions, who wrote not only in hopes of having a political impact but also in the deep conviction that they would. Mark Van Wienen, in his study of political poetry during World War I, eloquently states both this problem and the stakes involved: "[T]here remains a chasm between critics' commitment to politicize their readings of literary texts and their willingness to study (and therefore also to encourage the production of) literary texts that are themselves consciously fashioned to political ends. The difference between these two fields of study comprises . . . a continuing reluctance among scholars to engage in scholarship that is genuinely committed to political discussion" (239).

Happily, since the voluminous literary debates of the 1930s, a scholarly community devoted to preserving and understanding the "partisan political poetry" of the interwar period has existed. Daniel Aaron, whose *Writers on the Left* inaugurated the study of 1930s literary radicalism, admirably complicates the portraits offered by Phillips and Rahv and others, stressing that writers who joined or worked in concert with the Communist Party during the 1930s "did not come to the movement because they were broke or because publishing houses were failing. They became radicals because they thought the economic system had gone kaput, because they saw too many hungry and desperate people, and because men and ideas they detested seemed in the ascendant" (391). Aaron focuses the majority of his attention on fairly well-known writers like John Dos Passos, writers whose reputations are based at least in part on their less overtly political work. Walter Rideout, in his study of the proletarian novel, broadens the field to include a number of novelists whose reputations are almost nonexistent outside the limited field of "Left literature," and his work is built on and extended in Barbara Foley's exhaustive survey of proletarian fiction in *Radical Representations;* in Constance Coiner's thorough analyses of works by Meridel LeSueur and Tillie Olsen in *Better Red;* in Paula Rabinowitz and Charlotte Nekola's anthology of political writing by women, *Writing Red;* and in Rabinowitz's study of women's revolutionary fiction, *Labor and Desire.* These studies have often participated in a dialogue with works on working-class representation that range from the theoretical writing of Raymond Williams (*Culture*) and Peter Hitchcock (*Dialogics of the Oppressed*) and the historical research of E. P. Thompson (*The Making of the English Working Class*) to recent studies of English working-class fiction like Pamela Fox's *Class Fictions: Shame and Resistance in the British Working-Class Novel, 1890–1945.*

Poets of the American Left found an early champion in M. L. Rosenthal, whose Columbia University dissertation first worked through a set of issues and writers on whom Rosenthal went on to publish important articles. More recently, Alan Wald's study of the poetry of John Wheelwright and Sherry Mangan builds on Rosenthal's work to problematize the strict division between aesthetic and political discourses proffered by the New Critics and anti-Communist liberal critics like Irving Howe. And in perhaps the most important recent study of the modern poetry we have tried to forget, *Repression and Recovery,* Cary Nelson argues that poetry itself was a contested concept during the first half of the twentieth century, that it was the site of continuous struggle as political discourses sought to yoke its cultural value and energy to their own attempts to produce social meanings (251). Poetry between 1910 and 1945, Nelson writes, "became one of the most dependable sources of knowledge about society and one's place and choices within it. Indeed, for some people, poetic discourse was capable not merely of talking about but actually of substantially deciding basic social and political issues" (127). Nelson offers numerous examples of poetry in strategies of resistance and coalition building, from the efforts of individual poets to harness poetry's "power to define and alter human relations" in their political work to the compilers of anthologies who bring together poems by Mike Gold and Genevieve Taggard and, say, Frost, Eliot, and Pound, all under the rubric of "revolutionary poetry."[12] The political impulse in poetry and in what we do with it, Nelson insists, is enormously valuable to our literary institutions themselves and, perhaps more important, to the society of which those institutions are a part.

This book joins the growing number of studies, including Nelson's, Wald's, Coiner's, and Foley's, as well as more recent work like Kalaidjian's *American Culture between the Wars,* William Maxwell's *New Negro, Old Left,* Susan Schweik's *Gulf So Deeply Cut,* and Van Wienen's *Partisans and Poets,* that attend precisely to "partisan political" writers and their work. I examine poetry committed to a specific activist agenda, poetry that addresses a specific political question or issue and takes sides, presses its claims, and seeks to move its audience to action.[13] While all poetry might, under various contemporary theoretical rubrics, be seen as somehow political, the objects of scrutiny in this study are politically engaged in immediate, instrumental, even activist ways. I hope, in the chapters that follow, to illustrate what Van Wienen has called "a uniquely constructive poetics and politically engaged literary practice," one that challenges the still-prevailing romantic and individualist conception of the poet and "emphasizes the necessity of operating within, and upon, historical contingencies" (231–32).

In "Hugh Selwyn Mauberley" (1920), Ezra Pound had written that "the age demanded an image / Of its accelerated grimace" (*Personae,* 86). Classic literary models had lost all cultural purchase in the degraded postwar age, and readers wanted simply "a mould in plaster, / Made with no loss of time." But if the age clamored for, and perhaps deserved, nothing more than a portrait of its own fragmentation and chaotic speed, Pound thought he saw what the age really required. In place of either the "prose kinema" or the "'sculpture' of rhyme," figures for the popular culture and "genteel tradition" against which high modernism defined itself, Pound, in 1925, published his first installment of the remedy the age unknowingly demanded, *A Draft of XVI Cantos.* Opening with a disjointed rehearsal of the classical *nekuia,* the descent into the underworld crucial in epics, Pound begins both in medias res and at the end of a cultural epoch. He sketches that end in the first several cantos; in Canto 1, Pound takes up the mask of Odysseus to converse with Tiresias but throws the mask aside after Tiresias's dire prediction ("'Odysseus / Shalt return through spiteful Neptune, over dark seas, / Lose all companions'"). Speaking as the author of the poem, the compiler of its fragments, Pound steps away from epic voice and convention to lay bare the lineage of this conversation with the dead; he addresses his source, the 1538 translation of Homer by Andreas Divus: "Lie quiet Divus." The narrative and cultural coherence promised by the epic tradition fails.

The age demands a gathering of fragments to shore up the ruins of European culture, and Pound provides it, publishing the mosaic in Paris in a limited, deluxe edition complete with red illuminated capitals through William Bird's Three Mountains Press. *A Draft of XVI Cantos* is art for the ages, a publication event signaling, as the publication of Eliot's *Waste Land* had three years before, the beginning of a new literary era, though only the hundred or so readers who could buy and read the book might know it.

While the mid-1920s are marked on most literary calendars by the advent of *A Draft of XVI Cantos* and its formal experimentation, they also saw unfold the trial and appeals of Nicola Sacco and Bartolomeo Vanzetti, two Italian anarchists accused of murder and armed robbery in Massachusetts. The trial, with its highly politicized defense, revealed, as Edmund Wilson wrote, "the whole anatomy of American life with all its classes, professions, and points of view and all their relations, and it raised almost every fundamental question of our political and social system" (quoted in D'Attilio, 670). As Joseph Freeman, a member of the editorial board of the *Liberator,* recalls, the Sacco and Vanzetti case dominated the magazine's attention to the extent that it ignored "T. S. Eliot's *The Waste Land,* which appeared at this time but which we did not review" (quoted in Aaron, 92).[14] While they were the only literary intellectuals paying much attention to the case before its heavily publicized appeals, the *Liberator* staff members were not alone by the time of the execution; as Aaron has written, the execution of Sacco and Vanzetti "made the writer abandon his aloofness and enter, often hesitantly and without confidence, the conflicts of his day" (168). Well-known writers like Dorothy Parker, Mike Gold, John Dos Passos, and Edna St. Vincent Millay spoke out on the case's injustice. Millay's "Justice Denied in Massachusetts," which appeared in Lucia Trent and Ralph Cheyney's 1928 anthology *America*

Arraigned!, typifies the tone of much of the poetic outpouring over the execution:

> Let us abandon then our garden and go home
> And sit in the sitting room.
> Shall the larkspur or the corn grow under this cloud
> Sour to the fruitful seed
> Is the cold earth under this cloud. (106)

With stock images of death and a deadly change in the natural cycles of growth, Millay registers the despair many writers and intellectuals felt over the case's outcome; the very earth is, literally, appalled.

The adoption of causes célèbres by writers on the political Left, or by writers who gravitated to the Left because of these causes, continued throughout the 1930s. Eight young black men were convicted of rape and sentenced to death in Scottsboro, Alabama, in 1931, attracting the attention both of blacks and of working-class and Communist constituencies. Strikes broke out and were broken from Detroit to Gastonia, reinforcing the widespread view that state power served the monied interests and was being used to maintain, if not to worsen, the economic inequities exposed by the depression. Fascist parties took over crucial countries in central and southern Europe, threatening democracies throughout the continent, while Fascist demagogues in the United States drew ever-greater numbers into their groups. Of course, not all political poetry comes from the Left. When rebellious troops led by General Francisco Franco attempted to overthrow the popularly elected government of the Spanish Republic, writers of various political persuasions, from the Communist John Cornford to the Fascist Roy Campbell, entered the fray as observers and sometimes as combatants. And when war became general all over Europe, poets worked both to urge American entry on the Allied side (as Edna St. Vincent Millay did in "The Murder of Lidice," a radio-play in verse that treats the Nazi destruction of a Czech village) and to discourage American entry (as Ezra Pound did famously in prose and radio speeches but also, as I hope to show, in the cantos he wrote during the late 1930s). Poets participated in each of these causes, both as persons and as poets. Political poetry was everywhere, from the pages of *Poetry*, that founding little magazine of modernism, to those of *Esquire*, the new slick magazine for well-off American men.[15]

In this book, I closely examine four political poets—Edwin Rolfe, Langston Hughes, Ezra Pound, and Muriel Rukeyser—in an effort to understand how they sought to make something happen. My aim is to add to and flesh out part of the broad picture sketched by Nelson in *Repression and Recovery* with the sustained attention to individual poets paid by Wald, Schweik, James Smethurst, and others. But before turning to these specific cases, I will address three theoretical and methodological issues that arise at the intersection of poetry and political persuasion.

HOW DOES POLITICAL POETRY MAKE SOMETHING HAPPEN?

The answer to the question of how political poetry makes something happen lies in the concept of hegemony, in the hegemonic model of political struggle and change, and in the related notions of articulation and rearticulation. For Antonio Gramsci, the concept of hegemonic struggle shifts "the political" from electoral or state politics to the formations of the family, the church, educational institutions, the arts—to those social sites in which ideology operates.[16] To return briefly to Auden, hegemony broadens the political to encompass the locations that are affected by poetry, the "guts of the living" in which "the words of a dead man / Are modified" (248). Hegemonic struggles occur throughout "civil society." Articulation, disarticulation, and rearticulation are the modes by which hegemonic politics operate; they are the strategic means by which ruling blocs are formed in hegemonic struggles. Constituencies with widely divergent agendas must work through their shared antagonisms to forge temporary and shifting alliances through discourse, to create a network of discursively constituted spheres of political struggle. The construction of new hegemonies, as Ernesto Laclau writes, "is conceived as a differential articulation, not founded on the necessary centrality of any one sector, but which constructs a new popular historical subject, starting from the points of convergence of the numerous fragments generated by democratic struggles" (Laclau, 44). The constant joining of specific ideological elements with specific class positions accumulates an inertial force difficult to break in strategies of rational or expository disarticulation/rearticulation (Hall, "Signification, Representation, Ideology," 104–5).

It is precisely this inertial force that necessitates action in the aesthetic realm. In the presence of the artwork, we simultaneously direct our attention outward and inward. Attending to the formal properties, the execution, of the painting or symphony or poem, we submit to those properties' appeals to our senses. We are, for that moment, wholly ourselves, uniquely addressed by the work before us. And at the same time, we are at one with the community of viewers, hearers, readers. We unite with the "humanity" with whom we share both senses and values. The words we use to describe the moment of aesthetic experience testify to that moment's power. We are "enraptured." We "transcend," in that moment, our historical condition, our constraining circumstances. But the experience of aesthetic apprehension foregrounds what Terry Eagleton calls "the self-determining nature of human powers and capabilities" (*Ideology of the Aesthetic,* 9). The artwork is, after all, made; it is brought into existence through work. In the creation of the artwork, the artist imposes consciousness on the material world, molding it without regard to laws physical or governmental into the shape of individual conception. And in the experience of the artwork, in the multiple encounters with this re-creation of the world, viewers or readers find both the opportunity for individual reflection and sensuous joy and the potential for reconciliation with other individuals through the surrender of individual difference to the artist's vision. The aesthetic is, finally, a "markedly contradictory concept" (ibid., 415). In it lie "meanings and values . . . which are of vital importance" to revolutionary political goals as well as others that must be "challenged and overcome" (ibid.).

As Raymond Williams writes, the revolutionary aspects of the aesthetic come into play in strategies of rearticulation by bringing about a confrontation with hegemony "in the fibres of the self" (*Marxism,* 212). Grab subjects by the soul, which yearns for wholeness and transcendence, and their hearts and minds will follow. Some of the crucial work of counterhegemonic struggle, in other words, happens in the aesthetic realm. Literary texts can illustrate, embody, and perform identities, experiences, and relationships alternative to those prescribed by the dominant culture. They hail readers, invite them to join the "imagined community" of other readers, and combine, in the crucible of the aesthetic experience, values readers already hold with others readers should hold.

Some theorists of the aesthetic will claim that it is a domain characterized precisely by its uselessness, its utter incapacity to provoke action, to impinge upon the political, to soil itself in the mire of "the real world," while others will argue that there is no fundamental difference between the aesthetic and the political (or any other discursive realm). While I incline toward the latter view, I maintain a *functional* difference between the aesthetic and other discourses. That is to say, aesthetic artifacts *work* differently from nonaesthetic artifacts, though there is no inherent difference between them. They work differently because we, the viewers, readers, listeners, the receivers, treat them differently. We set them off from other objects and from ourselves. We establish certain expectations of them. An object, once ascribed aesthetic status, performs aesthetic functions. It invites distanced contemplation, it removes us from our atomized self-centeredness, it allows us to participate in meaning-making, to idealize conditions, to symbolically resolve problems or contradictions. At the same time, it works negatively, forbidding us to touch it, use it, be aroused by it.

But no object has only one function. Multiple functions and potentialities inhere in any object and any discourse.[17] After the rash of artistic avant-garde movements in the first three decades of the twentieth century, we tend to have no problem recognizing this possibility in one of its versions. Most college students now know about R. Mutt's "Fountain," the urinal Marcel Duchamp transformed into an artwork simply by calling it one and entering it in a show.[18] We see how the aesthetic function, or its potential, inheres in objects used for all kinds of other purposes. But we often resist the reverse assertion that other functions inhere in aesthetic objects and discourse, though we see demonstrations of this every day. Classic artworks are used to sell products, are themselves reproduced on and as products and sold. Their cultural capital is drawn upon or invested by entrepreneurs to generate real capital. A potential function always present in the object is, by its redeployment, its reshaped signification, its reception, made explicit, even dominant.

The same is true of literary texts. Intrinsic factors set such texts apart from other kinds of discourse. Poems tend to be broken into lines that leave an irregular right margin. Their rhythms, figurative language, and linguistic richness establish expectations among readers. As readers, we take note of these factors and ascribe a different status to poems than we do to, say, newspaper articles or textbooks. While other texts commend themselves through usefulness, the poem promises beauty. The relationship between poem and reader makes the aesthetic function dominate the others that inhere in the text. But to say that the poem's aesthetic function dominates is not to say that it precludes the operation of other inherent functions. Indeed, the complex interplay between functions, the tension between use and uselessness, attraction and distance, engagement and evasion, is precisely what criticism seeks to settle and resolve.

Texts that attempt both to achieve aesthetic status and to intervene in nonaesthetic realms use the productive tension between inherent functions to accomplish both aims at once. Functional dominance almost visibly oscillates in such texts so that at one moment we are distanced and invited to contemplate and at the next we are drawn in and exhorted to act. Contemplation and exhortation do not mutually exclude each other. To the contrary, new visions are dreamed, new possibilities suggested, new words made utterable and brave new worlds conceivable precisely in the simultaneity of aesthetic and political functions. The almost erotic energy of aesthetic experience is harnessed to the motor of political ideas through re-articulation and then works to reshape the popular imaginary, which in turn reweaves the hegemonic fabric. And *that* is cultural work.

THE IMPORTANCE OF BEING IN CONTEXT

Throughout this book, I focus on the textual acts that poets, as political agents, perform. These acts have their primary effects in the poems' aesthetic dimension—in the thematic development, rhetorical execution, and formal embodiment of the poems' political energies. When poets, responding to the multiple historical pressures that surround them as they contemplate a specific historical event, compose their response in the form of a poem, they act in the aesthetic dimension. Their goals in writing the poem—memorializing an event or individual, criticizing social institutions or forces, encouraging readers to act in concert for social change—are addressed aesthetically, through the organization of words into metrical feet and broken lines, the emphasis on language's materiality through rhyme and alliteration, the arrangement of images into a metaphorical or symbolic economy of meaning.

Poetry makes political ideas and agendas engaging by articulating them to culturally valorized judgments like "the beautiful" or the heroic. Through poetry's sensual pleasures and intensities, through its "liberatory concern with concrete particularity" (Eagleton, *Ideology of the Aesthetic,* 9), it effects political contemplation and perhaps action by contesting social meanings in aesthetically pleasing, compelling, or otherwise engaging ways. When, for example, Edna St. Vincent Millay poetically reacts to the execution of Sacco and Vanzetti in her 1927 poem, "Justice Denied in Massachusetts," she utilizes repetition, irregular rhyme and rhythm, complexes of images representing life and death, and a diction different from "everyday speech" to limn the significance of this historical event. Through a verbal construct shaped by the conventions of "the beautiful," she registers political outrage. Millay attempts to influence readers' perceptions of the meanings of the execution not by mounting an argument about those meanings but by drawing readers into a contemplation of them through their experience of the poem.

I am interested in acts that happen both in and around poems. On one hand, I want to examine the acts comprised by the poems themselves — things politically engaged agents do *in* poems.[19] On the other hand, it is important to recall the things politically engaged agents do *with* poems, for poetry elicits political engagement not only by harnessing the cultural capital of "beauty" or "power" but also by interpellating through its themes and forms the collective subjectivity required for political action, by constructing "imagined communities" of like-minded, or at least similarly subordinated, readers.[20] And this does not happen in a vacuum. The textual acts of poems occur in the context of other acts, textual and otherwise; a poem does its cultural work from the material location of the page, whether that page is made of heavy bond paper and stitched with similar pages between hard covers or is made of newsprint and folded with similar pages to be sold for three cents a copy. My arguments thus take into account such factors as where and in what context a poem appears and how, in what terms, a poet is discussed. My readings attend to what Jerome McGann, in *The Textual Condition,* has called the "bibliographic text," the various materialist aspects of a textual artifact (105). The spatial arrangement of a text on a page activates sets of semiotic codes that assist in the interpretation of the text. Perhaps more fully than other texts (or at least more obviously), poems signify in their spatial, as well as linguistic, dimension. Irregular right-hand margins call attention to poetic lineation and the cluster of conventions such lineation carries — enjambment or its absence, emphatic line endings, epiphora, perhaps rhyme. White spaces between blocks of text provoke consideration of stanzaic structures. The spatial dimension of a poem dictates to us a mode of reading, a heightened awareness of linguistic and rhetorical—as well as spatial—aspects of the text.

But we must also attend to less obviously significant features of the bibliographic text. Printers' colophons, paper quality, watermarks, and cover styles alert us to the character of the text and call out various interpretive strategies, thematic or generic expectations, and institutional associations. A publisher's name on the spine or title page arouses certain expectations in the knowledgeable reader, and the titles of publications listed in the acknowledgments can tell us even more. A specific comparison will clarify the importance of this attention to the broader set of signifying practices in which any poem appears. The mid-1920s are marked in most histories of modern American poetry by the completion and publication of T. S. Eliot's *Waste Land* and the publication of Pound's *Draft of XVI Cantos.* Eliot finished his revision of *The Waste Land,* with Pound's famous collaboration, in 1921, and the poem was published by *The Dial* in November 1922. Pound's first installment of *The Cantos* was published in Paris by William Bird's Three Mountains Press in 1925. The critical reaction to these works constitutes an important chapter in the development of literary modernism. But these years also saw the conviction of Sacco and Vanzetti on charges of robbery and murder in a heavily politicized Massachusetts trial and the first in a series of appeals in the case, which would occupy the American Left and many writers until the two men were executed in 1927. Poets as diverse as John Dos Passos and Edna St. Vincent Millay wrote and published poems about the two men and their trials in magazines as different as the *New Masses* and the *Greenwich Village Quill.* The critical reaction to these works was, for the most part, nonexistent. (Of course, critical reaction was not the goal of these poets' textual acts.)

Even a cursory reading reveals obvious differences between *The Waste Land* and the poems on Sacco and Vanzetti. On one hand, Eliot's poem is forcefully avant-garde and literary; it shifts voices, incorporates complex literary and cultural allusions, juxtaposes fragments in a way that demands compositional collaboration from its readers, and eschews any direct commentary on contemporary events. The protest poems, on the other hand, are coherent and accessible. They speak in simple, often very conventional, voices. They allude to the facts of the case, to persons involved in it, and only to very recognizable literary works. They present to the reader a finished facade, a verbal surface that neither requires nor invites participation. But an examination of the poems' bibliographic texts, of how and where they appeared, defines even more clearly the differences between these textual acts.

Eliot first published *The Waste Land* in *The Dial* in November 1922. He was, as part of his publication contract with both the magazine and Boni and Liveright, his American publisher, granted the Dial Award of $1,000 before the publication of the poem. As McGann has written, this circumstance meant that the poem's "artistic importance had already been institutionally imagined, if not actually and finally decided" (*Textual Condition*, 126).[21] The physical appearance of *The Dial* (and of the poem in *The Dial*) contributes to the poem's complex signifying practices and specifies in concrete ways the cultural work the poem was intended and expected to do, the kind of textual act the poem comprised.

The Dial was an irrefutably serious literary magazine. Its design and tone denoted sobriety. Within its pages, culture was taken very seriously and culture meant "Literature." Any poem published in this venue gained an aura, an authority, just by appearing on its mostly undecorated pages, between its dour covers, under the imprimatur of its heavily printed, somberly designed title. A poem appearing in this magazine, especially a poem as long as *The Waste Land* that had won the magazine's annual award, therefore, was presented as if accompanied by heraldic trumpets. This was *important* poetry. Its publication was a monumental occurrence.

Several weeks after *The Dial*'s publication of *The Waste Land,* Boni and Liveright brought out the first book version of the poem, and this was followed, early in 1923, by the Hogarth Press edition. These two book publications, even more than *The Dial*'s publication of the poem, define the textual condition of Eliot's poem, mark it as a key monument of modernism, and confer upon it an irresistible cultural authority. This is perhaps less true of Boni and Liveright's version, which carries the marks of a fairly typical commercially published book. The cover is a textured black pressboard on which only the title appears in serifed gold capitals. The title page gives Eliot's name and the poem's title in the upper third, with the poem's epigraph in smaller type in the middle of the page and the publisher's imprint at the bottom: "New York / Boni and Liveright / 1922." Full copyright information is given on the reverse of the title page, with usual rights reserved for the publisher and author. This page also includes a mark of the book's cultural importance, or at least of the publisher's expectation of it: "Of the one thousand copies printed of The Waste Land this volume is number —." The sentence is set in italics and is followed by a blank space in which a number could be written (though no number appears in the copy owned by Yale University's Beinecke Library).

The text of the poem in Boni and Liveright's edition is set in a fairly large, fairly simple typeface, and the lines are loosely spaced so that only about twelve appear on each page. Sections begin on new pages, with the section number (in roman numerals) and title at the top. Line numbers appear in the right-hand margin beside every tenth line. The poem takes up thirty-one pages, beginning on page 9 and ending on page 49. Eliot's notes, which do not appear in *The Dial,* fill pages 53 to 64. While the physical appearance of the book is similar to most commercial poetry collections, and to other books for that matter, the rather luxurious spacing draws our attention to the poem's value. Not many poems would be allowed to take up so much space, so much paper. Not many sets of twelve lines are graced, in publishing, with so much white space on all sides.

Leonard and Virginia Woolf brought out their Hogarth Press edition of *The Waste Land* in 1923, and this edition, more clearly than Boni and Liveright's, enhances the poem's standing as monumental art and publishing event. The cover is a beautiful marbled blue, and the deckled pages are thicker, more fully textured, than those in the American edition. A paper label bordered with stars gives the title and author. On the title page, Eliot's name, the poem's title, and the epigraph all appear, centered, on the top half. Two inches from the bottom, in capitals and centered, we find:

PRINTED AND PUBLISHED BY LEONARD
AND VIRGINIA WOOLF AT THE HOGARTH
PRESS HOGARTH HOUSE PARADISE ROAD
RICHMOND SURREY
1923

No copyright notice appears on the reverse. Like the book's breathtaking cover, the title page not only gives the necessary information but also establishes a specific aesthetic authority for Eliot and his poem. The Woolfs' names and the name of their already famous press confer on Eliot the considerable imprimatur of Bloomsbury, and the publishers' identification at the bottom of the title page, more effectively than the "numbered copy" indication in the Boni and Liveright edition, signals the reader that this book is a work of art. The book's physical form enhances the "high art" cues provided by the text itself. And this effect is only made stronger by the list of previously published Hogarth titles that makes up the book's last page. This publication makes Eliot a member of a group of other well-known authors, including Clive Bell, E. M. Forster, Roger Fry, Maxim Gorky, Katherine Mansfield, Anton Chekhov, and the Woolfs. By association, Eliot becomes the cosmopolitan author, a cultural force to be reckoned with.

Contrast this with the appearance of poems we might take to represent another story of modern poetry—poems that deal with the trial and execution of Sacco and Vanzetti that appeared in magazines like the *New Masses*. Compared to *The Dial*'s staid and subtly powerful design, its artifactual character, its look of something to be kept, the *New Masses* seems almost disposable. Its paper is certainly cheaper (it is less durable in the libraries where readers must now go to see it). And it cost less when first published (the price of twenty-five cents is often printed on the cover, whereas *The Dial*'s price is not). But this magazine, too, had value for its readers and subscribers. While printed on the same stuff used to wrap up fish or line birdcages, these issues, too, were meant to be kept. Indeed, the *New Masses* occasionally included an advertisement for "those who wish to keep *New Masses* in permanent form." For $2.50 a volume, dedicated readers could buy the magazine's annual volumes in "attractive craft bindings."

The *New Masses*' design is less subtle and less staid than *The Dial*'s, calculated less to communicate elevated taste and refinement than to evince concern with the pressing, the here and now. Cartoons, drawings, and lithographs on contemporary issues dominate the pages of the *New Masses,* and even its cover, with its boldly cubist or expressionist artwork, its Bauhaus block capitals, and the frequent sharp diagonals that separate black fields from white and even cross the letters of the title, as in the October 1927 issue, announces the magazine as a loud, dramatic, and committed set of voices. Like the frequent and very pointed cartoons, *New Masses*' parodies, articles, book reviews, and even advertisements share an aggressive tone and a fairly coherent, though by no means unified, point of view. No less than *The Dial*'s sense that its writers, editors, and readers form a community bound by "Literature," the *New Masses* conveys, even constructs, a community among its readership through layout, design, editorial policies and statements, and, of course, the texts the magazine circulates.

Among those texts, in the issue published a month after Massachusetts electrocuted Sacco and Vanzetti, was John Dos Passos's "They Are Dead Now." The poem appears on page 7, opposite the end of Max Eastman's article on the execution, "Sacco and Vanzetti: Anarchists and the Revolutionary Science" (Eastman argues that "unlike many martyrdoms, the death of Sacco and Vanzetti was of very great value to the cause they loved" [4]). Dos Passos's poem takes up the top half of the page; in the bottom half is the beginning of a four-page symposium on Sacco and Vanzetti, their execution, and their significance. Clearly, then, the poem participates not so much in a literary moment as in a political one. Much of this issue of the *New Masses* is devoted to figuring out what the execution means on various levels and for various interested parties. Dos Passos's poem is part of the magazine's long-running involvement in the controversy. Throughout its first two years (the *New Masses* began publishing in 1925), the magazine had run cartoons, usually by Hugo Gellert, about the trial's injustice and the need to free the two men. As Massachusetts governor Alvin T. Fuller considered appeals to commute the death sentences, the *New Masses* increased its attention to Sacco and Vanzetti. The May 1927 issue, for example, includes a call for readers to send letters and telegrams to Fuller demanding the men's release. After Fuller signed the death warrant in August, the magazine devoted one-fourth of its September 1927 issue to Sacco and Vanzetti, including a drawing by Art Young that compares the two anarchists to witches tried and executed almost 300 years before ("Same Old Massachusetts"), articles by Heywood Broun and Mike Gold, and a poem by James Rorty ("Gentlemen of Massachusetts"). Poetry, in this venue, in this context, is seen, then, not as something monumental, something removed by typeface, fine paper, and a judicious tone from the rough-and-tumble of political struggle and suffering. Rather, poetry, like cartoons, essays, exhortations, and analyses, demonstrates its utility as a tool with which readers (and, indeed, writers) might apprehend and understand significant events in their culture. Poetry takes part in a broader effort to make something happen, to make something not happen, to discover why something had to happen, and to figure out what ought to happen next.

Even when gathered in collections and published in book form, poems like Dos Passos's (or Millay's "Justice Denied in Massachusetts") function rather differently than *The Waste Land* because they appear to be a different kind of thing entirely. The marks of high value present in both the Boni and Liveright and Hogarth editions of Eliot's long poem are absent in Trent and Cheyney's *America Arraigned!* The first major difference, of course, is that whereas one book (in two different versions) presents the work of a single poet, the other collects and makes available the work of many. In place of the single poet doing different voices, *America Arraigned!* offers a range of poets speaking as if with one voice. Indeed, Trent and Cheyney include the periodicals in which many of these poems first appeared in the collective voice with which their book seeks to speak. But other differences signify as well. Both book editions of *The Waste Land* call attention to the poem's uniqueness and value. The Boni and Liveright edition, with its copy number on the title page's reverse, highlights the book's "limited edition" status, just as the Hogarth edition's brilliant blue cover and colophon do. These are books for a very limited audience. *America Arraigned!,* however, seeks simply to circulate. The book is cheaply printed on cheap paper and is bound in cheap covers. The press, New York's Dean and Company, does not announce itself loudly, and nowhere will we find a copy number. The poems are crowded, a distinct contrast to the ample white space in both Eliot books. This book is to be bought, read, lent out, passed around. Its poems are to be used. Trent and Cheyney make this abundantly clear in their foreword:

> This book is published with a three-fold function. It is a memorial tribute to Nicola Sacco and Bartolomeo Vanzetti, martyrs for world brotherhood and freedom. It is a protest against the rape of justice by Massachusetts in murdering these noble and innocent men and also by the Justices of the Supreme Court of the United States and by President Calvin Coolidge in not interfering. We hope that it will serve likewise as a clarion-call to participate in the labor movement for which Sacco and Vanzetti gave up their lives on the electric chair and which alone can prevent the repetition of such a tragedy. (9)

Trent and Cheyney explicitly address their moment. Indeed, the book's occasion is a historical event—the execution of Sacco and Vanzetti—and its purpose is a historical intervention. Their foreword to the book, their division of the poems according to their date of publication ("Before Governor Fuller and His Advisory Commission Refused to Intercede," "After the Intercession Was Refused but before the Crucifixion," and "After the Crucifixion"), and even the bright red cloth in which the book is bound all call attention to these poems' placement in time, their historical specificity, and their sense of utility.

POLITICS OF FORM AND VALUE

At the same time, poets strive to articulate to political action not only the self-reflexive moment of aesthetic apprehension but also the encrusted social meanings and associations of particular aesthetic complexes (forms). Marxist criticism has made available various ways to read politics in poetic forms. Among the most often cited of these is the model elaborated by Antony Easthope in *Poetry as Discourse.* Drawing at once on structuralist theories of language and on Louis Althusser's theory of ideology and interpellation into subject positions, Easthope argues that all poetic forms carry an ideological burden that complicates (and often forecloses) their political utility.

Insights like Easthope's have helped critics find, in Kalaidjian's phrase, "how a work's intrinsic form inscribes extrinsic politics" (*American Culture,* 8). Michael Davidson's recovery of objectivist poets George Oppen, Louis Zukofsky, and Charles Reznikoff is, in part, provoked and guided by Easthope's argument; Davidson concludes that "what makes poetry poetry is what makes poetry ideological" (22). Building on this sense of form's political content, Davidson sets out to chart "the ways [the objectivists] retained critical positions *by means of* formal strategies, both free verse and metrical" (25; emphasis in original).

Poetic forms for Easthope operate as "myth," naturalizing propositions that are in fact historical and ideological. Of iambic pentameter, for example, Easthope writes that this apparently natural (and neutral) dominant line in English verse "elides (and would conceal) *two* equations: (a) poetry consists of lines (the material nature of poetry); (b) pentameter is one historically determined form of line organization (and there are others). The metre can be seen not as a neutral form of poetic necessity but a specific historical form producing certain meanings and acting to exclude others" (64). A sonnet or poem in blank verse, Easthope argues, cannot effect radical social change regardless of its thematic treatment of, say, the plight of downtrodden workers because its form is inextricably bound up with the ideological networks that perpetuate bourgeois subjectivity and the capitalist economic structure on which that subjectivity depends.

But Easthope's arguments seem to foreclose the possibilities that Kalaidjian and Davidson raise. The Gramscian problematic of hegemony and the war of position in civil society opens the way to a more flexible account of forms' ideological contents. In place of Easthope's fairly fixed and schematic menu, which aligns each form with a specific set of ideological commitments, the Gramscian model (especially as developed and complicated by Stuart Hall and as applied to poetry by Cary Nelson) posits more fluid and changeable relationships between poetic form and political significance. These relationships are not structural or simply given; they are historical. The work of Raymond Williams is especially useful on this point. In his analyses (of pastoral and urban representations in *The Country and the City* and of bourgeois drama in *The Sociology of Culture* and *Problems in Materialism and Culture*), Williams demonstrates that specific forms of artistic practice (specific forms, for Williams, *are* practices) are inextricably bound up with the specific places and times in which they are developed and deployed. While it is true, on one hand, that "certain forms of social relationship are deeply embodied in certain forms of art" (as Williams puts something like Easthope's point), it is vitally important that we attend to "the immediate conditions of a practice—the signalled places, occasions and terms of specifically indicated types of cultural activity" (*Sociology of Culture,* 148). The political significance of an artistic form—the drama in this case—cannot be determined once and for all. The form changes over time, responding to shifts in the "determining factors" of "actual social relations" that a form mediates and expresses (166–67). We must take into account both the "determining factors" of context and motivation and the "actual productive institutions" that enable the text under consideration to signify (176).

So blank verse, for example, over time and through repeated association, becomes encrusted with a residue of bourgeois subjectivity and the maintenance of certain relations of subordination. Easthope points out a number of factors that give rise to this network of associations: the pentameter's "naturalization" and disavowal of "its own metricality," its constraints on "the activity of the signifier," and its insistent positioning of the reader as "subject of the enounced," which strengthens the illusion of individual subjectivity (or the ideological fiction of the unified speaking subject) (74–75). Blank verse, or any iambic pentameter verse form, is therefore, according to Easthope, *necessarily* and *ineluctably* "individualist, elitist, privatized" (77). But such a judgment requires, Williams would say, the effacement of history and context; it demands a level of abstraction that ignores the source, moment, and purpose of a given textual act. Against Easthope, then, it seems both more accurate and more useful to say not that blank verse *must* perform a specified social function but that this textual practice, this form—a decasyllabic line generally made up of iambic feet and tending not to rhyme—is *articulated* to specific social forces and cultural meanings.

Stuart Hall defines articulation as

> the form of the connection that *can* make a unity of two different elements, under certain conditions. It is a linkage which is not necessary, determined, absolute and essential for all time. . . . The so-called "unity" of a discourse is really the articulation of different, distinct elements which can be rearticulated in different ways because they have no necessary "belongingness." The "unity" which matters is a linkage between the articulated discourse and the social forces with which it can, under certain historical conditions, but need not necessarily, be connected. ("On Postmodernism and Articulation," 53; emphasis in original)

Or as Lawrence Grossberg has more succinctly put it, "[A]rticulation links this practice to that effect, this text to that meaning, this meaning to that reality, this experience to these politics" (54). To say that blank verse is *articulated* to Easthope's unholy trinity of individualism, elitism, and privatism is to recognize that this set of connections and associations is *not* "necessary, determined, absolute." Rather, it results from a historical connection between the poetic form and a model of subjectivity itself historically at odds with the collective or the popular or the intersubjective. Or, better, the connection results from a repeated and therefore deeply ingrained association. And this

Introduction [29]

recognition helps us see that the form might be *dis*connected from its associated social significances. Blank verse can be "rearticulated in different ways" because it has no *necessary* or *intrinsic* relation to any specific array of social forces. Its political meaning derives from its recurrent position within a formation, so its political meaning might be altered through its reorientation in a different formation. Hall's work on race and on the terms by which racial identities are ascribed has demonstrated the opportunity for rearticulation, the openness to redefinition, of quite powerfully charged elements of language. This suggests at the very least that the politics of poetic forms are contestable.

But this is not to say that the political meaning of blank verse is simply up for grabs, that a progressive poet working to advance a politics of collectivity can simply revise the ideological connotations the form has, over centuries, accumulated. Hall is often at pains to emphasize the limits, or at least the grave difficulties, of articulation. He argues that religion, for example,

> has been bound up in particular ways, wired up very directly as the cultural and ideological underpinning of a particular structure of power. . . . [T]here are powerful, immensely strong . . . "lines of tendential force" articulating that religious formation to political, economic and ideological structures. So that, if you move into that society, it would be idiotic to think that you could easily detach religion from its historical embeddedness and simply put it in another place. ("On Postmodernism and Articulation," 53–54)

Due to its repeated association with certain social forces and meanings, then, blank verse will *tend* to be articulated in the same ways, and it will take some hard poetic work to disrupt the "magnetic lines of tendency" (54).

This is precisely the work undertaken by numerous political poets, who, knowingly or not, bring the processes of disarticulation and rearticulation to bear in efforts to draft the cultural power of the form (which has, of course, dominated English prosody for centuries and is the form of such paragons of cultural force as Shakespeare and Milton) for a variety of political purposes and possibilities, some perhaps quite at odds with the agendas the form supposedly must serve. Many politically engaged poets of the 1930s sought precisely this sort of relationship with their medium's traditional resources, a complicated relationship that drew on forms' contractual expectations and historically accumulated power to attract and convince readers even as it aimed to dislodge those forms from the social structures that had, over the centuries, empowered them.

They undertake this project in three central ways that we might most clearly see through an examination of the sonnet, a form that Easthope finds at least as ideologically compromised as blank verse (97–109). First, poets exploit the possibility of turning forms against themselves by embodying in them "unsuitable" thematic content. In his careful and illuminating reading of Zukofsky's "Mantis," Davidson demonstrates Zukofsky's deployment of the "ideology of form," showing how he struggles with the traditional associations of the sestina as he subjects the form to "'ungainly' issues of poverty and alienation" (117, 120). Davidson's work, in fact, goes beyond Easthope's to make an important point about poetic form's ideological saturation. The "ideology of form," Davidson argues, is "the idea that formal procedures derive from and generate critical frames" (133). The apparent lack of fit between ostensibly conservative form (the overwrought and overdetermined sestina) and putatively radical political content is a potential resource for political poets to exploit (even as it presents a potential obstacle to the poet's immediate political aims).

Edwin Rolfe performs a similar operation on the sonnet in "Portrait of a Death," published in the 1933 anthology, *We Gather Strength*. The only sonnet in the book, the poem at first seems misplaced, perhaps even miscast. What is the role of this form in a book of "workers' poems" by the avant-garde Herman Spector, the Whitmanesque Joseph Kalar, and the modernist Sol Funaroff? No less odd is the scene described in the sonnet's three quatrains. The death portrayed here is that of capitalist society, depicted as a "slowly-sinking octopus," its "tentacles in greedy disarray." Rolfe reworks images of capitalist prosperity—the ticker tape and the radio—transforming them into symptoms of the system's fatal illness:

The ticker-bandage on his wrist connotes
arterio-sclerosis of his veins;
no longer can the wireless call for votes
to speed false dawn when day already wanes.
(*Collected Poems,* 266)[22]

The last line of the poem concludes the long description with the expected radical prognosis: "His the swift death! and ours again the earth!" The sonnet's compression and its strictness allow Rolfe to explore the grotesque image of dying capitalism and guard against a poetic growth and overindulgence that would strangle the poem as its economic counterpart does the octopus. At the same time, though, the sonnet, awkwardly closing its rhyming, metered lines around the bloated image and the bombastic exhortation, comes to seem part of the dying system, an example of the inefficacious speech Rolfe thematically depicts.

But "Portrait of a Death" also exploits aspects of the form it seems to strain against: the enormous popularity and familiarity of the sonnet, its immediate recognizability among audiences. While it is outnumbered in Francis Palgrave's *Golden Treasury* and E. C. Stedman's *American Anthology, 1787–1900* by poems in hymn meter and quatrains, the sonnet is well represented in these two most common volumes in American poetry readers' libraries. Moreover, among the middle-brow mass-circulation magazines that published verse in the late nineteenth and early twentieth centuries—*Century, Harper's, Scribner's,* and *Atlantic*—the sonnet is a popular form.[23] While the form does not appear as frequently in the pages of newspapers, which also, it must be remembered, regularly published verse, it is not uncommon to see the occasional sonnet in the *New York Times, Boston Globe* or *San Francisco Examiner.* And perhaps even more important a factor in the sonnet's familiarity was the place of poetry in American education during the last decades of the nineteenth century and the first decades of the twentieth.[24] Prominent in that poetic education was the sonnet, as practiced by Spenser and Shakespeare and, more often, Emerson and Bryant.[25]

On one hand, it is precisely this familiarity that makes it so difficult to rearticulate the sonnet to a specific set of social aims. The form's presence in anthologies like Palgrave's and Stedman's locates it in an institutional formation that certainly works to foreclose, or at least hinder, any attempt to detach the sonnet and, in Hall's phrase, "simply put it in another place." But on the other hand, the sonnet's recognizability, its place in just this formation of tradition, literary publishing, and educational institutions, grants it the cultural capital a politically engaged poet might want to invest in the specific agenda he or she advocates. Rolfe is up to just this sort of attempt when, during the anti-Communist inquisition of the early 1950s, he writes "In Praise Of" about a victim of political persecution:

> Therefore I honor him, this simple man
> who never clearly saw the threatening shapes, yet fought
> his complex enemies, the whole sadistic clan,
> persistently, although unschooled. Untaught,
> he taught us, who could talk so glibly, what
> the world's true shape should be like, and what not. (*CP*, 223)

Readers (of the *California Quarterly* in this case) schooled in the "genteel tradition" as well as the political poetry in traditional forms that so often graced the last page of the *Daily Worker* would recognize in Rolfe's sonnet a culturally sanctioned discourse. It is this discourse that Rolfe mobilizes to shape and reflect on a lesson taught during difficult times. It is in part on the form's familiarity and assumed elevation and authority that he depends for the lesson's impact.[26]

But there is more than one tradition of the sonnet, more than one set of institutions through which its popularity and prominence were secured and exploited, and political poets setting out to rearticulate the form are aided in their efforts by the multiplicity of traditions available to them, the variable histories through which a particular form descends into their hands. The form has a dominant and familiar tradition that begins with Dante and Petrarch; crosses the English Channel with Wyatt; gradually shifts under the hands of Surrey, Sidney, Spenser, Shakespeare, Donne, and Milton; drops out of sight until rescued by Wordsworth and Keats; and wends its way through Meredith, Hardy, Hopkins, Frost, and Yeats. Within this tradition, the form tends toward a fairly limited set of thematic associations, a fairly limited range of cultural functions. The sonnet typically treats love ("Whoso List to Hunt," "Love that doth reign and live within my thought," *Astrophil and Stella, Amoretti,* "Let me not to the marriage of true minds"), religion (Holy Sonnets, "When I consider how my light is spent," "The Windhover"), or fate and mortality ("No longer mourn for me when I am dead," "How Soon Hath Time," "When I have fears that I may cease to be," "Carrion Comfort," "Hap"). But a political strand is twined through even this dominant braid. Some of the poems I list here treat, in coded ways, political pressures, problems, anxieties, and agendas. But many more sonnets take up politics much more explicitly.

In 1802, when William Wordsworth feels compelled to write a poem critical of his contemporary society, he finds in the sonnet not only the supple and powerful means for condensing political vision into complex figures and logical schemes but also the example of Milton. He exploits this whole range of resources to justify and empower his social critique:

> Milton! thou should'st be living at this hour:
> England hath need of thee: she is a fen
> Of stagnant waters: altar, sword, and pen,
> Fireside, the heroic wealth of hall and bower,
> Have forfeited their ancient English dower
> Of inward happiness. We are selfish men;
> Oh! raise us up, return to us again;
> And give us manners, virtue, freedom, power. (172)²⁷

The sonnet's political possibilities run through the English poetic tradition as a sometimes buried seam, revealed anew when poets return to mine it, as both Milton and Wordsworth did.²⁸ And poets writing after the likes of Milton and Wordsworth—like those whose work is gathered in Brian Maidment's anthology of nineteenth-century workers' poetry and Peter Scheckner's *Anthology of Chartist Poetry*— have the earlier poets' use of the sonnet for political purposes behind their own deployment of the form. When, in mainstream and partisan American newspapers of the early twentieth century, from the *New York Times* and *Boston Globe* to the *Daily Worker* and *The Masses,* we find numerous sonnets on such subjects as the Spanish-American War, the plight of workers, and women's suffrage or when, in *America Arraigned!,* we find fourteen sonnets on Sacco and Vanzetti—one-third of the poems gathered to protest the execution (including Countee Cullen's "Not Sacco and Vanzetti" and Alfred Kreymborg's "August 22nd: A Red-Letter Day")—we see poets using the alternative tradition of the sonnet as they work to rearticulate the form, to decouple it from one meaning-granting formation of social forces and join it with another.

The variable traditions manifest themselves in varying institutions as well. The institutional formations through which the sonnet typically circulated—the moralizing popular magazines, the schools— provide a sense of poetry's cultural work that is at once available for rearticulation and a factor in the rearticulation of the sonnet. As Van

Wienen writes, "[O]nce poetry was defined as a field of social and moral practice, it was not so difficult for writers, publishers, and even political activists to connect poetic production to a more comprehensive program of social action" (10). Poetry is put to work in those comprehensive programs in a variety of ways, from party-aligned or independent publishing ventures to magazines (associated with trade unions, political parties, and, later, the John Reed Clubs of the Communist Party), from poetry readings to the poetry cards distributed at rallies and the International Workers of the World's *Little Red Songbook*.[29] Politically committed poets throughout the decades between the wars (and throughout history) avail themselves of all of these resources and resistances to claim through poetry a powerful authority for their specific engagements.

This book attempts to put some of the political poetry written and published between 1920 and 1950 back into circulation, albeit the very limited circulation afforded a book of this kind. More important, though, it argues that this poetry has value to us. To read the poems collected in *America Arraigned!* or periodically published in the *Daily Worker* or the *New Masses* is to remember the sorts of cultural work expected of this supposedly most personal and inwardly turning genre, to see the variety of ways in which poetry was made to participate in very public and externally focused struggles.

We are trained and accustomed to evaluate poems in formal terms, to prize formal perfection. Such evaluative terms, though, simply do not fit much of the work surveyed in the chapters that follow or much of the partisan poetry published between the world wars (or ever published). Indeed, trying to claim value for such poetry on the basis of formal perfection opens the door to a quick dismissal of partisan poetry as formally flawed (to say the least). In his work on Edwin Rolfe, Cary Nelson has claimed that Rolfe's poetry meets the criteria for poetic excellence established by formalists like the New Critics. While Nelson's arguments for Rolfe's importance do not depend on this claim, his rationale for why Rolfe has been repressed from American cultural memory is bolstered by his sense of Rolfe's quality as a poet: "Rolfe is one of the politically committed poets whose work largely meets New Critical standards for producing formally coherent, metaphorically inventive, fully realized, and self-sufficient poems. That he is almost wholly excluded from our cultural memory demonstrates that political—not merely purported disinterested aesthetic—criteria have helped determine what poets we honor in our texts and literary histories" (*Repression and Recovery*, 114). Rolfe's latter-day reception—poems published in *Triquarterly*, a full-page rave in the *New York Review of Books* for the 1993 *Collected Poems* that Nelson edited—seems to support Nelson's claim. But the argument on New Critical grounds invites attacks like the one Marjorie Perloff makes on Rolfe in her reading of the 1930s journal *Pagany*. Perloff singles out Rolfe's "Entreaty at Delphi" to show that New Critics like Cleanth Brooks and Allen Tate might have legitimate aesthetic complaints about Rolfe's poetry and need never address his politics; they "would have complained of the laxity of the poem's diction and the self-indulgence of its tone," she writes (*Poetry on and off the Page*, 80). Later in the same essay, Perloff quotes Rolfe's "Poem for May First," which appeared in the first issue of the *Partisan Review* (1934), only to tar it with the "genteel" and "echo of Longfellow" brushes (81). It is worth pointing out that Perloff not only dismisses the unironic, the sentimental, and the nonmodernist but also chooses two poems to represent Rolfe that were published fairly early in his career, two poems he chose not to include in his first book (or any subsequent collection), two poems, in other words, that he knew did not measure up aesthetically. Judging Rolfe on the basis of these poems is something like judging Ezra Pound on the basis of "Salutation the Third." But Perloff is able, through her choices, quite easily to make a case that answers Nelson's claim.

Perhaps more important, arguments for the aesthetic quality of political poems miss the point of the poems' "way of being." To paraphrase Karl Marx, the poems Rolfe wrote during the bleak early-depression years, the poems Muriel Rukeyser wrote in the aftermath of a labor disaster that took hundreds of lives, were intended not only to explain the world but also to change it. They were intended not to stand as well-wrought urns amenable to scrupulous rhetorical and formal analysis, bearing their ironic ash within seamless and burnished tropes and metrical patterns, but to energize an audience, to articulate a program for social change through values held by many of their readers, to expand the range of imaginable political possibilities, the "common sense" that is the terrain of what Gramsci calls the "war of position" in "civil society."

Perhaps the most eloquent expression of this sense of cultural work and the attendant shift in criteria for quality is Jane Tompkins's in *Sensational Designs:*

> When literary texts are conceived as agents of cultural formation rather than as objects of interpretation and appraisal, what counts as "good" . . . changes accordingly. When one sets aside modernist demands—for psychological complexity, formal ambiguity, epistemological sophistication, stylistic density, formal economy—and attends to the way a text offers a blueprint for survival under a specific set of political, economic, social, or religious conditions, an entirely new story begins to unfold, and one's sense of the formal exigencies of [literature] alters accordingly, producing a different conception of what constitutes success. (xvii)

Tompkins's formulation is taken up by Van Wienen in his discussion of partisan poetry of World War I and by Susan Schweik in her treatment of women's poetry of World War II, and it remains a clear statement of the need for alternative evaluative criteria for literary works whose aims are the kind of "cultural formation" she describes.

We might, therefore, judge the works of partisan political poets on their salutarity, on how well a given poem achieves its own aim inasmuch as that aim might be determined and described. Success, then, might not be seen as such according to New Critical canons or protocols, which demand the irony and intricacy that give rise to elaborate close readings. But if our standard is the generally accepted and shared taste developed by and evinced in such publications as mass-circulation magazines and newspapers, the very vehicles through which much of the poetry under discussion in this study circulated, many partisan poems measure up. A successful poem, given this understanding, is one that deploys poetic conventions—figurative language; heightened attention to the materiality of language through rhyme, assonance, consonance, and alliteration; and meter and rhythm—to link its political significance to an inviting, pleasurable, and compelling verbal texture that grants readers an opportunity to reflect on, in an affectively fraught textual environment, the poem's thematic burden.

The partisan political poetry at the heart of this study invites us to reflect not only on how we evaluate poems but also on what we value in poems and, on that basis, what kind of poems we value. Paul Lauter, in *Canons and Contexts,* values the literary production of working-class writers and other writers outside the political "mainstream" because it helps us see "how art has functioned in historically specific situations to develop and sustain marginalized communities" (65). This art, produced and circulated in the social space of "a particular group of people facing particular problems at a particular moment in time," aims not at timelessness or transcendence but precisely at its time, and it helps us realize a wider variety of art's or literature's usefulness and value to the communities in which and for which it is produced (65). Such art, Lauter argues, "aimed to inspire consciousness about and actions within the world, indeed to enlarge the world" its readers could experience (66). Its value to us, readers removed by time and circumstance, by training and values, from the work's initial audience, is to show how "cultural activity . . . becomes part of a process for transforming people from passive sufferers into activists" (67).

Lauter also notes the collective character of much working-class artistic production, and this production and circulation in group situations gives rise to another potential value such writing can have for contemporary readers. At the most pragmatic level, the romantic ideal of the individual writer at work in privacy is challenged by the competing ideal of a communal author (literally a group or a writer sustained by and writing for a group). The aim of individual self-expression is similarly challenged by an ambition to express a larger consciousness (65–67). It is this ideal that Kalaidjian finds operative in much leftist political poetry of the 1930s. Writing that we need to "consider how depression-era poetry actually functioned as a potent catalyst for changing views of self and society," Kalaidjian singles out as especially important the "transpersonal" poetics manifest in collective efforts like anthologies and choral chants (*American Culture*, 52–53) and in individual poets' attempts to speak as and for the collective (56–57).[30] Such poetry, Kalaidjian argues, should help us "see how our own contemporary allegiance to possessive individualism is not so much a 'natural' as it is a historically contingent credo" (57).

The values Lauter and Kalaidjian locate in 1930s political writing, as well as Kalaidjian's echo of Barbara Herrnstein Smith's *Contingencies of Value*, point to a final reason for recovering and valuing the partisan poetry I treat in this book: it casts into relief the contingency and constructedness of our criteria for evaluating poetry, denaturalizing what we might all too easily take for granted as the commonsense values of poetry. As Kalaidjian effectively makes the point, "The shock of radical difference that we confront in proletcult verse—a difference that violates nearly everything we have been disciplined to expect from poetry—highlights how our personal reading habits are themselves not just 'normative' but always already positioned in relation to particular critical genealogies" (*American Culture,* 58).

It is perhaps useful to clarify this point with an example. Of Rolfe's "Kentucky—1932," a poem that certainly does not measure up to formalist criteria for aesthetic excellence, Eric Homberger writes that Rolfe is "scarcely using the medium" (113). While "Kentucky—1932" is admittedly a "bad poem" under dominant evaluative criteria, it *is* a poem:

> Out of darkness, out of the pits now—
> foreigners only to the light of day—
> claiming the mountains in the sudden glow
> of battle, welded in mass array,
> shouting!
>> This is our land, we planted its first seed!
>> These are our mines, our hands dig the coal!
>> These roads are ours, the wires across the land
>> are ours! THIS IS OUR EARTH! (*CP,* 71)

Rolfe figures a workers' rising as a resurrection. His lines are propelled by rhythmic regularity. The language's physical properties are foregrounded through repetition—assonance, alliteration, occasional rhyme. The poem "scarcely [uses] the medium" only if we define "the medium" not by such things, then, but instead by reference to some essence not apparent in its visible properties. The medium is essentially transcendent and nonpropositional, divorced from exhortation, distinct from such instrumental political discourses as the smear, the slogan, or the battle cry. It is a unified mode of language entirely segregated from the propositional or persuasive. But "the medium" is in fact inextricable from those discourses against which it is often defined. Rolfe is "scarcely using the medium" because he addresses poetry's "fixed 'other,'" writing on a political event and attempting to galvanize an audience, to urge political action, instead of turning language on itself in an attempt to achieve transcendence. He puts poetry's linguistic and rhetorical tools to work for purposes other than strictly literary idealization. He blurs the line of demarcation between poetry and its "others." According to one contingent set of values, this makes the poem worthless. According to another set of values, admittedly no less contingent, the poem's aims are precisely what render it valuable.

Each of the four chapters that follow takes up an individual poet, but the four divide into two pairs. Edwin Rolfe and Langston Hughes both illustrate the powerful political potential of traditional verse forms in the hands of gifted political poets. Rolfe develops a fairly conservative poetics and draws on traditional tropes of postromantic lyric in his poetry, but he adapts these to meet the changing historical pressures of the Popular Front, the Spanish Civil War, and postwar anticommunism. Rolfe's resourcefulness enables him to articulate a radical politics of both force and beauty, to exercise poetic options that partisan accounts of the period have claimed were unavailable to poets on the Left. In a similar way, Langston Hughes's effectiveness as a political poet rests on his ability to reach out from his complex cultural position to fashion temporary tactical alliances between such diverse communities as, for example, Harlem writers and the Communist Party of the United States. Faced with the Scottsboro trial, the Spanish Civil War, and the example of the Soviet Union, Hughes constructs and draws on a distinctively African American literary tradition to advance his deep commitment to the Left and to perform his articulation of revolutionary politics through considerations of race.

The experimental poetics of literary modernism present a quite different set of resources for the political poet. In the cantos of the late 1930s, the poetry Ezra Pound wrote as Europe moved inexorably toward another war, we find Pound working to imagine a community of like-minded Americans, working to construct a common sense that supported American neutrality. In Chapter 3, I read this poetry, especially Cantos 62–71, the Adams Cantos, alongside Pound's prose of the period to show how Pound articulates not only social credit economics but also Fascist politics and isolationist polemics through the juxtaposition of fragments drawn from his source texts. Muriel Rukeyser attempts to work out a political praxis through experimental verse heavily influenced by such modernists as Pound. In her 1938 poem-sequence, *The Book of the Dead,* Rukeyser combines the allusive and fragmentary modernist poetics of Pound with a documentary practice informed by photographers and filmmakers. Deploying the documentary tropes of case study and exposé quotation, Rukeyser lays bare the devices by which corporations and their allies in the courts and the government conspire to evade their culpability for workers' deaths. She then works through these same means to construct a new version of "the truth," a version that offers workers and those who sympathize with them the means for change.

Pound's and Rukeyser's projects suggest not only a continuum of the political uses to which modernist poetic practice could be put but also a range of Americas or American histories available for deployment in poetic (and prose) attempts to imagine communities for political change. Pound's articulation of Adams to the cause of American neutrality foregrounds the nation's Enlightenment birth, its institutions' establishment of order. In her evocation and invocation of John Brown, Rukeyser proffers an America at whose core lies rebellion and devotion to ideals of freedom and equality. Both poets' visions are shaped by, and at the same time seek to shape, the America of the 1930s.

The institutional supports for partisan political poetry between the world wars largely disappear during the late-1940s transition from global war to Cold War. The awarding of the Pulitzer Prize to Robert Lowell in 1947 and of the Bollingen Prize to Pound in 1949 signals a decisive depoliticizing of mainstream American literary institutions. Those tendencies, which came to dominate literary study in the 1950s, constituted a complex response to changing political pressures in the postwar United States, pressures most clearly represented by the domestic anticommunism epitomized by Joseph McCarthy. This forced segregation of literature from politics ultimately resulted in the retreat of many politically engaged poets into an underground of small magazines and private publishing, while it encouraged others, especially a younger generation, to explore new means and new myths through which resistance to the dominant political culture might be expressed.

I

Tradition and the Political Poet

EDWIN ROLFE

"No poet . . . has his complete meaning alone." T. S. Eliot wrote this, and as his readers know, it is as true of Eliot as of anyone. Indeed, it is, at least in part, to justify his own allusive poetics, his elaborate demonstrations of literary erudition, his gathering of poetic fragments, that Eliot composed "Tradition and the Individual Talent" and published it in the *Egoist* in 1919. The essay is, of course, one of the landmark publications in Anglo-American literary modernism, a famous and influential defense of the impersonal in poetry, a manifesto for the modernism Eliot is teaching readers to accept, a primer in the aesthetic judgment of new poetry. And it is a brief for a sort of qualified novelty, a newness in poetry that comes, paradoxically, from poetry's relationship with the very old. "If we approach a poet without this [antitraditional] prejudice," Eliot writes, "we shall often find that not only the best, but the most individual parts of his work may be those in which the dead poets, his ancestors, assert their immortality most vigorously" (48).

Literary critics have, ever since, used Eliot's essay (just as he intended) to explain the practices of famous modernist poets, and the essay really does illuminate and rationalize the sometimes bewildering welter of allusion and fragmentary reference in *The Waste Land* or *The Cantos*. On the surface, it might seem as though "Tradition and the Individual Talent" has nothing to do with the work of partisan political poets writing in the wake of its famous publication. Political writers themselves provide a basis for this claim, at least when they are read selectively or superficially. Mike Gold, after all, did use his position as editor of the *New Masses* to urge writers to leave behind "the dead horses of Bible mysticism, Greek fatalism, Roman decadence, and British snobbery" ("Let It Be Really New," 26). But critics writing about political poets from the outside tend more frequently to segregate political poetry from Eliot's concerns. As early as the mid-1930s, William Phillips and Philip Rahv argued that political poets had a very different relationship to history from that envisioned and urged by Eliot. Instead of the "historical sense" that acknowledges "not only the pastness of the past, but . . . its presence" (Eliot, "Tradition," 49), Phillips and Rahv claim that poets on the Left attempted to "become the conscience of history spurring on the working class to its 'inevitable' tasks" (171). Political orthodoxy demands a dissociation from the "ideal order" that, Eliot claimed, was formed by the "existing monuments."

There is ample evidence in the voluminous political writing and the energetic theorizing of political literature in the 1920s and 1930s to challenge this assumption. James Murphy quite effectively shows both the incorrectness of this interpretation, in which all proletarian literature and criticism is "leftist," and the important fact that Phillips, Rahv, and others in the *Partisan Review* circle had themselves written "leftist" criticism during the early 1930s. While Phillips and Rahv lambaste Mike Gold, Granville Hicks, and other proletarian critics for leftism, they fail to recognize the antileftist writings of Joseph Freeman, for example, who published critiques of leftism in the *Daily Worker* as early as 1933, as well as important changes in the thought of critics like Gold, who by 1933 was also questioning his earlier positions on proletarian literature and criticism (Murphy, 133). At the same time, the orthodox account overlooks writings by Rahv from the early 1930s, in which he argues that writers on the Left should only selectively place themselves in positive relation to the literary tradition, writing in 1932, for example, that from the "symbolists and the romantics . . . the proletarian writers can learn little" (quoted in ibid., 151).

In this chapter, I want to revise the conventional wisdom about political poetry's relationship with "the tradition" through the example of Edwin Rolfe, an indisputably "political" poet. Rolfe's career is shaped by a relationship to literary tradition quite similar to the one Eliot recommends. A lifelong Communist, Rolfe both argued for and practiced an informed and informing relationship to the bourgeois/romantic literary tradition and the lyric aesthetic concomitant with that tradition in ways that challenge the still-dominant view recently summed up by Eric Homberger: "Within the notoriously humorless Communist Party, and on the American Left as a whole, bourgeois culture was viewed with contempt. The atmosphere within the party was aggressively philistine" (109).

While Rolfe's aims remain constant throughout his career, his specific poetic strategies shift in important and illuminating ways. Historical changes forced alterations in the specific political ends toward which the poetry worked and in Rolfe's ideas of what poetry could actually accomplish in the political world. Confronting the widespread misery caused by the economic depression of the 1930s, Rolfe works through the lyric in an effort simultaneously to represent the suffering of individuals and to overcome the atomization sustained by a cultural insistence on individual experience. In the International Brigades, in the concerted effort to defend democracy and resist fascism in Spain, Rolfe found the collective political response his poetry of the 1930s had sought, explored, and urged. But when the Spanish struggle ended in defeat for the republic and when his own country betrayed its citizens in a McCarthyite spasm of cultural hysteria, Rolfe was forced to rethink the political potential of his chosen medium, to search the repertoire of the tradition for a means to memorialize Spain, to preserve for a more propitious moment the values the republic stood for. In his last years, Rolfe found in the tradition the resources for a poetry at once critical of the censorious political climate of the United States in the 1950s and dedicated to the memory of those whose lives were warped by that climate.

In 1935, sixteen years after the publication of "Tradition and the Individual Talent," Rolfe published his own manifesto in the *Partisan Review*. Rolfe's essay is a substantial statement on political poetics, a statement that adapts Eliot's view of the poet's proper relationship with tradition. Rolfe argues for the importance of a complete integration of political thought with personal emotion, the necessity of poetic form, and the usefulness of an appropriate relationship with the English poetic tradition. The poetry renaissance America has hoped for, Rolfe begins, has not happened, though the necessary elements are present in the American literary scene. Rolfe's list of these prerequisites is revealing, for in it he links political radicalism and a "clear sense of tradition, of continuity, of exciting living in the midst of profound social and spiritual change" ("Poetry," 32). Significantly, though, Rolfe castigates those poets whose relationship to the tradition is one of simple, slavish imitation, whom he calls the "little half-dead lyricists who ape and thereby insult what they regard as 'tradition.'" His sense of the importance of poetic tradition echoes Eliot's: the poet must, in some ways, measure himself against the tradition but must, in the spirit of those poets whose work makes up the tradition, also alter it through his or her own efforts. "Only the poets who announce change," Rolfe writes, "can herald a new day in American poetry." But Rolfe does not want poetry to affect only poetry, does not want the work of contemporary poets simply to jostle with the "great works" in some ethereal realm where "the tradition" floats, a celestial book-case into which new works seek admission. "To be significant in the most real sense," he argues, "a poet must affect not only other poets, as some of these older poets have influenced us; he must leave his mark on the world in which he lives and in which other men live" (33). The poet's relationship to the literary tradition must be one out of which the poet fashions work that will contribute directly to the lives of people other than poets.

The tension between these requirements runs throughout Rolfe's article. He recalls, for example, the early work of political poets like himself and the difficulty they found in bringing their political thought to poetry: "Every poem was a call to action: an exhortation to the reader to awake from his political lethargy and join the class-conscious forces of the working class. Other poems described accidents in shops, bemoaned the trials and miseries of long hours and slavish conditions in the factories. It was, in short, journalistic verse that we wrote—serving the same purpose as a polemic, although far less effectively. It was not literature" (37). These poets' poems failed to function *as poems* rather than polemics because the poets tried to isolate themselves from their work and to isolate their work from other poetry; the poets tried to "sit down and say 'I am going to write a revolutionary poem.'" In spite of the wealth of poetic examples and forms readily available in "the great literary tradition of history," these poets, Rolfe among them, tried to make their way without regard for form, without recourse to the tradition's resources. Politicized poets failed to make vital poetry of their themes precisely because and to the extent that they neglected "the great literary tradition." Rolfe offers, as the solution to this isolation, the advice he received from Joseph Freeman: "Stop thinking of yourselves . . . as poets who are also revolutionists or as revolutionists who are also poets. Remember that you are *revolutionary poets*" (38; emphasis in original). The two roles, political and poetic, must be fused, just as, Rolfe writes, the intellectual political commitment of the artist must itself be fused with the other aspects of the artist's life.

An emotional and ideological identification with the working class, Rolfe writes, will partly, but only partly, address these shortcomings. But revolutionary poets must also resist the tendency Rolfe saw in himself and others to reject the poetic tradition. This rejection is not a necessary corollary to the complete identification with the working class: "Such an identification, again, does not mean that the poet will discard the great historical traditions with which he has become acquainted in the bourgeois world. Quite the contrary: it means that he will perceive traditions in clearer, more understandable terms" (39). Contrary to these poets' earlier ideas, attention to formal execution and the literary tradition is not simply the province of bourgeois writers and is not incommensurable with politically committed writing. Rather, Rolfe argues, these aspects of writing are themselves revolutionary, and the revolutionary poet's duty is to "work hard at your poetry," to produce work that is vital because it grows out of an integration of the political and the poetic, out of a relationship with the tradition that finds and foregrounds the tradition's own radical potential.[1]

Rolfe's assertion that political poetry must emerge from the actual experience of the individual writer, must embody the unity of the writer's philosophy and experience rather than the abstract historical consciousness of a class, aligns him with a faction of writers on the Left who during the early 1930s began to argue that proletarian writers needed to abandon the easy abstraction of polemics and slogans (an abstraction, it must be admitted, toward which much of Rolfe's own early work often tends) and to address the importance of literary form. Murphy shows the emergence of this position in the writings of Mike Gold, Joseph Freeman, and others in the *Daily Worker* and *New Masses.*[2] He characterizes the approach to proletarian literature that begins, around 1933, to appear in these periodicals as a new "insistence on artistic quality . . . coupled with the demand for thematic diversification" (122). Writers, Rolfe and others began to argue, must expand the scope of their political awareness to take in those parts of their lives not immediately recognizable as political (thereby bringing into their work the entirety of social reality) and must work to succeed in terms of literary form.[3]

Early reactions to Rolfe's poetry locate it firmly at one end of a continuum of aesthetic choices available to poets on the Left. In his introduction to *We Gather Strength,* the 1933 collection of poems by Rolfe, Herman Spector, Joseph Kalar, and Sol Funaroff, Gold writes that, more than the other poets in the volume, Rolfe has "a marked sense of design; he has been affected by all the influences of modern bourgeois poetry, T. S. Eliot, Ezra Pound, William Carlos Williams. One watches in him a conflict between these influences and the crude primitive material of revolution. . . . Rolfe is spectator; he is critic; his judgements are cool and accurate" (8). On the jacket of Rolfe's first solo effort, *To My Contemporaries,* Horace Gregory writes in a similar vein: "Edwin Rolfe's poetry combines, with unusual integration, the major forces in the contemporary literature of the west. It stems from the romantic tradition which is our common heritage, and which, in its greatest protagonists, Shelley, Byron, Heine, is intransigent and revolutionary." Gregory continues by finding in Rolfe's poetry similarities to Whitman and to the "renaissance of 1912," the poetry of Sandburg and Lindsay, and to offer, as Rolfe's "most immediate heritage," the poetry of the contemporary revolutionary movement. From these disparate traditions and their components, Rolfe "has fashioned a poetry of his own which is as original as it is melodious, as lyrical as it is revolutionary."

An index of Rolfe's commitment to what Cary Nelson has called "lyric politics" is Rolfe's devotion, throughout his career, to the sonnet. In the Introduction, I briefly touched on one of Rolfe's earliest sonnets ("Portrait of a Death"). While this poem, rightly, fails to make it into Rolfe's 1936 *To My Contemporaries* (whereas all of the other poems Rolfe published in *We Gather Strength* do appear in the later volume), the book includes three other sonnets: "Faces No Longer White," "Unit Meeting," and "Definition." Of these, only "Definition" comes close to succeeding even according to the criteria Rolfe establishes in his *Partisan Review* essay (though "Unit Meeting"—a valiantly doomed effort to romanticize, through poetic form, the drudgery of real work for social change—might take the prize for oddest subject matter approached through the sonnet). And while imperfect in its execution, "Definition" does marshal the sonnet's history as a love and seduction poem to both castigate the false comrade who hails the speaker and prize the great "love for fellow men that motivates our kind" (*CP*, 96). *First Love and Other Poems*, Rolfe's second book, includes nine sonnets and a poem ("At the Moment of Victory") whose three stanzas are sonnets (the poem was originally published in 1946 in the *Saturday Review of Literature* as "Three Sonnets"). And *Permit Me Refuge*, Rolfe's last book, published posthumously in 1955, gathers six sonnets (seven if one counts "Poem," an unrhymed poem in two seven-line stanzas), including "Bon Voyage," the final poem in the volume and the poem from which it draws its title.

At the end of his career, Rolfe still found it useful to explore political terrain in a sonnet, to bring the associative networks of the form to bear on the contemporary scene. This is evident in "In Praise Of," first published in 1954 in the *California Quarterly* and later collected in *Permit Me Refuge:*

> To understand the strength of those dark forces
> phalanxed against him would have spelled surrender:
> the spiked fist, the assassin's knife, the horses'
> eyeless hooves above as he fell under.
> To understand the sum of all this terror
> would *a priori* have meant defeat, disaster.
> Born of cold panic, error would pile on error,
> heart and mind fall apart like fragile plaster.
> Therefore I honor him, this simple man
> who never clearly saw the threatening shapes, yet fought
> his complex enemies, the whole sadistic clan,
> persistently, although unschooled. Untaught,
> he taught us, who could talk so glibly, what
> the world's true shape should be like, and what not. (*CP*, 223)

While some of Rolfe's earlier sonnets find him, as Homberger writes of "Kentucky—1932," "scarcely using the medium" (113), this late example gives us a mature poet's use of form against itself, a cannily ironic deployment of a form's associations. In it, Rolfe encapsulates both the menace of postwar anti-Communist paranoia and the only strategy left with which to fight against that menace—stubborn, unreflective resistance. The octave sets out the problem any leftist would encounter in 1950s America; at all levels, in all places, lurk dangers as threatening as marauding armies. More dangerous than these, though, is the awareness of them. To know all that one is up against can lead only to paralysis. The forces arrayed against the poem's protagonist are so numerous, so powerful, so inexorable and ineffable, that an accurate appraisal, a recognition of their strength and multiplicity, would on its own crush him. In the sestet, Rolfe finds in the protagonist's partial ignorance the ground for praise. Unable to assess his enemies, this "simple man" fights on. His example takes on powerful, though paradoxical, significance. "Untaught, / he taught us, who could talk so glibly"; laboring without benefit of subtle understanding, the protagonist compels the speaker to understand. Schooled in subtleties, the speaker talks in the face of those dark forces; his glibness masks a willed impotence, a version of the surrender elaborated in the octave. Blind and untaught, the protagonist teaches the speaker not the truth of things as they are but how they ought to be. More important, the speaker learns what "the world's true shape" ought *not* to be. From blindness, insight; from ignorance, imaginative resolution.

Rolfe plays on the sonnet's two-part structure to explore this paradox and on the form's forced compression to give it added sharpness. In altering the traditional rhyme scheme of the last three lines, Rolfe calls our attention to the poem's ultimate message: "taught," "what," "not." The protagonist's example provokes a recognition of the present's distance from "the world's true shape." But the Petrarchan sonnet's traditional associations give force to yet another paradox at work here. The vehicle for praise of the distant and unattainable beloved, the sonnet is not simply a poem of love; it is an exercise in seduction, a dense cluster of verbal strategies by which the poet hopes to realize love's true shape. Thus burdened with conventions both formal and rhetorical, the sonnet is a "schooled" form, harbor and home to glibness through its centuries-long career. A sonneteer in "In Praise Of," Rolfe enacts the glib talk he decries and exemplifies the protagonist's paralyzed counterpart. But at the same time, Rolfe's educated, practiced formal exercise enables the protagonist to endure. Without the poem, "this simple man" disappears, perhaps overwhelmed after all by those phalanxed forces. In the political realm as well as in the wider world of love, Rolfe's formal choice implies, poetry attempts to draw the "is" and the "ought" together.

Early on in Rolfe's career, and through the 1930s, his poems reflect his belief in the ability of lyric poems on political topics simultaneously to work as closed, independent entities and to intervene in concrete political struggles. Through the depiction in his poetry of the plight of workers, of mass political actions in which individual consciousness is superseded for a broader social good, Rolfe attempts to connect his poems directly to political action. Rolfe deploys traditional poetics to construct poems whose political messages are enhanced by their poetic compression and density.

One of Rolfe's most accomplished early political lyrics, for example, is "Asbestos," which was first published in the *Daily Worker* as "The 100 Percenter" on September 22, 1928. In this poem, we find the kind of grimly fascinating representation of the exploited and alienated worker typical of Rolfe's 1930s poetry. A simple laborer, John, works like an animal; he cannot imagine a different state of affairs. A workhorse whose sweat binds the granite stones of a tower, John becomes what he builds; he is dehumanized by the circumstances in which he works. Ignorant of alternatives to his demeaning work, incapable of communicating with those who share his fate, John makes himself a monument to his own misery—"the edifice his bone had built." In Rolfe's hands, though, the transformation of man into monument is reversed as the poet answers the challenge his first stanza poses. Knowing how men act when "roused from lethargy" and, unlike John, having something to say, Rolfe builds an edifice of his own from the resources of lyric poetry—compression, extended metaphor, meter, and rhyme—to rouse readers, to show how "dead workers are dead before they cease to be." Whereas the first two stanzas' figures transform John into things, the third stanza's conceit humanizes an object:

> John's deathbed is a curious affair:
> the posts are made of bone, the spring of nerves,
> the mattress bleeding flesh. (*CP*, 62)

Rolfe condenses man and mattress to render alienated labor's abject death-in-life. And the metrical regularity, along with the quatrains' rhymes, intensifies the drama Rolfe's images enact. Squared like the corners of the deathbed's mattress, these lines lead inexorably to the poem's epigrammatic conclusion.

Such conceits, though, are far less common in Rolfe's poetry than a more sustained attempt to articulate revolutionary political ideology through the tropes of a revisionary romanticism. In "Brickyards at Beacon," which first appeared in the *Daily Worker* on June 22, 1929, Rolfe describes anonymous toilers in a way that records their struggle and labor with a bleak beauty that turns romantic contemplation of landscape against itself. The natural prospect that someone with leisure might enjoy is tainted by the brickyard's atmosphere of misery:

> Here, on the rivershore, the edge of music,
> of water flowing, melodious, to sea,
> they work: and the rainbow is obscured;
> the sunshower seen through smoke-haze seems
> unreal, repellent;
> the west wind rolling across the Berkshires
> meets inferno heat here
> and is absorbed into heat, becomes heat.
> They who work here know no other things;
> only heat and smoke and fumes of baking bricks. (*CP*, 63)

Rolfe interrupts what seems in the first lines a romantic contemplation of the beauty of nature by focusing on the hellish prospect of the brick factory, implicating, thereby, not only the factory for despoiling the scene of the rivershore and the rainbow but also the poetry that would ignore that wreckage; indeed, the "west wind," which seems to recall Shelley and which symbolizes the powerful forces of nature apostrophized by the romantic poet, is annihilated by the heat of the brickyard. Romantic contemplation is absorbed by the production of commodities. Rolfe resists the Wordsworthian tendency to aestheticize the suffering of the workers, to ground an independent poetic resolution in the plight of, say, a leech-gatherer, by showing the suffering without romantic palliatives. But he provides a compensatory beauty radically (in two senses) different from the tradition's conventional consolations. The poem recalls a night when "I heard them singing" and compares the beauty of the workers' songs to the natural beauty of the river: "slow, beautiful and melodious as the river / when it is arced with rainbow color." This beauty is built on suffering, for the workers' songs are "outlets / for a million pains." The difference between the painful beauty of the workers' songs and a more traditionally evoked beauty that would obscure their suffering is that the beauty is won through the workers' own recognition of their suffering and their determination to end it, for it is the end of such suffering that Rolfe ultimately desires. And it is the desire for the end of the workers' suffering that is coded in the poem as the *most* beautiful and the *most* meaningful:

> And many times (most meaningful of all)
> I have heard them at their work,
> bent under heavy burdens,
> wet with rivulets of sweat,
> utter two words, a beginning:
> "Some day . . ." (CP, 64)

"Brickyards at Beacon" sets out first to preserve the human beauty of the workers even under inhuman and degrading conditions and then to rearticulate the category of beauty to the conscious recognition of suffering under these conditions.

Both of these poems show not only how Rolfe articulates a worker-focused political vision through the resources of lyric but also how he articulates the lyric to the specific political agendas of the Communist Party during the late 1920s and early 1930s. Each poem appeared in the party's newspaper, the *Daily Worker,* so each set out to perform its cultural work in the context of nonlyric and nonliterary discourses aimed at class-based revolutionary change. The conceit that seeks to overturn John's dehumanization under capitalism condenses and focuses the narrative of news stories, the fragmentary experiences submitted by "worker correspondents," and the rhetoric of editorials. The discovery and shaping of the brickyard workers' "Some day" song make available a resource for imaginative transformation of laboring life not unlike the other resources typically included on the last page of the *Daily Worker:* recipes, listings for cultural and educational programs, and humor. The poems, circulating to a Communist and labor-oriented readership, cheaply available (the *Worker* sold for three cents a copy), generally disposable, and positioned so as to comment on and be commented on by the rest of the paper, put lyric to work in quite specific ways, ways different from both the other discourses included in the paper and poems circulating in other ways (in Rolfe's

1936 book and in his *Collected Poems*).[4] They value work and workers by attending to them, by linking them with a tradition and its values, by at once finding them and seeking to make them beautiful.

But the individual realization recorded in "Brickyards at Beacon" is not, on its own, a sufficient poetic response to the misery the poem depicts. The "I" who hears the workers' songs must transform itself into a "we." This is, of course, more easily said than done. Rolfe acknowledges the difficulties of political struggle and collective consciousness in "These Men Are Revolution." The poem thematically addresses the intractable differences between people, differences that prevent the "we" necessary for broad political resistance from forming. Again, though, literary form offers resources for the creation of a new popular imaginary. Rolfe attempts to chart a course through class- and race-based differences, to suggest a way over them, by drawing on revolutionary rhetorics embedded in English ballads and the contemporary workers' songs that are their descendants. "These Men Are Revolution" begins with a statement of the theory of mass action, cast in the metrically irregular but generally rhymed quatrain Rolfe often uses:

> The power in men and leaves and all
> things changeable is not within themselves
> but in their million counterparts—the full
> accumulation. (*CP*, 79)

But instead of moving directly to a representation of the class struggle actualized in armed insurrection—a tactic often employed in Rolfe's 1930s poetry—Rolfe seeks to persuade readers, as much through his poem's formal resemblance to popular cultural discourses as through its thematic representation of "the people." In roughly dactylic, inconsistently but frequently rhyming quatrains, Rolfe addresses the "million counterparts" that make up the nation's exploited masses. His stanzas take up, in turn, workers, students, and soldiers and finally combine these groups into a multifaceted whole. As a strategy for building a counterhegemonic coalition, this mechanical procedure alone is doomed to failure. But the combination of the quatrains' form, the serial construction of a community for action, and Rolfe's hortatory rhetoric evinces similarity to workers' songs that were popular from the beginning of the labor movement in the 1880s and circulated in such sources as the International Workers of the World's

(IWW) *Little Red Songbook* as well as a host of books and pamphlets in which, as Cary Nelson writes, "genteel values often struggle with socialist or Marxist commitments" (*Repression and Recovery*, 135).[5] Compare, for example, two stanzas from "These Men Are Revolution" to a verse of Joe Hill's "Workers of the World, Awaken!":

> Come brother—millhand—miner—friend—
> we're off! and we'll see the thing through to the end.
> Nothing can stop us, not cannon not dungeon
> nor blustering bosses, their foremen and gunmen.
>
> We will return to our books some day,
> to sweetheart and friend, new kinship and love,
> to our tools, to the lathe and tractor and plow
> when the battle is over—but there's fighting on now! (*CP*, 80)

> Join the union, fellow workers,
> Men and women, side by side;
> We will crush the greedy shirkers
> Like a sweeping surging tide;
> For united we are standing,
> But divided we will fall;
> Let this be our understanding—
> "All for one and one for all."
> (*I.W.W. Songs*, 8)

The labor songs circulated by the IWW and other labor organizations, with their simple, often repetitive structure, their familiar derision of "bosses" and calls for togetherness and action, and their setting to the tunes of popular or traditional songs—usually ballads, as the meter of "Workers of the World, Awaken!" shows—were intended to be easily remembered and passed along.[6] They were often sung at rallies, at meetings, and on picket lines during strikes. The songs functioned to raise the spirits of workers often endangered by their union activities and to bring the individual workers attending rallies or meetings together as one voice. The familiar songs and the communal singing that is their primary mode of circulation construct a multiple but provisionally unified identity. In casting this part of his poem formally and rhetorically like workers' songs, Rolfe reaches out to the tradition of labor songs and the role of *that* tradition in the history of the labor movement. In so doing, he also incorporates the entire political history of the ballad form on which the workers' songs were based.

The sonnet, the extended conceit, the romantic landscape poem, the popular ballad—these make up the toolbox with which Rolfe hoped to build a new way of thinking collectively, a new world built by what Rolfe calls, in "Credo," "bodies phalanxed in a common cause" (*CP,* 59).[7] In his first book, in this first phase of his poetic career, Rolfe availed himself of the resources he saw in "the great literary tradition" to effect very specific political changes. Poetry makes something happen after all. It calls readers into collective revolutionary consciousness. It lays bare the base that poetry alchemically transforms into aesthetic gold and reworks that metal into a politics made beautiful through metaphor and language's materiality. More than the contemporaries he hails in the book's final poem—fellow poets Sol Funaroff and Alfred Hayes—Rolfe aligned himself with that tradition, with its stockpile of forms and cultural associations.

In February 1936, the people of Spain elected a progressive, Popular Front government that promised land reform, which might ease the crushing poverty of the nation's many landless peasants; cultural reform, which would relax the Catholic Church's hold on most of the institutions of civil society; and military reform, which could ensure the democratic determination of national priorities and the peaceful exchange and exercise of state power. While the government itself advocated a moderately left-wing agenda, the landowners, church hierarchy, and military officers whose position was threatened feared broader changes that might completely strip them of their power. Almost immediately, a group of military officers began to plan a coup, and on July 18, they led the majority of the Spanish army against the five-month-old republic. Soon joined by church leaders and landowners, the army of General Francisco Franco moved quickly, gaining control of one-third of the country in less than a week.[8]

While the regular army had largely abandoned the republic, the government continued to be supported both by a majority of the Spanish people and by the progressive political communities of Europe and the United States. The governments of Britain, France, and the United States, however, maintained a neutral stance toward Spain and refused (aside from minor assistance by France early on) to intercede on the republic's behalf. The defense of democratic Spain was left to the Spanish, at least at first. Local militias fought the rebels in the field and in the streets, defending the mountain passes to the nation's capital, Madrid, and finally mounting barricades to defend the city itself. The International Brigades, organized by the Communist International (Comintern) in Moscow and comprised of volunteers from Europe and the United States, arrived in November 1936 to add their men and matériel to the defense of the republic, and especially the defense of the capital, which managed to hold off the rebels through intense street fighting and which, though heavily bombarded by the rebels, stood for more than two years.[9] By early 1937, the battle lines were drawn; the country lay divided, with Madrid and Barcelona in Republican hands but important territory possessed by the superior forces and armaments of the right-wing rebels.

To My Contemporaries charts Rolfe's continuing, and only occasionally successful, efforts to find in the romantic lyric a way to capture without compromise the violence and exploitation inherent in the American economic system and a way to explore and enact the collective resistance necessary to change that system. Two years after that book's publication, Rolfe traveled to Spain to join the International Brigades in the fight for the Spanish Republic. In the early months of his sojourn in Spain, Rolfe brings to fullness the rhetorical gestures of *To My Contemporaries;* he finds, in the collective voluntarism of the International Brigades, a satisfying model for revolutionary community. But the poems collected in Rolfe's second book, *First Love and Other Poems,* elaborate a narrative of Rolfe's changing expectations for poetry. Early in the war, Rolfe works to capture the war and the men fighting it so as to provoke awareness of the conflict, its necessity, and its costs. By the end of his first year in Spain, though, Rolfe's poetry takes on an elegiac tone that signals a change in his poetic agenda. No longer do the poems seem calls for action. Rather, they become attempts to memorialize both the people and the ideals Rolfe associates with Spain. This shift registers not only in the elegiac subject matter and tone but also in the intensified lyricism of the poetry, which pervades much of *First Love and Other Poems.* It is here, in the turn from exhortation to elegy, that Rolfe finds his most powerful and persuasive voice as a political poet.

The poems collected in *First Love and Other Poems* span the fifteen years after Rolfe's publication of *To My Contemporaries.* Poems written just before Rolfe left for Spain, poems he wrote in Spain, poems about Spain written after his return, and poems about events occurring after World War II are included. They are not, though, presented chronologically in order of composition or periodical publication. Rather, the four parts that make up *First Love and Other Poems* chart the complicated transformation both of Rolfe's poetry and of his conception of the roles and possibilities for poetry in the changing world. Lia Nickson's illustrations for the book offer signposts for the shift; they establish the tone of each of the book's four parts, so it is to these that I now turn before looking at the poems themselves.[10]

Nickson's drawing for Part 1 depicts, in the foreground, three figures. A woman, apparently dead, lies on the cobblestone street. A man, his face in his hands, kneels in grief beside her, and another woman, her arms raised over her head and her eyes turned to the sky, stands beside her in an attitude of grief and terror. In the background lie the ruins of houses and buildings, their roofs and walls destroyed by bombs and shells. Amid the rubble, a dog barks at the sky. The arched windows and doorways, tiled roofs, and cobbled street locate the scene in Spain, and the dress of the three figures marks them as civilians. The setting seems to be Madrid or another Spanish city after bombardment. Nickson's drawing captures, in its twisted figures and stark outlines, the destruction wrought by the war and the suffering of those who must endure it. This illustration establishes the expectation that the poems in this section will deal with the war, with destruction and suffering. The poems, all about the Spanish war and most written while Rolfe was actually in Spain, fulfill that expectation. Within the section, though, the treatment of these themes changes so that, by the last poems of the section, we have already moved from calls for action and a rhetoric of exhortation to a subdued and elegiac tone.

That tonal shift is followed by Nickson's illustration for Part 2, a pastoral scene depicting, in the foreground, grazing sheep and their sleeping keeper beside a river. Across the river, we see a farmhouse and, in the distance, rows of crops. This illustration is appropriate, for the poems included in the section it precedes are generally lyrics, some written before Rolfe left for Spain and some after his return. Spain and war are largely absent in these poems, and politics are submerged, appearing overtly only in "The Ship" and "Prophecy in Stone." Beneath the surface, though, lie reminders of Rolfe's pur-

Lia Nickson's illustration for Part 1 of Edwin Rolfe's First Love
and Other Poems *(1951). Reprinted by permission of Estate of
Edwin Rolfe.*

pose for writing poetry. In "Pastoral (2)," for example, he conjoins the
coming of spring with a subdued political prophecy, a prophecy that
tells us something of Rolfe's changing poetics as well:

> This is true season's end, true quest's beginning:
> man discards artifice of ice, becomes artist
> of natural summer, mature, eyes set on winning
> the warm world entirely, to the farthest horizons. (*CP,* 149)

Lia Nickson's illustration for Part 2 of Edwin Rolfe's First Love
and Other Poems *(1951). Reprinted by permission of Estate of
Edwin Rolfe.*

Still present is the vision of a new world; the way to that world,
though, has changed from the apocalyptic battles of "Credo" and
"These Men Are Revolution." Here we find a slower transformation,
a long revolution imagined through the setting, through a political
but nonpolemical art. The poet's eyes are on the victory, but it lies
somewhere far ahead. Part 2 of the book records an experiment, run-
ning through Rolfe's experiences in Spain and after; it traces an at-

tempt to retreat from the revolutionary poems of the early and mid-1930s into a poetic stance more personal and oblique, to read in the natural world, in the body of the beloved ("Night World"), or in artworks ("Prophecy in Stone") some assurance of coming changes in the world.

But Lia Nickson's illustration for Part 3 shows us that the experiment has failed. A man writhes in pain, clutching a mortal wound in his abdomen. His open eyes and mouth scream shock and pain. Beside him, beneath the remains of a blasted and blackened tree, sits another male figure, his head partially hidden under an arm thrown over as if to protect it. The eyes of the figure are empty—black holes in the emaciated face—and the face turns both toward the dying man and away from a bomb blast in the background, beyond the twisted strands of barbed wire that mark the battle's front. The lyric retreat of Part 2 has not escaped the horrors of the war, the suffering wrought on the bodies of men in combat. In a series of poems here, Rolfe works to clarify the significance of the Spanish struggle from the distance of several intervening years. The section juxtaposes bitter attacks on the forces of appeasement and isolation that kept the Allies from joining the Spanish cause ("Biography") with contemplations of the guilt felt by survivors of the battlefield ("War Guilt"). Most important, we find in these poems Rolfe's recognition that he cannot, in his voice alone, adequately remember Spain or account for its significance. He begins, in poems like "Survival Is of the Essence" and "May 22nd, 1939," to include other voices and fragmentary memories.

Nickson's drawing for Part 4, with round arches, wrought iron, and cobblestones, places us once again in a Spanish city, or what is left of one. Here, too, we find rubble and destruction—a wall is reduced to bricks haphazardly stacked, a gate or window has fallen partway down a wall, bullets mar the white space around the ruined architecture. Before this scene, though, stands a peasant woman carrying an armful of grapes. Unlike the woman in the first drawing, she wears a placid expression that creates a quiet peace in the midst of this destruction. Hers is not, though, a peace retained through ignorance of destruction and suffering. The woman has walked through the ruined city. Her expression exudes the peace earned through suffering, through lived history. The grapes she carries are the fruits borne through that experience, the beauty and nourishment that redeem human suffering. Together, the woman and the grapes symbolize the

Lia Nickson's illustration for Part 3 of Edwin Rolfe's First Love
and Other Poems *(1951). Reprinted by permission of Estate of
Edwin Rolfe.*

poetic resolution to which Rolfe, through the book's fitful progres-
sion, has come—a lyrical beauty and intensity bought at the cost of
witnessing and bearing suffering and constituting the refuge of his-
torical memory.

The narrative of *First Love and Other Poems* is, in part, a narrative
of failure. It runs from "Entry," the book's first poem (which Rolfe
wrote just after his arrival in Spain in 1937) to the book's final poem,
"First Love," through a series of attempts to find the poetic strategies
that must replace those on which Rolfe relied in his earlier work. The

Lia Nickson's illustration for Part 4 of Edwin Rolfe's First Love
and Other Poems *(1951). Reprinted by permission of Estate of
Edwin Rolfe.*

attempts to create a collective through the mechanical strategies of *To My Contemporaries* are rejected for the representation of an actual collective in Spain. But that collective is both constantly embattled and very short-lived. It fails in its mission and is overrun by historical circumstance. Rolfe's poems register the struggle and defeat, resolving to remember and offering memory as a resource for political change. But memory, too, is threatened by history's inexorable progress and by forces arrayed against Rolfe's political ideals. It is, ultimately, through an engagement with the failures of exhortation and even of witness that Rolfe finds a poetry whose way of happening holds out some hope of making something happen.

In "Entry," Rolfe continues to use some of the techniques that were effective in his best depression-era poems. He speaks, for example, as a plural subject powerfully to evoke the forging of community both in shared politics and in opposition to and struggle against "the enemy." The voice recalling the illegal nocturnal entry into Spain and the physical entry into the struggle that this border crossing entails is always "we" in the poem, never "I." "We whispered," he writes early in the poem, and later "we relaxed" (*CP,* 128). Writing in 1937, Rolfe is in the middle of a community forged by struggle, a community in which differences of nationality are elided and the International Brigades, made up of Communists and other anti-Fascists from all over Europe and North America, fight alongside each other and alongside the Spanish people. This experience imbues "Entry" with a power to speak collectively.

But "Entry" is the only "Spain poem" as optimistic and rhetorically assured as the revolutionary poems of the earlier 1930s. The experience of the war makes it impossible for Rolfe to continue in the poetic vein he had mined before arriving in Spain. We see the beginnings of a turn in Rolfe's poetry in "City of Anguish," a 1937 poem that complicates "Entry"'s depiction of warfare. Rolfe records the carnage of the siege of Madrid, tours the city and witnesses its destruction through the narrative of one night under bombardment.[11] The realistic and matter-of-fact account of these actions and of the ebb and flow of the bombing itself comprises the poem's first section. In the second, we witness the collapse of consciousness as it confronts the wholesale destruction of a city. Rolfe's images take on a strangeness, a shimmer of unreality:

The headless body
stands strangely, totters for a second, falls.
The girl speeds screaming through wreckage; her
    hair is
wilder than torture.
    The solitary foot,
deep-arched, is perfect on the cobbles, naked,
strong, ridged with strong veins, upright, complete . . .

The city weeps. The city shudders, weeping. (*CP,* 132)

From his rooftop vantage, Rolfe scans the city, surreal in this night lit
by scattered fires and the lightning flashes of exploding shells. Rolfe
captures this eerie scene in lines that move from a weird lyrical de-
scription to the underlying suffering:

And closer. There. The Puerta del Sol exudes
submarine glow in the darkness, alive with
strange twisting shapes, skyfish of stars,
fireworks of death, mangled lives, silent lips. (132)

With the "o" and "a" assonance, and especially with the almost obses-
sive sibilance of this passage, Rolfe captures the sounds, as well as the
sights, of the bombardment's fiery aftermath and figures the destruc-
tion in the simple out-of-place quality of his images. What, though,
are we asked to do here? Whereas in, say, "Brickyards at Beacon" Rolfe
deploys such a scene to rehumanize the mechanical workers, here he
can do no more than record or re-create the bombing. Bodies are
rendered in their dehumanizing partiality; the scene expresses only
horror. But the sound play here does more than simply call attention
to the poem's artifice. It forces our concentration onto pronuncia-
tion, onto phonetics, onto the very mechanisms of spoken language.
Rolfe brings the body into play, not merely working to mimic the
sounds of bombardment and burning but to invite readers into bodily
participation in the horrors he evokes.

Once we are there, Rolfe keeps us there with a cyclic repetition
that turns time into time without end. Just as he does in "These Men
Are Revolution," Rolfe turns to popular song in "City of Anguish."
Here we hear the song of a "beggar among the ruins," a song in which
the headless body, the dogs of war, the trees lighting the avenues like
torches, the images of the nightlong bombardment are reworked in a

lyrical lament. The beggar's song, with its occasional rhyme ("night," "bright"; "lifeless," "childless"), its startling figures of speech ("spilled like brains from the sandbag's head"), and its circular structure, its closing return to the opening gesture, attempts to enclose the carnage and destruction, to transform the grisly reality of the shattered walls and bodies into the mere aesthetic. But it fails. The song ends in repetition—"all night, all night"—and ellipses that trail this chorus off into infinity. Whereas work songs weave difference into tactical unity, the beggar's song evinces isolation and meaningless repetition. The poetic transformations work backward, as mundane objects symbolize death and destruction. Just as the "trees became torches," so too are the dreams of those who have endured such bombardments invaded by nightmare images; waking life becomes a constant ritual of recognition, a constant confrontation with the bombing's destruction.

By the spring of 1938, Rolfe's poetry begins to move away from the hortatory rhetoric of "Entry" and toward the elegiac and philosophical stance that "City of Anguish" only begins to explore. The reasons for this are easy to surmise. During the writing of "Entry" and "City of Anguish," the Spanish Loyalist forces and the International Brigades had been fairly successful in fighting Franco's insurgents. While the battles at Jarama in the spring of 1937 and at Brunete that summer had been indecisive and had incurred huge numbers of Spanish Republican and international casualties, and while the bombardment of Madrid had continued, with vast devastation, throughout the year, the late summer of 1937 had seen the somewhat successful Aragon offensive, in which the Loyalists and internationals had taken the cities of Quinto and Belchite, partially diverting rebel forces from Madrid.[12] Rolfe had himself participated directly in the preparations for the Aragon offensive, working to gather the international troops scattered throughout Madrid and to equip their truck convoy for transport to the front.[13] "Entry" and "City of Anguish" reflect a period that, in spite of the terrifying and destructive bombardment of Madrid, saw advances on the part of the Loyalists and internationals, saw the possibility of success even in the face of Franco's superior numbers, superior armaments, and assistance in the form of tanks, planes, and troops from Germany and Italy.

Of course, to read "Entry" and "City of Anguish" as the first two poems in *First Love and Other Poems,* published more than a decade after the war had ended and the republic had fallen, or to read them in Rolfe's collected poems half a century later, is to abstract them from the contexts of their composition and, more important for the purposes of this study, of their initial reception. These poems are written not, or not chiefly, for retrospective critical reading but for more immediate purposes. And those purposes at once direct and affect the cultural work that "Entry" and "City of Anguish," the latter in excerpts, performed. The fourth and fifth parts of "City of Anguish" first appear, as "Madrid," in a collection of poems published in Madrid in 1937; they are published, then, almost immediately after their composition and while the bombardment is taking place.[14] These sections follow the description of bombardment and begin "Come for a joyride in Madrid." They describe the aftermath of bombing, the deprivation and inconvenience experienced in a city under attack. Food is scarce and bad. The power is out. They explain the importance of poetry in such a scene: "words to pull / the war-weary brain back to life from forgetfulness." Rolfe offers, as an example of such words, those of the Republican activist Dolores Ibarruri, La Pasionaria, "her voice a symphony, / consoling, urging, declaiming in prophecy." His poem, circulating here along with other poems on the war's first year, circulating to and for readers who have already experienced the realities that the poem's earlier parts describe, aims to perform the same work he ascribes to La Pasionaria: to console and urge, to declaim in prophecy, to solidify and hearten a population under fire.

When Rolfe publishes the very end of "City of Anguish" as "No Man Knows War" in the *New Republic* in 1939, he is up to something quite different.[15] Nine lines long, this excerpt is surrounded not by other poems on Spain, other poems by combatants in Spain, but by advertisements and the stories and reviews composed for the magazine's smart-set readership.[16] The poem circulates here not to fellow sufferers of Madrid's bombing and deprivation but to Americans who chose not to go to Spain. Rolfe aims, in this instance, not to urge or console but to rebuke:

No man knows war or its meaning who has not
stumbled from tree to tree, desperate for cover,
or dug his face deep in earth, felt the ground pulse with
the ear-breaking fall of death. No man knows war
who has never crouched in his foxhole, hearing

the bullets an inch from his head, nor the zoom of
planes like a Ferris wheel strafing the trenches . . .

War is your comrade struck dead beside you,
his shared cigarette still alive in your lips.

The advertisements, the stories and gossip, the sophisticated tone
and artistic focus of the magazine, and especially its isolationist posi-
tion regarding foreign affairs are all implicitly devalued by this poem
in their midst. Rolfe's "No man knows" means, to the magazine's
readers (most of them anyway), "You don't know." And this sharpens
the last two lines' second-person pronouns: "your comrade . . . be-
side you . . . your lips." Written and published for one audience and
one purpose in 1937, the poem finds a quite different audience and
performs a quite different task two years later, after the Republican
cause is lost and as Europe gears up for a much broader war. Thus
circumstance makes elegy of exhortation.

The winter and early spring of 1938 found the Loyalists and inter-
nationals bogged down in the grim battle of Teruel, a battle Rolfe
calls "Spain's Valley Forge" (*Lincoln Battalion*, 158). After initial suc-
cesses against the city in December 1937, the Republicans were over-
powered by Franco's concerted counterattack, which was largely as-
sisted by massive aerial bombardment. In addition to the bombing
and artillery, the Republicans had to endure a terrible blizzard that
struck the area on January 1, 1938. The International Brigades were
sent into battle in mid-January, and their entry provoked a new round
of fierce bombing. By mid-February, after sustaining heavy casualties,
the internationals were forced to retreat, fighting to keep open the
route of escape for the Republican troops still in Teruel. By March, it
had become clear that the battle was a major loss for the Republican
side.[17] This led to a series of retreats over the next several months,
and by April 1938, the internationals had retreated all the way to Gan-
desa, near the sea. Madrid was almost completely cut off by rebel
forces, and the Republicans had lost the gains they had won through
the Aragon offensive.[18]

In July 1938, the Loyalists and International Brigades launched the
Ebro offensive, and out of the early days of that fight comes a poem
that exemplifies the new direction Rolfe's work takes.[19] In "Epitaph,"
he meditates on the death of his friend, Arnold Reid, in combat at

Villalba de los Arcos. Reid, whom Rolfe first met during his year at the Experimental College of the University of Wisconsin, was a friend of eight years, a fellow Communist, and perhaps Rolfe's closest friend in Spain.[20] "Epitaph" records Reid's death and, more important, develops it through the conventions of the pastoral elegy and the resources of poetic form into a figure for the meanings of the Spanish war:

> Deep in this earth,
> deeper than grave was dug
> ever, or body of man ever lowered,
> runs my friend's blood,
> spilled here. We buried him
> here where he fell,
> here where the sniper's eye
> pinned him, and everything
> in a simple moment's
> quick explosion of pain was over.
>
> Seven feet by three
> measured the trench we dug,
> ample for body of man ever murdered.
> Now in this earth his blood
> spreads through far crevices,
> limitless, nourishing vineyards for miles around,
> olive groves slanted on hillocks, trees
> green with young almonds, purple with ripe figs,
> and fields no enemy's boots
> can ever desecrate.
>
> This is no grave,
> no, nor a resting place.
> This is the plot where the self-growing seed
> sends its fresh fingers to turn soil aside,
> over and under earth ceaselessly growing,
> over and under earth endlessly growing. (*CP*, 142)

Visiting the site of Reid's death three days after it happened, Rolfe begins his meditation on this individual death by setting it in the context of all of the deaths that have happened in the world, the repetition of "ever" recognizing the vastness of that context even as it works to set Reid apart — "deeper than grave was dug / ever, or body of man ever lowered." Reid, from the poem's beginning, is seen as part of something larger than himself, both the earth and the "we" who, in the second sentence, buried him. Though he is buried at this specific point in space, the location's importance reinforced by the repeated "here where" of lines 6 and 7, Reid is not limited to that space. Rolfe provides the exact dimensions of the space the body inhabits — "seven feet by three / . . . ample for body of man ever murdered" — but the appearance of "ever" here, as in the first stanza, holds out the promise that Reid, one of the "ever murdered," will overcome that spatial limit. "Now in this earth," the earth on which Reid's blood was spilled, Reid is dispersed through that spilled blood; he becomes "limitless," transformed into the olive groves, almond trees, and fig trees that the blood nourishes. Reid's blood goes on to nourish the people of Spain, to feed the brigades, who harvest and eat the fruits of these "fields no enemy's boots / can ever desecrate," contributing to the struggle after his death. As the seed planted in this field, Reid branches out in the roots without which the fight cannot continue, without which it is meaningless. In the memories of those who live to fight, as example and provocation, Reid lives "over and under earth ceaselessly growing / over and under earth endlessly growing." Only against the backdrop of that struggle does Reid's individual death take on larger significance. "Epitaph" marks a transitional node in the narrative of Rolfe's changing poetics, taking, as it does, an elegiac stance but retaining the impulse to make of this individual death a collective experience and a ground for collective action.

The elegiac impulse of "Epitaph" dominates much of *First Love and Other Poems.* Even in poems not predominantly elegiac, lines like "We remember" and "I will remember" recur.[21] "Catalogue" presents, in rhyming quatrains, "the simple enumeration of losses," listing by name the wounded and resolving that "nothing more" than such a list is needed. On the basis of "the undying fact" of these men's sacrifice, the struggle carries on (*CP,* 138–39). "Elegy for Our Dead" memorializes the "Men of all lands [who] here / lie side by side" and offers their example for others: "Deeds were their last words" (143). First published in 1938 in *Volunteer for Liberty,* the International Brigades' English-language magazine, the poem honors not only those who had already given their lives but also those who, in the trenches or on leave, in bivouac or in a hospital, might well give theirs up soon.[22] Reprinted later that year in the *New Republic,* the poem honors the fallen, calls like-minded Americans to do their bit for Spain, and shames those who do nothing.[23] And when reprinted again in the *Daily Worker* on October 1, 1939, the poem memorializes not only the fallen individuals but also the lost cause for which they fell.

"Elegia," the book's penultimate poem, casts the fallen Madrid as a lost beloved, always to be remembered, someday to be restored:

Madrid Madrid Madrid Madrid
I call your name endlessly, savor it like a lover.
Ten irretrievable years have exploded like bombs
since last I saw you, since last I slept
in your arms of tenderness and wounded granite.
Ten years since I touched your face in the sun,
ten years since the homeless Guadarrama winds
moaned like shivering orphans through your veins
and I moaned with them. (*CP,* 186)

The city's fall entails the poet's fall—from the intimacy of touch and shared breath to the absence that leaves only the name to be repeated, "savor[ed]," chanted in an effort to effect communion. Rolfe goes on to catalog the sights and sounds, persons and places, experiences and meanings of Madrid, building up through the sustained act of recollection a continuing presence for the city and what it symbolizes for Rolfe.[24] And he resolves, here as in the other elegiac poems, to keep the memory alive; he offers it as the ground for action:

Madrid Madrid Madrid Madrid
Waking and sleeping, your name sings in my heart ˙
and your need fills my thoughts and acts
(which are gentle but have also been intimate with rifles).
Forgive me, I cannot love you properly from afar—
no distant thing is ever truly loved—
but this, in the wrathful impotence of distance,
I promise: Madrid, if I ever forget you,
may my right hand lose its human cunning,
may my arms and legs wither in their sockets,
may my body be drained of its juices and my brain
go soft and senseless as an imbecile's.
And if I die before I can return to you,

or you, in fullest freedom, are restored to us,
my sons will love you as their father did
Madrid Madrid Madrid Madrid. (189)

May lost memory bring with it loss of strength and sense. If this memory, a lyrically manifested provocation to continued action, fails, then may the rememberer fail as well. Cary Nelson writes that "Elegia" forcefully demonstrates the interdependence, for Rolfe, of lyricism and polemicism ("Lyric Politics," 42). The value of Rolfe's poetry resides, in part, in this interdependence, in the "historically occasioned" character of Rolfe's lyricism. And this quality accounts for the impact "Elegia" had on Spanish exiles, American anti-Fascists, and Ernest Hemingway.[25] But the lyrically purchased confidence in memory here, the assuredness that enables the speaker to promise not only his own but also his sons' memory and to seal the oath with the psalmist's vow, is problematized elsewhere in *First Love and Other Poems*.

Indeed, among the most important rhetorical practices Rolfe discovers in his Spain poetry is the confrontation with memory's failure. The sense of memory's fragility, of the difficulty of keeping promises like those of "Elegia," is, over the course of the volume, intertwined with the injunction to remember. "We must remember cleanly why we fought," Rolfe writes in "Postscript to a War" (*CP*, 160). And in "Biography," which follows it in the book, he writes: "It is hard to be victorious, / to seek, find / and in the search remember" (161). Rolfe's poems in Part 3 of *First Love and Other Poems* place a premium on memory in a paradoxical way—by forcing readers, through the inclusion of unexplained narrative fragments and allusions, to recognize the poems' incompleteness without lost referents. The poems are not simply repositories of memory; they are provocations to a remembrance of things past and repressed, reminders of the fragility of memory. This strategy is partly a result of the Left's loss in the Spanish conflict. But it is also a consequence of Rolfe's recognition that, in the rush of historical time, the people and ideals that animate Spain for him will be lost as well.

In "Song for a Birthday in Exile," which Rolfe wrote eleven years after the fall of Spain as an answer to Yeats's "Prayer for My Daughter," Rolfe cryptically alludes to a speech by Miguel de Unamuno, the well-known philosopher and rector of the University of Salamanca who died under house arrest by the Spanish Nationalists after the speech.[26] After wishing the newborn daughter of his friend and translator, Spanish Socialist José Rubia Barcia, well in the first three stanzas, Rolfe offers:

> May she never live apart
> from the life her people live
> in their passion to survive,
> nor forget, through joy or grief,
> the deep and tragic sense of life:
> the words that Unamuno spoke
> before his heart, confused with wisdom, broke. (*CP*, 177)[27]

The passage is an easy one to miss, to skip over. We might not recognize Rolfe's reworking of Yeats's wish ("May she become a flourishing hidden tree / That all her thoughts may like the linnet be") (93). In the same way, we might register Unamuno as just another Spanish name, if, indeed, we register it at all. It reaches out from the poem, though, to recall a narrative related to the poem's themes. Unamuno, a philosopher and writer, was perhaps best known for the book Rolfe mentions, *The Tragic Sense of Life*, in which he subjected traditional concepts of faith to critical scrutiny and arrived at a rather existentialist view.[28] Only further suffering will end the suffering of humanity on earth, a suffering that brings consciousness into constant collision with unconsciousness in order to raise consciousness: "[T]he evil of suffering is cured by more suffering, by higher suffering. . . . [T]o be, that is imperative" (Unamuno, 283). This is the tragic sense of life that Rolfe hopes young Elena will remember.

The "words that Unamuno spoke," though, are not from his famous book. Rather, they are from the speech in which Unamuno dramatically demonstrated his shift in sympathy away from the Nationalists. Attacking General Millan Astray, founder of the Spanish Foreign Legion, Unamuno concluded: "You will win, because you have more than enough brute force. But you will not convince. For to convince, you need to persuade. And in order to persuade you would need what you lack: reason and right in the struggle" (quoted in Thomas, 503).[29] This speech landed Unamuno in the house arrest under which he died two months later (Jackson, 301). In hoping that Elena will not forget this speech or Unamuno's exacting and painful prescription for existence, Rolfe deploys a brief allusion to bring into the poem a great deal of information, narrative and philosophical, that resonates through his other wishes for this child of exiled Spaniards.

Only two lines later, Rolfe, in another brief allusion, brings Pablo Picasso into the poem in a way that amplifies Unamuno's resonance. He hopes that Elena will not forget

> the prodigious canvases
> of that other Spaniard who,
> brush in hand, in Paris's
> teeming streets still comes and goes,
> illumining man's agonies.

Picasso's famous *Guernica* commemorates the destruction by German and Spanish bombers of a civilian Basque village. The most famous artwork to come from the Spanish Civil War, the painting is seen as a monument to all who were killed in the bombings of civilians in this war, the first in which that practice became widespread. Another thing for Elena not to forget, then, is the carnage wrought by the Axis military force at Franco's disposal during the civil war, a force the Allies failed to match in their obstinate refusal to back "leftists" against Fascists. Through the allusions to Unamuno and Picasso and the juxtaposition of these two figures, Rolfe replaces Yeats's values — custom and ceremony — with a set of values tied to Spain and the memory of the Spanish cause.

None of these references is explained in the poem; all require historical backing and filling on the part of the reader. By the time of *First Love and Other Poems*' publication, a decade and a half had passed since the Spanish Civil War; a world war had been fought, leaving its own new vocabularies in the memories of survivors; and a long anti-Communist inquisition had been resumed. References like those in "Song for a Birthday in Exile" would have had little purchase in the culture. The lack of explanation in the poem seems to ensure that most readings would remain fragmentary. Indeed, the poem's power *depends* on that referential opacity. The puzzlement most readers experience foregrounds the poem's incompleteness, Rolfe's inability truly to render the lived community of Spain. Rolfe could not speak community into being in the years before the war forced a communal consciousness on the international Left, and he cannot recover in speech the community that lasted only as long as the struggle to keep Spain from the Fascists.

In "First Love," Rolfe's most anthologized and readily recognized poem, we find his most powerful commemorative act inextricably bound up with resignation in the face of memory's eventual failure:

> Again I am summoned to the eternal field
> green with the blood still fresh at the roots of flowers,
> green through the dust-rimmed memory of faces
> that moved among the trees there for the last time
> before the final shock, the glazed eye, the hasty mound.
>
> But why are my thoughts in another country?
> Why do I always return to the sunken road through corroded
>   hills,
> with the Moorish castle's shadow casting ruins over my shoulder
> and the black-smocked girl approaching, her hands laden with
>   grapes?
>
> I am eager to enter it, eager to end it.
> Perhaps this one will be the last one.
> And men afterward will study our arms in museums
> and nod their heads, and frown, and name the inadequate dates
> and stumble with infant tongues over the strange place-names.
>
> But my heart is forever captive of that other war
> that taught me first the meaning of peace and of comradeship
>
> and always I think of my friend who amid the apparition of
>   bombs
> saw on the lyric lake the single perfect swan. (*CP,* 190)

The poem's lyricism depends on the historical and moral specificities both of the moment Rolfe commemorates and of the moment in which he writes. If such moments as the end of "First Love," Nelson writes, are "explicit triumph[s] of literariness, [they are] not . . . exclusively textual. Rolfe's point is that the poetic lyricism is historically warranted" ("Lyric Politics," 37). But Rolfe's poetic lyricism in this, the closing moment of his book devoted to Spain and all it stands for is not only historically warranted; it is historically *necessary* if he is even partially and problematically to preserve the significance of the moments of which he writes under the ideological pressures operating during and after World War II to erase those moments from the American cultural memory. Writing during his military service in World War II, Rolfe sees Spain disappearing under the huge historical impact of this war against fascism, sees the specific political commitment that brought him and the other internationals to Spain disappearing under the massive and indiscriminate mobilization of troops to stop Hitler and Mussolini. He is pressed to remember Spain, to memorialize its significance, to meet the monumental "responsibilities of the medium" (Phillips and Rahv, 174). "First Love" results from this pressure.

"Again I am summoned to the eternal field," Rolfe begins, summoned again to take part in military struggle, to fight fascism on the battlefield "green with the blood still fresh at the roots of flowers." The poem's first strophe, though its lines bear a rhythmic regularity, is held together not by meter or rhyme but by the repetition of words and sounds. The eternal field is twice green, Rolfe writes, not only green with blood that nourishes the flowers (as Arnold Reid's blood nourished the olive groves in "Epitaph") but also "green through the dust-rimmed memory of faces." The land's vitality continues; the field is eternal. More important, though, are the repeated sounds in these opening lines. "Field," "fresh," "flowers," and "faces" are conjoined not only through their obvious thematic resonance (especially apparent where "flowers" and "faces" end consecutive lines) but also through the audible alliteration. We see and hear how those who fought for the land lost themselves in it, became a part of it. The alliteration of "m" sounds—"memory," "moved," "mound"—effects the same connection along another vector, as the soldiers who moved in battle rest at last in mounds, living on in memory.

Rolfe deploys the resource of repetition in the poem's third stanza as well, from the alliteration of the first line—"I am eager to enter it, eager to end it"—through the repeated "one" in the second—"Perhaps this one will be the last one"—to the almost obsessive "and" that joins the phrases of the last three lines' long sentence in a syntax of coordination. That sentence is a pivotal one; last one or not, this war will recede into history just as the Spanish war has begun to. The weapons with which Rolfe and his fellow soldiers train will become artifacts, objects to be found in museums, to be studied by people for whom the "strange place-names" and "inadequate dates" are the last and insufficient vestiges of these all-important conflicts. Rolfe knows that Spain carries more significance than the names of Brunete or Teruel or the dates on which those battles were fought, carries more significance even than the names—Arnold Reid's and many others—he has memorialized. But no matter how many conjunctions he deploys, no matter how he stacks "and"s in an anaphoric column, Rolfe cannot forge any link between the past and future that will sustain the vow of "Elegia" and preserve Spain's significance.

Against forgetting, Rolfe can pose only the sensuality of lyric language and the gripping image. Training on the arid Texas plain, Rolfe's mind slips from the present conflict to "thoughts in another country." Why, though, do the field on which he trains and the field for which he prepares continually give way to the field on which he fought before? His recollections of Spain are not the result of an unwillingness to fight the present war: "I am eager to enter it, eager to end it." Rather, Rolfe is lured by the historical specificity of Spain, rendered here in the image of the Moorish castle and the figure of the girl carrying grapes. Spain must be recalled, for it was in that conflict, with its basis in fundamental political and ethical values, that Rolfe first learned "the meaning of peace and of comradeship," and it appears on the training ground as a miragelike figure on another battlefield. With a new and larger war effort, though, with the passing of time and the receding into more and more distant memory of Spain and its significance, Rolfe cannot count on the country at large or on the memories of individuals to preserve the historical moment so crucial for him; he holds to Spain, though, as the beautiful image of a girl bringing life and sustenance back to a landscape marred by death, by ruins, by history's long shadow.

The poem's final lines repeat this hoped-for solution to Rolfe's problem. Against the insufficient institutional memories of museums and history books, Rolfe places a startlingly beautiful image: "and always I think of my friend who amid the apparition of bombs / saw on the lyric lake the single perfect swan." While the conflict's ordnance will soon be nothing more than "arms in museums," while the bombs are rendered ghostly, the insubstantial "perfect swan" gets the last word and promises to outlast "the apparition of bombs." Nelson has explained the autobiographical significance of this image for Rolfe but argues that "Rolfe raises the image to a more general meaning. For it is the special justice of the Spanish cause . . . that justifies the lyrical vision at the poem's end" ("Lyric Politics," 37).[30] We might, though, justify the poem's lyrical conclusion not only by the "moral specificity" of Spain but also by the historical necessity Rolfe confronts in

1943. Threatened with obliteration by the overwhelming historical spectacle of World War II, Spain must be preserved in the breathtaking beauty of the poem's final image just as "first loves" often live on in the lyrics that commemorate them. The swan on the lake allows us to read back to the poem's title, to find in Rolfe's recollection of Spain the intensity of romantic love and in that intensity the means for preserving the moral and political significance of Spain. Amid bombs that, though lethal, are ghostly and insubstantial, the "single perfect swan" takes on a reality, a concrete character that allows it to hold, for as long as is necessary, the political potential Rolfe found in Spain.

It might be argued that the political commitments that guide Rolfe's poetry from beginning to end, the commitments signaled by his continuing membership in the Communist Party from 1925 until his death, severely compromise the value even of his best poems. The revolutionary poems, after all, are written to the specifications of a limiting (and shifting) cultural bureaucracy, itself in thrall to a repressive Soviet regime. The view of Spain that Rolfe sometimes movingly renders is a partisan and therefore necessarily partial one. Nowhere in Rolfe's poems do we find, for example, the liquidation of the Partido Obrero de Unificación Marxista (POUM) by Communist forces, the burning of churches and shooting of priests by left-wing forces, or the internecine struggles that plagued and fragmented the Republican coalition.[31] And Rolfe's poems on postwar American anticommunism neglect to mention the murderousness of the Stalinist regime that American Communists continued to support. There is some justice to the charge that Rolfe's commitment to certain political ideals, to specific vectors and goals of radical social change, poses some ethical problems. But the charge can be answered in three ways.

First, we should remember that *any* political position entails ethical compromise and sacrifice. Dedication to the grossly uneven distribution of wealth that existed before and during the depression of the 1930s (and that exists as I write this sentence) carries with it *at the very least* the acceptance of widespread poverty and its concomitant suffering and, in some cases, the exacerbation of poverty and exploitation for the maximizing of individual and corporate profits. Support for American and Allied neutrality in Spain amounted to tacit support for the right-wing rebels who sought to overthrow a democratically elected government and of the Fascist regimes of Germany and Italy, both of which supplied Franco's forces with men, money, and matériel. No politics are untainted, and to choose not to take a political position amounts to a de facto endorsement of things as they are, a position itself awash in ethical problems.

Second, we would do well to historicize our judgments of political positions and their problems. The crash of the American stock market in 1929 cast millions of Americans into dire economic straits and seemed to spell the failure of capitalism. The American government's stance toward the working classes, at least for two generations prior to the election of Franklin Roosevelt in 1932, was overwhelmingly hostile. Communism reasonably seemed, to many, not only a viable alternative but, given the depth and severity of the depression, a necessary one. And the rise of fascism in Europe posed a threat that seemed to warrant association with an international Left that stood in opposition to it. Spain presented an opportunity to confront fascism, and against that right-wing threat, the repressive tactics of the Communists might have seemed a lesser evil. (This is, in effect, the position the U.S. government adopted during World War II when it made common cause with the Stalinist Soviet Union against Hitler and Mussolini; it is, in that instance, a position against which few would now argue.)

Third, Rolfe's work keeps alive before us, even if we recognize the blindnesses that underlie his insights, two things well worth remembering: the ideal of a community devoted to democracy and the memory of the human costs of the United States' own political persecution of its citizens after World War II. We have seen the first of these in Rolfe's poetry of revolution and Spain. In his final work, the poems gathered in *Permit Me Refuge,* we find the second. After discussing Rolfe's later, McCarthy-era poetry, I want to return to "First Love," Rolfe's signature poem, to examine the cultural work it was positioned to do not at the moment of its composition or first publication (in *Yank: The Army Weekly*) but in 1951, at the end of the volume it names. The placement of the poem at the end of the book becomes part of its signifying practice and comprises a reaction to historical pressures related to but distinct from those to which the poem reacts in 1944.

Contrary to the popular view that Senator Joseph McCarthy was responsible for the anti-Communist activities of the U.S. government after World War II, Red-baiting, surveillance of people involved in left-wing causes, and other forms of political censorship lumped together by Carey McWilliams under the rubric of "witch hunt" predate (and in some ways enable) McCarthy's election to the Senate.[32] These activities predate World War II itself, in fact, and were put "on hold" because of the wartime alliance between the United States and the Soviet Union.[33] The House Un-American Activities Committee (HUAC), which we associate with Richard Nixon and the Communist witch-hunts of the late 1940s and early 1950s, was actually formed (as the Special Committee to Investigate Un-American Activities) by Congressman Martin Dies of Texas in May 1938.[34] But even before these government initiatives, Red-baiting was a widely popular activity among what Peter Buckingham calls the "anti-Red nativists" (34) and was not, as Kenneth O'Reilly claims, "favored only by the far right fringe and a scattering of respectable publicists" (36). Dies, though, was able to forge a relationship with the Federal Bureau of Investigation (FBI) (whose director, J. Edgar Hoover, had been a committed anti-Communist since his participation in the Palmer Raids of 1919), which, though it did not result in a broad anti-Communist consensus, secured for the anti-Communist constituency a respectability it had heretofore lacked (ibid., 37).[35] The formation of this committee was not the only government action against Communists in the late 1930s. In 1939, Congress passed the Hatch Act, which prohibited the employment by federal agencies of persons belonging to political parties or organizations that advocated the overthrow of the American form of government (Steinberg, 23).[36] Moreover, from 1940 onward, Congress added a rider to every appropriation bill that prevented the use of federal money for the employment of persons belonging to similar organizations.[37]

Among the organizations that fell under this rubric were the Veterans of the Abraham Lincoln Brigade (VALB) and other organizations that had supported the Loyalists. The offices and homes of supporters of the Spanish Republic were raided during 1939, and financial records and correspondence were turned over to the Dies Committee (O'Reilly, 44). In 1940, the FBI led predawn raids in three cities (Detroit, Milwaukee, and New York) to arrest veterans of the Spanish Civil War (ibid., 70). By 1944, the HUAC was investigating the Joint Anti-Fascist Refugee Committee, a group founded in 1942 to assist refugees from Spain. The committee's investigative tactics threatened to reveal not only the names of 30,000 American supporters of this supposedly Communist-infiltrated group but also, through committee member J. Parnell Thomas's relationship with Franco's government, the identities of Republican activists still operating in Spain (ibid., 119). By the 1950s, members of the VALB had to register with the attorney general as members of a Communist-front organization (Brome, 247).

Because of their activities in Spain, their assumed affiliation with the Communist Party, veterans of the conflict had difficulties serving in the military (over 500 veterans, including Rolfe, served in the U.S. military during World War II) and finding and sustaining employment after World War II.[38] The experience of Alvah Bessie is in many ways exemplary of the fate of veterans of the Spanish conflict:

> I tried vainly to find work in my former field—newspaper editorial and critical work. I couldn't. I finally was given a job on the old *New Masses* as drama critic and remained there from January 1940 to December 1942 as drama, film and book critic and feature writer. . . . So I became a freelance writer throughout 1946 and 1947, until the subpoena arrived from the House of Representatives' Committee on Un-American Activities in October of that year. (quoted in Brome, 247–48)

Rolfe's own experiences are quite similar to Bessie's. Upon his return from Spain, he worked first on his history of the Lincoln Battalion, which, though critically well received, did not sell well (Nelson and Hendricks, *Edwin Rolfe,* 41). Rolfe then took a position with the Soviet news agency, Tass, after searching for several months for a writing or editing job. He worked for Tass until 1943, when he was inducted into the U.S. Army. When he reported to Camp Wolters, Texas, for basic training, Rolfe was interrogated by FBI agents.[39]

After his discharge from the army in 1944, Rolfe joined his wife, Mary, who had found work in California. They would live in and around Los Angeles for the rest of Rolfe's life. Rolfe worked on several film projects through the late 1940s and attempted to find a publisher for a new book of poems (originally titled "Two Wars") without success. He also worked, with Lester Fuller, on a mystery novel, *The Glass Room,* the film rights to which Warner Brothers purchased in 1945; Rinehart and Company published the book in late 1946. In spite of such successes, though, the last ten years of Rolfe's life became a grim narrative of difficulties that resulted from Rolfe's unpopular political views. In September 1947, nineteen film-industry members were called to testify before the HUAC. Almost immediately, Rolfe's opportunities for work seemed to vanish. He wrote that this was probably due to "the witch-hunting atmosphere here," an atmosphere that continued for several years, leaving Rolfe "jobless, aimless, and unhappy" through the end of the decade.[40] In 1951, after trying for years to find a publisher for his book of poems primarily dealing with the now unpopular cause of Republican Spain and the International Brigades, Rolfe published the book himself through the Larry Edmunds Book Shop in Los Angeles.

The repressive political climate of the late 1940s and early 1950s makes its way into Rolfe's poetry (most of it published after his death, if at all, and much of it collected in *Permit Me Refuge*) in a variety of forms. Nelson writes that "a range of voices and styles is necessary to negotiate these oppressive years" ("Lyric Politics," 47). At some moments, especially as the inquisition intensified, Rolfe tapped the satiric traditions of the quatrain and ballad (in "Ballad of the Noble Intentions," "Little Ballad for Americans," and several unpublished individual quatrains like "1949 [After Reading a News Item]"). At others, he tried the resources of noirish mystery or surrealistic science fiction (in "Mystery," "All Ghouls' Night," "Mystery II," and "A Poem to Delight My Friends Who Laugh at Science Fiction"). Most often, he elegized the victims of what Nelson calls "America's Walpurgisnacht" (ibid.). In all of these modes, Rolfe turns to the tradition as a resource, but one whose strength is limited, whose utility at moments like this is questionable. "Ballad of the Noble Intentions," for example, stages a mock dialogue between an interlocutor and an overly self-confident victim of the inquisition:

What will you do, my brother, my friend,
    when they summon you to their inquisition?
I'll fire from the heart of my fortress, my brain,
    my proudest possession

. . . .

I'll read them bold pages from Areopagitica,
    quote Milton and Marvell to rout and abuse them.
The best words of men of all ages will rise
    to my tongue to confuse them. (CP, 224)

The individual talent who is called to testify, certain of himself be-
cause he is backed by the tradition of Milton and Marvell, breaks
before the committee and names names. Rolfe puts in his mouth the
standard defenses—that he named only dead men or men on whom
the committee already had incriminating testimony. But Rolfe's tar-
get of derision also finds in the seventeenth century of Milton and
Marvell traditional sanction for his compromise:

> I decided that boasting like Milton were vain,
>   or refusing, like Marvell, their guineas with anger.
> I patterned myself after Waller, who lived
>   more richly—certainly longer. (225)

The tradition is a resource without guarantees, available to support
and enrich any position one might choose. Rolfe's speaker, Rolfe him-
self, can only affirm the testifier's choice of Waller as model and rather
impotently flail the "dear stranger, lost friend" with the Milton and
Marvell the friend has disavowed, with the singsong regularity of the
ballad's meter, and with the ballad's history of satiric use.

It is as a preservative that Rolfe ultimately finds traditional form
and lyricism useful. For all the anger and shock in his late poems,
Rolfe's last work is dominated by the elegiac impulse that first comes
into his poetry as Spain falls. A number of sonnets in Rolfe's final vol-
ume aim to remember, to preserve in meter and rhyme, assonance
and alliteration, and metaphor and image, victims and ideals threat-
ened by political repression, by the Hatch Act, by loyalty oaths, by
the Smith Act and the prosecutions carried out under it, by the con-
struction of concentration camps in which, under the McCarran Act,
Communists and other political undesirables could, in case of war,
be interned.[41] *Permit Me Refuge* ends with such a sonnet, "Bon Voy-
age," in which the speaker explicitly hopes not only to be remem-
bered but also to serve, in memory, as the spark that might "rekindle
. . . the dying candle-light" of threatened political ideals (*CP,* 248).
And in this light, even the aggressive quatrains Rolfe wrote but did
not (could not) publish—poems like "A Letter to the Denouncers" or
"1949 (After Reading a News Item)"—might be read as sibylline leaves
or Dead Sea scrolls, notes left for a future generation to discover and
learn from.

In this context, "First Love," as the final poem in a book inti-
mately bound up not only with Spain but also with memory, with

the proper poetic relationship to history, as the final poem in a book whose timing during the rise of anti-Communist forces ensured its limited reception, and as the exemplum of Rolfe's turn to an earned lyricism, is most pressing and poignant. In this context, the poem marks the poetic position at which Rolfe, by the early 1950s, had arrived. Among the discarded notes for an essay on American political writing that Rolfe worked on during the late 1940s is the sentence, "If art is a weapon—in the thoughtless sense that many think it is—how could Republican Spain have lost?"[42] On another page of handwritten notes for future projects, Rolfe writes, "Write as if you lived in an occupied country."[43] This question and this imperative underlie Rolfe's attempts to think through the relationship between politics and poetry after he is forced to abandon his own version of the art-as-weapon position during the early months of the Spanish Civil War. Rolfe has witnessed too many defeats, chief among them the defeat of the Spanish Republic (and with it the loss of an ideal community) and the defeat of the American Left, which becomes more consolidated and definite with each year between 1947 and 1951. Rolfe's early awareness of the latter defeat is apparent in an unpublished review of contemporary literature that he wrote late in 1947. "Persecuted men live hunted lives," he begins, and he goes on to explain the process of persecution from attacks on ideas to "actual physical persecution," adducing Socrates, Galileo, and the autos-da-fé of the Inquisition. His own moment in history, Rolfe indicates, is a time of such persecution: "The inquisitor's name may be Torquemada or Thomas; the century the 15th or the twentieth. But persecution of ideas, unless it is vigorously opposed and the ideas themselves strengthened by staunch defense, leads to the destruction of the people who hold them."[44] Literature, in this "period of stress," has an important function. It can "gladden the hearts" of those whose ideas are currently persecuted, those who are in danger of physical persecution, by crafting from those ideas literary works that carry them.

In order to accomplish this work, though, poetry must go beyond "theoretical clarity" or "good communist intentions," and Rolfe's writings of the late 1940s and early 1950s repeat some of his aesthetic arguments of the early 1930s—politics in poetry must be integrated with the entirety of the individual writer, and effective political poetry must work as poetry, as formally accomplished and rhetorically compelling verbal art. In a paper Rolfe wrote for a *Main-*

stream magazine conference in 1947, he reminds the magazine's editors and contributors that "a novelist or poet writes out of compulsion far more than out of desire . . . , out of a morass, a jungle of memories, experience, feelings and impressions which are more often unconscious than conscious."[45] Poetry must, as Rolfe writes in an undated manuscript from the same period, be a "human revelation," must reflect a complete human response to "the complexities, contradictions and clashes of real life." To be such a revelation, a poem must "be intense, heavy with many meanings, charged with emotion," and as Rolfe had learned by the time he wrote his manifesto for the *Partisan Review* in 1935, "the meaning and tension should burst from the package of the verse form" ("Poetry," 33). Rolfe articulates, through these essays and notes written over several years, parts of the poetic position at which he has arrived after twenty years of his career as a political poet. Poetry must be political; it must embody ideas persecuted in their historical moment. That political component, though, must arise out of the experience of the individual in history, must be integrated with the emotional, spiritual responses of that individual. Finally, this complex individual response must itself be integrated with the form of the poem, for poetic form lies at the heart of the poet's vocation. As Rolfe writes, "[C]ontent is the coupling of subject matter, the poet's view, and the poet's method as combined in a particular poem."[46] Poetry depends on the integration of the poet's experience (subject matter), politics (the poet's view), and form (the poet's method).

If we read "First Love"—the final poem of Rolfe's collection of Spain poems and the culminating moment of a book whose political commitments are among the ideas persecuted during this historical moment—as a poem that integrates the poet's experience and politics with compelling poetic form, we find in it a conclusion only obliquely hinted in Rolfe's prose writings on poetry and politics.[47] "Again I am summoned to the eternal field," he writes. This is, as we have seen, the battlefield that was Spain, constantly renewed for Rolfe by his memory and by his continuing commitment to the ideas underlying the Republican cause. In 1951, though, and at the end of this book, the eternal field seems also to be the battlefield on which those ideas now suffer attack. Blood is still "fresh at the roots of flowers" because it is newly spilled in the persecution that intensifies almost daily. The girl, dressed in a black smock, "her hands laden with grapes," comes now to symbolize not only Spain but also poetry. Amid ruins, she carries nourishment, amid destruction, beauty. She is the woman depicted in Lia Nickson's illustration for the fourth part of *First Love and Other Poems,* the image of lyric beauty earned through personal experience of the pain wrought by history.

And what of the "single perfect swan" on the "lyric lake"? Here, Rolfe brings to bear a handful of his chosen medium's peculiar resources. This line, alone in the poem, scans almost perfectly (except for the first foot's trochaic substitution) as iambic hexameter. Sight, singularity, and swan are joined alliteratively, as are the lake and the lyricism that the line exemplifies. And thanks to this happy accident of history, the bird present "amid the apparition of bombs" is not just any bird but that most lyrical of waterfowl, a swan. Rolfe alludes to Yeats in a number of his poems, from the title poem of *To My Contemporaries* to "Song for a Birthday in Exile," and here too Yeats lingers just beneath the surface of the image. Yeats's swans, in "The Wild Swans at Coole," "Leda and the Swan," "Among School Children," and other poems, carry a complex set of symbolic resonances: embodied wisdom or sentience, supernatural or divine power, a life that promises to outlast merely human spans. Rolfe's swan carries these significances through the bombardment, lands with them on the lyric lake. And through the Yeatsian conduit, Rolfe's swan bears in its wings and feathers Yeats's own antecedent swans, the legendary children of King Lir, transformed by a jealous stepmother and doomed to live on lakes and seas for 900 years. Outliving their stepmother, the swans bear their father's story and their own long-forgotten names through the ages, through the disappearance of Druidic culture and the rise of Christianity in Ireland, to utter the inadequate dates, the strange names, once and finally at the moment of their death, to read into the record of legend what otherwise would be entirely forgotten.[48]

Like the girl who carries grapes, the allusive swan at the poem's end completes the transformation of the "eternal field" from the location of apocalyptic struggles over political power to the location of historical memory. Deploying the resources of the medium against the repressive force of history, "First Love," finally, completes the progression of Rolfe's political poetics from exhortation through elegy to a hard-won ground on which political commitment and personal experience coexist in the carefully constructed poetic vessels that hold them in productive and protective tension.

2

All Together, Black and White

LANGSTON HUGHES

In a 1926 *Nation* article, "The Negro Artist and the Racial Mountain," the first substantial work in which he published his thoughts on social art, Langston Hughes foregrounds the crucial interdependence of poetic form and political expression. He argues forcefully for the integration of political commitment and poetic accomplishment, defining that accomplishment in terms of the black artist's independence both from the white-influenced black middle class and from white readers who try to limit black literary expression. The successful merging of politics and poetry depends, for Hughes, on the reconciliation of the poet and "the lowdown folks, the so-called common element." Maryemma Graham has written that "The Negro Artist" is "a statement about social commitment, and about the solidarity between the artist and the masses of people, in the form and through the process of social art" (213). Hughes develops, in the essay, a strategy through which the poet can "reestablish his relationship with the struggling masses . . . [and] realize his critical revolutionary task" (216).

This goal is a crucial one for Hughes's "adventures as a social poet" (as he calls such work in the title of a 1947 essay). Hughes puts his poems to work on behalf of all kinds of political aims, seeking continually to articulate racial protest to broader political agendas throughout his career. As James Smethurst writes, "Hughes was, with the exception of Richard Wright, the black writer most identified with the Communist Left during the 1930s" (93). The decade certainly finds Hughes the single most frequent poetic contributor to the *New Masses,* the magazine of the Communist Party of the United States of America (CPUSA). (This is not to say that Hughes's career as a political poet began in the 1930s, though; his earliest poems reflected his political interests and passions, from "Steel Mills," a labor-centered poem he wrote in high school, through the politically pointed poems on colonialism and other issues Hughes published in the mid-1920s in magazines like the *Messenger* and *Workers Monthly.*) And while he was in all likelihood not a member of the CPUSA, Hughes participated in various allied organizations, even serving briefly as president of the Communist-affiliated League of Struggle for Negro Rights. He agitated and wrote poems on behalf of the "Scottsboro boys" ("Scottsboro," "Christ in Alabama," "Scottsboro Limited"), an obvious cause célèbre for a black poet, but also poems on behalf of Tom Mooney ("Mass Chant for Tom Mooney"), the Industrial Workers of the World (IWW) member long imprisoned in San Francisco. He traveled to Spain to cover the civil war for the *Baltimore Afro-American* and, while staying at the Alliance of Anti-Fascist Intellectuals in Madrid, wrote poems in support of the republic and the International Brigades. Hughes's simultaneous political and poetic effectiveness results from his ability to work in a variety of poetic forms in different contexts, his canny choices of forms and venues. From his position in the American cultural landscape, he draws on the entire range of positional and poetic resources at hand—writing as the black artist, the black Communist, and the Communist artist and adapting the forms of the blues, the ballad, and the belletristic meditation—to fashion or maintain politically necessary coalitions.[1]

Arnold Rampersad has written that Hughes was "a divided man," and these internal divisions position Hughes almost uniquely to perform the cultural work of effecting solidarity; Hughes was born athwart a set of cultural divides. For example, while neither of Hughes's parents were white, his ancestry was racially mixed. Rampersad characterizes both of Hughes's parents as "of French, Indian and some African blood," and Hughes's grandfather, Charles Langston, was the son of a white father and black mother (*I, Too, Sing America,* 5). Hughes himself was so light-skinned that, on his first trip to Africa in 1923, he was not accepted by Africans as a black man: "They looked at my copper-brown skin and straight black hair—like my grandmother's Indian hair, except a little curly—and they said:

'You—white man'" (*Big Sea,* 73). The Africans' response emphasizes the variability of Hughes's cultural position. Stuart Hall has argued that cultural position results from social structures, from "the given conditions of existence," and not from racial (or sexual or any other) essence. For Hall, the social structures that determine or limit the position of a subject can, against more rigid structuralist arguments, be understood as "simply the result of previous practices" ("Signification, Representation, Ideology," 104). At the same time, though, "social relations do exist . . . independent of our will. They are real in their structure and tendency" (105). Social position consists of a set of discursive relations; that set does not necessarily correspond to specific ideological formations, but repeated articulation with those social relations results in a cultural weight difficult to shrug off (106). While there is play in the system, the historical encrustation of social relations limits the flexibility of positional identity. To echo Marx's famous statement in "The Eighteenth Brumaire," we might see these structures as the anterior conditions not of our making in which we make history (245). Hughes's poems speak from specific cultural positions because throughout his life he occupied them, sometimes by (socially circumscribed) choice and, more frequently, by default; we cannot always choose the crosses we must bear.

Moreover, as Ernesto Laclau and Chantal Mouffe have argued, we can consider none of these positions primary; all of them participate in interlocking social relationships.[2] While his racial identity was probably the most crucial for Hughes and while it has certainly dominated critical attention to his work, we occlude much of Hughes's political identity and the poetry that draws on that identity if we define Hughes *only* by his racial position or commitments to race-based political positions.[3] Hughes stands at several cultural crossroads, placed at the juncture of multiple discursively created and maintained fields. Thresholds, of course, are meant to be crossed. They are ways through; they provide communication, however tenuous, between enclosed spaces, hostile territories, divergent priorities.

In his 1935 address to the First American Writers' Congress, Hughes himself recognizes the importance of crossing thresholds, of reaching out to complex and multiple audiences. While black writers must, he argues, "reveal to the Negro masses . . . our potential power to transform the now ugly face of the Southland into a region of peace and plenty," they must also reach white readers if they are to accomplish necessary cultural work. Most important, Hughes writes that "Negro writers can seek to unite blacks and whites in our country, not on the nebulous basis of an interracial meeting, or the shifting sands of religious brotherhood, but on the *solid* ground of the daily working class struggle to wipe out, now and forever, all the old inequalities of the past" ("To Negro Writers," 140; emphasis in original). Hughes sought to unite blacks and whites on this solid ground through his poetry, which drew on the tropes of proletarian literature and the tradition of African American literature both to construct that ground and to bring various readers together on it. Writing from his complex position in the American political culture of the 1930s and 1940s, Hughes intervenes in several political crises precisely by working toward a broader, temporary and tactical solidarity. In his poems on revolution, on the 1931 Scottsboro case and its years of appeals, and on the Spanish Civil War as it happened and in retrospect, and in these poems' various sites of publication and through their various networks of circulation, Hughes appealed across racial, class, aesthetic, and political lines for provisional political unity among often bitterly opposed factions. He did so by mobilizing a variety of literary and cultural traditions and by developing a set of rhetorical strategies to make his revolutionary poems' speakers multiple, producing a rich and various partisan poetry.

While many critical accounts of Hughes's career dwell on the number of his poems that have "Blues" in the title or the text, it is startling to see the number with "Revolution" in the title or the text: "Song of the Revolution," "Good-Bye Christ," "Advertisement for the Waldorf-Astoria," "Letter to the Academy," "One More S in the USA," "A New Song," "Wait," "Revolution," "Ballads of Lenin," "Let America Be America Again." Throughout these poems and Hughes's poetry of the 1930s and 1940s more generally, we find Hughes working in a variety of ways to articulate racial and class or revolutionary politics.

In "Union," for example, a poem Hughes published in the *New Masses* in 1931, Hughes elaborates the title's multiple meanings through a set of figures intended to draw together blacks and other oppressed people, especially workers, to offer these disparate communities of readers an image of collective effort toward revolutionary social change. "Union," of course, contains both its standard lexical meaning—the *Random House Un-Abridged Dictionary* defines it as "the act of uniting two or more things, the state of being unified"—and the specific historical freight of a workers' organization, an association of workers designed to protect their rights and interests precisely through the process of *collective* bargaining. In the poem's opening lines, Hughes deploys sound to effect the transformation of an individual speaker into a member of such a collective:

Not me alone—
I know now—
But all the whole oppressed
Poor world. (*CP,* 138)

While the consonance of "n" sounds highlights the speaker's recognition that he is not an isolated worker, the assonance built around "o" sounds links him to a community of similarly positioned people. The last two lines, with their rhythmic echo of a blues conclusion, enhance this sense of communal identification. His growing or newly revealed awareness of membership in this "union" enables the speaker to connect "White and black" under the rubric of "Poor" and to envision collective action. Evoking the biblical hero Samson, Hughes casts his vision in the imperative:

Must put their hands with mine
To shake the pillars of those temples
Wherein the false gods dwell. (138)

Betrayed, blinded, and enslaved, Samson, the strong-man judge of the Israelites and scourge of the Philistines, is brought into the temple to be ridiculed during the Philistines' sacrifice to their god, Dagon, and there, while the house is packed, he calls on God to restore his famous strength so he can topple the pillars and destroy the temple and the Philistines in it.[4] Through a story in the Hebrew Bible about an easily recognizable figure in the Judeo-Christian tradition, Hughes both positions the "oppressed / Poor world" and imagines the mode of its resistance. Powerful enough to withstand any kind of frontal assault ("Too well-defended"), the temple and its altars and its false gods must instead be brought down through the quiet exercise of unexpected strength, a strength latent when the workers are dispersed but manifest in their union. Sounds once more cinch Hughes's point. The last lines are more metrically regular than the rest of the poem, and end-rhymes suddenly appear:

And worn-out altars stand
Too well-defended,
And the rule of greed's upheld—
That must be ended. (138)

Here, in the premier left-wing magazine of its time, in a deft allusion presented through taut verbal structure, Hughes not only elaborates "union" but also models, justifies, and urges it. The poem captures, in its few lines and its single central image, themes Hughes would spend the 1930s and 1940s exploring, expressing, and expanding.

In a poem published less than a year later, again in the *New Masses*, Hughes once more takes up the image of the hand both to critique one dominant African American vision—a sort of "separate but equal" philosophy—and to articulate in its stead one of cross-racial collaboration, of at least provisional unity. "Open Letter to the South" begins with an address to "White workers of the South" and elaborates and specifies this object with a roll call that recalls Edwin Rolfe's attempts to hail readers through their specific occupational or regional identities:

Miners,
Farmers,
Mechanics,
Mill hands,
Shop girls,
Railway men,
Servants,
Tobacco workers,
Sharecroppers,
GREETINGS! (*CP*, 160)

Workers are differentiated first by race and region and then by the specificities of their work. But for the rest of the poem, Hughes attempts to overcome the divisions he has indicated. The collective Samson-hand of "Union" here rebuts Booker T. Washington's famous prescription for racial separation. As separate fingers, white workers and black workers, northern workers and southern workers, industrial workers and farmworkers, cannot wrest from the "bosses" any of what Hughes calls "the tools of power." But gathered in "One single hand," in a communal fist, they can, Hughes writes, "smash the old dead dogmas of the past / —[and] kill the lies of color / That keep the rich enthroned" (160).

The poem foresees an end to racist violence and racial oppression when people of all colors become "red." Blacks will no longer need to migrate north. The South's black colleges will be renewed. Lynching will cease; the trees once used as gibbets will support posters advertising freedom. Indeed, by joining together under the workers' banner, blacks and whites will overcome racial difference (and the long-standing, legislated prohibitions of miscegenation, the very prohibitions used to sanctify white womanhood and to sanction lynching) and become brothers and sisters: "'You are my brother, black or white, / You are my sister—now—today!'" This family of workers, though, will reap still greater benefits as the means of production, listed almost litany-fashion, fall into their hands and the proletariat arise to take over the world. Hughes's vision of revolutionary apocalypse, effected through the repetition of "union" in the long sixth stanza, ends as it begins—with the hand. The speaker offers his to the white workers; implicit in this handshake is no less than the humanity of workers of all races: "Today, / We're Man to Man."

But Hughes's most effective explicit attempt to invite readers of various types into this revolutionary collective must be the two-page, illustrated "Advertisement for the Waldorf-Astoria," published in the December 1931 issue of the *New Masses,* just in time for Christmas. Here the roll call that began "Open Letter to the South" becomes the structuring device for the whole poem, as Hughes reaches out serially to "Hungry Ones," "Roomers," "Evicted Families," "Negroes," and, finally, "Everybody" in sections titled for their audiences. The poem is structured around these different groups (note that "Negroes" is fourth in the progression; as he often does in his 1930s poems, Hughes subordinates race to highlight his emphasis on class, poverty, and revolution), but each section is built around the device of antithesis, as if this collective cannot be composed except in opposition to a common enemy. Again and again, Hughes contrasts the hotel's luxury with the living conditions of the poor. The hotel's gourmet menu and its well-appointed rooms are set alongside the scraps and the flophouses of the poor. More powerful still, Hughes writes into each section a *human* contrast between those outside the hotel (the people Hughes wants to unite) and those inside (the ground of and provocation for their union, the basis for their collective identity). And this contrast is based not on race or other aspects of identity, even in the section addressed to "Negroes," but on work and living conditions.[5] To "Roomers," for example, Hughes writes:

> Dine with some of the men and women who got rich off of
> your labor, who clip coupons with clean white fingers
> because your hands dug coal, drilled stone, sewed gar-
> ments, poured steel to let other people draw dividends
> and live easy. (*CP*, 144)

And to "Negroes":

> (A thousand nigger section-hands keep the roadbeds smooth,
> so investments in railroads pay ladies with diamond
> necklaces staring at Sert murals.)
> *Thank God A-mighty!*
> (And a million niggers bend their backs on rubber planta-
> tions, for rich behinds to ride on thick tires to the
> Theatre Guild tonight.) (145; emphasis in original)

One's position inside or outside the new luxury hotel depends on what one does for a living, what one does with one's hands, and whether one produces or consumes. The distinction holds regardless of race. Although, of course, the people inside are exclusively white, Hughes's poem never mentions this; it implies it only in the speaker's assumption, in the "Negroes" section, that the "downtown folks" who patronize the hotel and enjoy Paul Robeson are, unlike Robeson, white.

The serial interpellation in "Advertisement for the Waldorf-Astoria," so similar to the practice deployed by Edwin Rolfe, culminates in an apostrophe to "Everybody" that implies that the collective has been forged. Hailed by the appropriate "advertisement," all of the oppressed communities come into place. As in the earlier sections, Hughes structures this one around antithesis. The "Everybody" addressed consists of those left out. Their identity derives from the "n't" in Hughes's verbs; it depends on their negative relation to those on the inside: "You ain't been there yet? . . . You haven't seen the ads in the papers? Didn't you get a card?" And like the others, this section culminates in an imperative: "Come on out o' that flop-house! Stop shivering your guts out all day on street corners under the El" (*CP*, 145).

But neither the section nor the poem is over at this point. With the mob of outsiders rhetorically assembled, it remains for Hughes to clarify their task, to lift them into pointedly political significance. And to this task he brings a tool oft-used in certain sectors of the Left: the re-articulation of Jesus into a figure of revolution.[6] The "Everybody" section's final line — "Jesus, ain't you tired yet?" — functions both as an exclamation implying the speaker's own weariness and frustration and as a question posed to Christ himself (Jesus, aren't you tired of seeing the rich conspicuously profit at the poor's expense? Jesus, aren't you ready to come back and set things right?). The latter reading allows the line to function as a link to the poem's final section, titled "Christmas Card":

> Hail Mary, Mother of God!
>> the new Christ child of the Revolution's about to be born.
> (Kick hard, red baby, in the bitter womb of the mob.)
> Somebody, put an ad in *Vanity Fair* quick!
> Call Oscar of the Waldorf—for Christ's sake!!
>> It's almost Christmas, and that little girl—turned whore because her belly was too hungry to stand it anymore— wants a nice clean bed for the Immaculate Conception.
> Listen, Mary, Mother of God, wrap your new born babe in the red flag of the Revolution: the Waldorf-Astoria's the best manger we've got. For reservations: Telephone EL 5-3000. (*CP*, 146)

We can now retrospectively see all the groups Hughes hails as avatars of Mary and Joseph, as poor and weary travelers denied the shelter of an inn in midwinter. And like that couple, these carry within them a figure for radical change. Hughes's phrase, "the new Christ child of the Revolution," transforms the oppressed into the vehicle for a second coming, an apocalyptic return of Christ as warrior, intent on destroying evil and bringing the Kingdom of God into earthly existence. This elevation of the mob to the "bitter womb" out of which the warrior Christ of the Revolution will be born comes hand in hand with a rereading of Christian miracle as capitalist malfeasance. The "virgin" is impregnated by economic forces that turn her to prostitution. Insiders of the Waldorf have sown the seed of their own destruction, and that seed will come to fruition inside the hotel itself—"the best manger"—when the oppressed come from their "street corners under the El" to claim the rooms that they've reserved at "EL 5-3000."[7]

On March 25, 1931, a fight broke out among men illegally riding a freight train through Alabama. The train stopped at Paint Rock, and nine black men, one white man, and two white women dressed as men were taken into custody. When the black men were arrested for vagrancy, one of the women, Ruby Bates, told the arresting officer, Charles Latham, that the men had raped her and the other woman, Victoria Price. The "boys" were immediately charged with rape and taken to jail, their trial date set for early April (Dan Carter, 8–9). At the trial, in spite of the defendants' testimony that they had not known there were women on the train, in spite of a doctor's testimony that the women had not been raped, and in spite of Bates's unwillingness to testify against the defendants, all nine defendants were quickly convicted, and all but thirteen-year-old Roy Wright were sentenced to death (ibid., 50). The International Labor Defense (ILD), a Communist-affiliated group of attorneys, convinced the defendants to let them handle the appeal instead of the attorneys provided for them by the National Association for the Advancement of Colored People (NAACP), and the case drew the national spotlight largely through the efforts of the CPUSA (ibid., 54–56).[8]

Hughes's most effective (and best known) poetic contribution to the debate over the Scottsboro case is probably the short poem "Christ in Alabama." This poem captures, in thirteen lines, the insoluble complexities of the racial, sexual, regional, and religious tensions touched off by the case and the verdict:

> Christ is a Nigger,
> Beaten and black—
> *O, bare your back.*
>
> Mary is His Mother—
> *Mammy of the South,*
> *Silence your mouth.*
>
> God's His Father—
> *White Master above,*
> *Grant us your love.*

Most holy bastard
Of the bleeding mouth:
Nigger Christ
On the cross of the South. (*CP*, 143; *Contempo*, December 1931, 1)

The inflammatory opening line specifies and historicizes Christ as a dark-skinned man and ironizes traditional portrayals of the pale savior, but it also deflates the Christ image by rewriting the Immaculate Conception. The poem radically reinscribes the divine creation of the biblical Jesus as the profane creation of the mulatto; the savior becomes the unwanted issue of a white man's rape of a black woman, a version of the issue Hughes famously treated in "Mulatto" and to which he often returned throughout his career. Perhaps most important, Hughes aggressively deploys the trope of the Black Christ familiar from, especially, Countee Cullen's work of the late 1920s.[9] The lines in roman type through the rest of the poem define the image: Mary is Christ's mother, God his father. The final stanza's two roman lines bring together the basis of Christ's divinity, his unique parentage ("Most holy bastard"), and the suffering through violence ("the bleeding mouth") that, tracking back to the first stanza's "Beaten and black," refigures the crucifixion, the heart of Christ's mission and Christian belief. These lines ironize a Christianity that has become either passive or complicit, a Christianity whose apotheosis of suffering seems to justify and (super)naturalize racial oppression. The overt critique of Christianity works simultaneously as a covert critique, a "signifyin(g)" repetition of the popular Black Christ constituted by passive suffering.[10]

We can read Hughes's religious critique here more specifically as a pointed attack on aspects of black religious culture. In "My Adventures as a Social Poet," Hughes writes that his adventures began when, after the publication of *The Weary Blues,* he gave a reading at a black church in Atlantic City. During the reading, a deacon brought him a note signed by the minister that read, "Do not read any more blues from my pulpit." Hughes writes that this was his first experience of censorship and in the next paragraph of his essay links the pastor to Charlotte Mason, whose patronage Hughes lost over his increasingly political poetry in the late 1920s (151). The linkage is telling; the black churches represented by the Atlantic City minister, like Hughes's onetime patron Charlotte Mason, would allow only certain kinds of poetic expression under their auspices, and Hughes would not tolerate either brand of censorship.

Hughes's ironic use of the Black Christ challenges both religious and cultural norms.[11] As William Maxwell points out, the poem charts "an apocryphal Christian Trinity" whose "iconoclastic political moral . . . is that the South's champion miscegenationist—'White Master above'—has fingered his black sons for his own sins and chastised them in Scottsboro" (141). But the italicized lines throughout "Christ in Alabama" complicate and destabilize any easy reading.[12] Following the roman lines in each stanza, set off by dashes in the first three stanzas and a colon in the last, and—except for the last stanza—cast as imperatives, the italicized lines appear to be antiphonal responses to the roman lines' nominative calls.[13] But the relative familiarity of antiphonal structures (in hymns, work songs, field hollers) in African American culture and in Hughes's own work is challenged here by the impossibility of determining the speakers of each set of lines.[14] Both roman and italic lines make available multiple subject positions that, like a Union Square protest rally, are crowded with potential speakers. The italic imperatives in the first three stanzas, for example, seem directed at black hearers by white speakers. The Black Christ is ordered to submit to a beating ("O, bare your back"), while Mary is commanded to remain silent ("Silence your mouth"). Mary's identity as a black woman is reinforced by her italicized colloquial appositive—"Mammy of the South." This pattern breaks down in the third stanza, in which the speaker implores the "White Master," God, for his love. This is a puzzling moment. Perhaps the descriptor here, marking the usually unmarked cultural position of the white person, emphasizes the italicized speaker's identification with the white god. But italics, conventionally indicating a stressed or unusual tone, can lead us to read these lines as the ironic habitation of a white subject position by a black speaker or speakers. The commands to "bare your back" and "Silence your mouth," in this case, struggle against themselves, rhetorically illustrating the deplorable conditions of black life in the South. The invocation of the "White Master," the plea for his love, rings with an irony made more bitter still by the poem's final two lines. Whereas in the New Testament "God so loved the world he gave his only begotten son," the speakers of the italicized lines receive the "Nigger Christ / On the cross of the South." The unique suffering of the Gospel is replaced by the repeated suffering of the lynched black man; the black masses are continually forced to partake in this outward and visible sign of the White Master's cruel "love."

The rhetorical instability of "Christ in Alabama," enacted through its compression, its irresolvable typography, its redefinition of the Black Christ trope, and its multiply refracting irony, makes the poem available for various political readings; the cross might support numerous structures. Reading the poem in its initial publication, we can see how context shapes those structures, partially foreclosing some meanings while throwing others into sharper relief. Hughes first published "Christ in Alabama" in the December 1, 1931, issue of *Contempo*, a magazine published by Anthony Buttitta and Milton Abernethy in Chapel Hill, North Carolina. Buttitta and Abernethy had published a poem of Hughes's in September, and when they heard of the poet's plans to make a reading tour through the South, they contacted him about appearing at the University of North Carolina and solicited work about the Scottsboro case (Rampersad, *I, Too, Sing America*, 222). Hughes responded with "Christ in Alabama" and an inflammatory essay, "Southern Gentlemen, White Prostitutes, Mill-Owners, and Negroes." The *Contempo* editors published both pieces on the front page of the December 1 issue, timed to coincide with Hughes's arrival in Chapel Hill on November 19. Anticipating the furor Hughes's appearance would cause, they printed an extra 5,000 copies (ibid., 223). As a final affront to white Chapel Hill society, they took Hughes to lunch the day after the reading at what Buttitta called "the snappiest cafeteria in town," where Hughes was served, according to Buttitta, because "the cheap, southern soda jerker took [him] for a mexican or something and let it go at that" (Buttitta, 141). Needless to say, the outcry was tremendous; Hughes was attacked in the North Carolina press, and when news of the controversy reached the North, he was implored by his mother to abandon his plan to visit the Scottsboro defendants (Rampersad, *I, Too, Sing America*, 225).[15]

The visually rich field of *Contempo*'s front page draws the eye away from the poem, though it occupies the center of the page and is set off from the surrounding columns of print by white space. Zell Ingram's illustration looms immediately above the poem: a stylized silhouette of a black man's head and upper torso, his hands raised next to his face, palms out. The figure stands in deep shadow—"lit" from behind and to its right—so that its features are indistinguishable. In fact, the figure is completely black except for the stigmata on each

Front page of Contempo, *December 1, 1931, including Langston Hughes's "Christ in Alabama" and Dell Ingram's illustration.*

hand and the lips, which are white. Almost half as long and a third again as wide as the text of the poem, the illustration dominates the page, casting the poem below in its shadow. The stigmata reinforce the poem's Black Christ image, but the stylized figure also supports Hughes's apparent ironic distance from aspects of that trope. Ingram's spare design, though, maintains a quiet dignity for the figure, rescuing Hughes's Christ from the poet's own irony. The featureless face atop the poem substitutes for Christ's uniqueness the ubiquity of black suffering.

The texts that surround the poem on the page simultaneously echo and limit that ubiquity. Scottsboro governs the 11- by 19-inch page: an essay by Lincoln Steffens ("Lynching by Law or by Lustful Mob North and South: Red and Black") runs along the left-hand side, and Hughes's polemical piece runs along the right-hand side. These prose pieces amplify and complicate the poem's political significances. Steffens mounts a political critique of the case, drawing a distinction between justice and righteousness to argue that the South has simply legitimized its lynchings, clothed them in the trappings of courtrooms and juries: "The righteous people of the South have been gradually waking up to the idea that they can save their face by taking justice out of the rude hands of the mob and putting it in the delicate hands of the lawyers, and judges and a few representatives of the better people in a jury" (1). Steffens's view of the Scottsboro tragedy as a triumph of propriety for the righteous South echoes Hughes's antagonistic stance toward a complicit white Christianity personified in the poem by the White Master. But Steffens also articulates a political linkage Hughes does not touch on in his *Contempo* pieces (though he does elsewhere)—the linkage of race and class, of lynching and Red-baiting, of southern blacks and northern Reds: "That is to say, they [southerners] can lynch their blacks the way the superior North, West and East get their Reds [that is, through the justice system]" (1). Steffens's essay, assigning blame squarely and emphatically to southern whites and northern anti-Communists, reverberates with some of the textual energies of Hughes's poem. The sympathetic echoes of blacks under southern oppression and the ironic portrayal (Steffens) and invocation (Hughes) of white Christian society link the two texts in a relationship of mutually amplifying echoes.[16]

At the same time, though, Hughes's own essay pulls the poem's surplus meaning across the page, away from Steffens and into a different congeries of political critiques. "If the 9 Scottsboro boys die," Hughes begins his polemic, "the South ought to be ashamed of itself—but the 12 million Negroes in America ought to be more ashamed than the South" ("Southern Gentlemen," 1).[17] Throughout the brief essay (450 words), Hughes lays ironic blame as much on blacks (the defendants and American blacks generally) as on whites, working to equate the two races under the rubric "American": "The 9 boys in Kilbee Prison are Americans. 12 million Negroes are Americans too. (And many of them far too light in color to be called Negroes, except by liars.) The judge and the jury at Scottsboro, and the governor of Alabama, are Americans" (1).

The racial distinction, Hughes implicitly argues here, is an impossibly complex one. Not only are blacks and whites equally American in Hughes's formulation; the categories themselves are fluid and un-stable.[18] Hughes amplifies this point later in the essay, modifying the phrases "black populace" and "dark millions" in order to break down a strict and easy racial demarcation. Hughes follows "black populace" with the parenthetical redefinition "(and for the half-black, too—the mulatto children of the Southern gentlemen)" and alters "dark mil-lions" to include the "black and half-black, brown and yellow, with a gang of white fore-parents—like me." These cases, taken together, point up the poem's indictment of interracial rape (White Master and the Mammy of the South), teasing from across the page a particular strand from the poem's fabric.[19]

While Steffens articulates a critique of southern "justice," Hughes, weaving strands of the poem with the strong cords of his essay, braids his own heavily ironic critique of southern race and gender relations. Stripping away the proper white suit and black string tie, Hughes flails the suspect mores of "Southern gentlemen," laying bare the economic skeleton beneath. Establishing his position as an interracial speaker ("with a gang of white fore-parents"), Hughes links the implied rape in the poem with the accusation of rape at the center of the trial. While the Scottsboro defendants face death for simply sharing space with white women, unwittingly riding on the same train that carried them, white men enjoy unquestioned mastery over women of both races because they control women's economic horizons. In both the essay and the poem, Hughes writes these power dynamics onto the figurative bodies of black men; the Scottsboro defendants will burn in the state's electric chair for the amusement of Alabama's southern gentlemen, and the "Nigger Christ" will be continually crucified "On the cross of the South."[20]

The front page of *Contempo* grounds "Christ in Alabama" in one set of the Scottsboro case's historical specificities. Ingram's illustra-tion resists sentimental readings of the poem's Black Christ trope while recapitulating, in its featurelessness, the infinite repeatability of racist violence; it contributes to the poem's universalizing impulse, its stylized figure representing every black man prey to southern preju-dice. The dialogue between the poem and Hughes's essay further re-defines the trope, drawing it from rhetorical heights to bitter realities. Hughes powerfully locates the case's political significance in the web of intertwined racial and gender exploitation that makes possible the southern caste system.

The poem works quite differently in its other contemporary publication, the pamphlet *Scottsboro Limited,* which Hughes published with the assistance of Carl Van Vechten and Prentiss Taylor through their Golden Stair Press. The pamphlet includes Hughes's one-act play, "Scottsboro Limited," and the short poems "Justice," "Scottsboro," "The Town of Scottsboro," and "Christ in Alabama." Taylor illustrated the pamphlet with original lithographs. Thirty copies were printed on fine paper, signed by Hughes and Taylor, and sold for $3, while the rest were printed on cheaper paper and sold for fifty cents. Proceeds from the sales were donated to the ILD to help pay for the defendants' appeals. Shaped by the texts and illustrations that surround it in the pamphlet, "Christ in Alabama" voices a political statement here at variance with the one it makes in *Contempo.* The difference provides an index to Hughes's positions in the aesthetic and political communities in which he participated during the late 1920s and early 1930s.

Born into poverty, Hughes worked throughout his youth to attain and maintain financial security without sacrificing his intention to live by writing. For much of his early life, he hovered between the poverty of his childhood in Lawrence, Kansas, and the relative security his fame as a writer eventually brought.[21] Working at odd jobs—as a seaman, waiter, farm laborer, and florist's deliveryman— the young Hughes inhabited the world of the working class. At the same time, his intelligence, his dedication to writing, and his family's expectations separated him from much of that class's culture.[22] Once Hughes began to "make it" as a writer, he left the working class. Living on the proceeds of the poems and stories he published (and on the patronage of Amy Spingarn and later Charlotte Mason), Hughes could count himself among the intelligentsia, the class that created and participated in "high culture." His poverty, though, complicated that social position just as the gentility of Hughes's family had complicated his working-class position.[23] A college-educated and widely published poet, Hughes suffered, as late as the early 1940s, the humiliations of eviction and financial dependence.[24]

Perhaps partly because of his marginal class situation, Hughes took up a similarly marginal aesthetic position among his Harlem colleagues in what George Cunningham calls "the black artists' fragmenting constituency" (177). Cunningham reads much of Hughes's Harlem Renaissance–period poetry as reflections of Hughes's "doubts about the middle-class values of his family," and, we might add, the aesthetic choices of such "middle-class" black poets as Countee Cullen (58). Hughes's own pronouncements in "The Negro Artist and the Racial Mountain" seem to reinforce this impression: "This is the mountain standing in the way of any true Negro Art in America—this urge within the race towards whiteness—the desire to pour racial individuality into the mold of American standardization, to be as little Negro and as much American as possible" (175).

Hughes's work resists the trend in black poetry characterized by Cullen's work. Whereas Cullen hoped that black writers would attain "the austere circles of high literary expression which we call poetry" (73), especially by mastering the forms of "traditional" (white) poetry, Hughes's work focused on racial subjects and drew on an alternative tradition of black folk culture. These aesthetic choices drew mixed reactions from other Harlem writers. Jessie Fauset, for example, in her review of Hughes's 1926 book *The Weary Blues,* had stretched the bounds of her taste to find aspects of the book to praise. While she had enthusiastically promoted Hughes's early work, she had difficulty with his newer, blues-influenced poems and his free verse. Cullen, while he praised Hughes's "spontaneity," called the jazz poems "interlopers" and appraised the book negatively:

> Taken as a group the selections in this book seem one-sided to me. They tend to hurl this poet [Hughes] into the gaping pit that lies before all Negro writers, in the confines of which they become racial artists instead of artists pure and simple. There is too much emphasis here on strictly Negro themes; and this is probably an added reason for my coldness towards the jazz poems—they seem to set a too definite limit upon an already limited field. (73)

On the other hand, some younger black writers applauded Hughes's formal choices, his use of black folk forms. Alain Locke, reviewing *The Weary Blues,* defends Hughes's work as "poetry of a vitally characteristic racial flow and feeling that is the next step in our cultural development" (26). Hughes's poetry, like the work of Zora Neale Hurston, recognized the richness and importance of black folk culture.[25] But Locke was not necessarily pleased with the direction Hughes often took in his use of folk forms. He shared the reservations Cullen and Fauset had expressed to Hughes himself about Hughes's friendship with Carl Van Vechten, his apparent acceptance of Van

Vechten's exoticizing and eroticizing stance toward black culture, a stance many in Harlem, according to Cunningham, found "hostile to a literature of racial responsibility" (159).[26] Not firmly part of any aesthetic camp, Hughes found himself in the middle, working somewhere between the competing generations and styles in Harlem.

By the early 1930s, Hughes's difficulties in Harlem were exacerbated as he began to find himself caught not only between the shifting and fractious aesthetic alliances of the Renaissance writers but also between competing political factions. The African American community was riven by divisions like those summarized in the shorthand of Bookerite accommodationism versus W. E. B. Du Bois's program for racial uplift as well as by varying attitudes toward nationalism and communism (or socialism). The political map of Harlem in the 1930s is a complicated one indeed, and apparently incommensurable programs competed for adherents and power. While the NAACP remained a dominant and popular organization for "advancement," other more aggressive organizations drew a great deal of attention and support. On one hand, followers of Marcus Garvey and members of his Universal Negro Improvement Association organized along racial lines regardless of class, pressing for a new black nation and, in some cases, expatriation and the foundation of that nation outside the United States.[27] On the other hand, Socialists and Communists in African America, especially in New York, had been organizing along class lines, both within and across racial communities, for decades and were represented by such magazines as the *Messenger* and the *Crusader,* as well as groups like the African Blood Brotherhood, the American Negro Labor Congress, and the League of Struggle for Negro Rights.[28] Recent scholarly accounts have brought these two hands productively together. Robin D. G. Kelley's examination of changing membership in the Communist Party during the 1930s at once undermines "the common assertion that Communists imposed integrationist values on black artists" and demonstrates that "ethnic nationalism and internationalism were not mutually exclusive" (*Race Rebels,* 104–5). Kelley argues that Garveyism actually prepared the way for Communist involvement in African American politics by radicalizing its adherents. James Smethurst's and William Maxwell's excellent studies of African American writing and communism both elaborate and enrich the portrait of black nationalist and Communist interpenetration that Kelley begins to sketch.

Hughes's location on this map, like the location of his hometown, Lawrence, Kansas, on the map of the United States, is somewhere right around the middle. His early career had been aided by the NAACP and the organization's magazine, the *Crisis,* in which many of Hughes's early poems appeared, and by the Urban League, which published *Opportunity,* another home to much of Hughes's early work. The annual contests both magazines held during the mid-1920s had provided Hughes with needed money and recognition. Both organizations, though, were politically cautious in orientation, and Hughes's growing political consciousness during the late 1920s led him to seek other comrades. Hughes never joined the Communist Party, but by 1930, his sympathies lay with the Communists' revolutionary program for bringing about social change. When, in 1930, the previously inactive American Negro Labor Congress re-formed as the Communist-affiliated League of Struggle for Negro Rights, Hughes joined the league; by 1934, he was its president (Rampersad, *I, Too, Sing America,* 217). When the Scottsboro case gained national prominence and the ILD took up the case for the defendants' appeals, Hughes tacitly sided with the party and against the NAACP, which opposed the ILD's involvement. Of the poems Hughes published on Scottsboro, none appeared in the NAACP's organ, the *Crisis.* Instead, Hughes published in *Opportunity* and, more radically, in the *New Masses* (ibid., 217–18).[29]

Scottsboro Limited gives us this aesthetically flexible, politically energized Hughes. The cover illustration (Taylor's lithograph for "Scottsboro Limited") includes a black figure on off-white paper; the title is printed in red, and heavy red lines border the illustration's vertical edges. The illustration molds the booklet's texts quite specifically around the impending fate of the Scottsboro defendants. Crowded onto a platform that could be a railroad flatcar or a place of execution, the nine black men stand or kneel, some gesturing for help from the viewer, others stoically awaiting death. Power lines stretch over them, but the illustration's perspective draws the lines in the foreground down to the defendants. The contact with high-voltage lines and an apparent radiance along the left-hand side of the illustration suggests the electrocution of the men, the punishment they were sentenced to by the Alabama courts. But the lines disappear at the head or neck of two of the black figures, and the angles of the figures' heads suggest the posture of hanged men. The state-sanctioned execution of the men is depicted in Taylor's illustration as just another lynching. Clearly, the pamphlet aims to prevent that lynching.

Taylor's illustration for "Christ in Alabama" focuses our reading of that poem as well. While Ingram's illustration in *Contempo* generalizes from the specific case and enhances Hughes's apparent irony regarding the Black Christ trope, Taylor's illustration resists that irony and more clearly draws out the trope's implications. Taylor's lithograph depicts suffering grimly but sentimentally. In the foreground, a black man is crucified on a stark, white cross. To the man's right, an older black woman sits, apparently crying. The figures are detailed with relative realism. The man wears jeans or work pants and no shirt, and his muscled torso and woolly hair partake of the stock black worker of contemporaneous illustrations. The woman wears a simple dress and apron as she sits beside the crucified man. Opposite her, cotton grows beside the cross. The illustration's sincere depiction of a Black Christ figure resists the poem's irony regarding the trope; Taylor enhances a reading of "Christ in Alabama" as a straightforward representation of black suffering in the racist South, a reading compatible with the pamphlet's fund-raising and publicizing aims.[30]

While Taylor's illustrations gear this poem and the pamphlet as a whole as humanist appeals for justice and clemency, Hughes's other texts in the pamphlet elaborate the cover's red border and lettering; they align racial injustice with the broader injustices of American capitalist society and link the Scottsboro defendants with the Communist cause. In all five of the pamphlet's texts, but especially in the short poem, "Scottsboro," and the play, "Scottsboro Limited," Hughes explicitly makes the defendants representatives of and grounds for an interracial politics.

The short poem, "Scottsboro," knits a variegated coalition from the diverse threads spun by the Scottsboro case. "8 BLACK BOYS IN A SOUTHERN JAIL," the poem begins, "WORLD, TURN PALE!" Whites, responsible for the fate of the defendants, should become whiter still, and the next line glosses this color contrast: "8 black boys and one white lie" (*Scottsboro Limited,* 5). The defendants, "boys" in both references, are innocents condemned by white mendacity. The body of the poem, though, complicates and ultimately undercuts such easy, racially coded judgments. Writing that it is "much to die when immortal feet march with you," Hughes provides, for the heart of the poem, a list of those immortal feet, figures from various backgrounds

Prentiss Taylor's illustration for Langston Hughes's "Christ in Alabama" in Hughes's Scottsboro Limited *(1932).*

and social positions who share a dedication to justice and equality. Christ appears here alongside John Brown, the two of them followed by "That mad mob / That tore the Bastille down." The poem suggests a progression from individual struggle ("Christ . . . fought alone"), through the actions of the small band behind John Brown, to the "mob" in the French Revolution; Hughes generalizes, thus, from the Scottsboro defendants to the larger body of which they are part. Next, Moses, Jeanne d'Arc, the Haitian revolutionary and emperor Jean-Jacques Dessalines, and Nat Turner come together as, in a summary line, "fighters for the free." Hughes elides differences of religion, culture, race, and historical moment to present a broad historical category linked metonymically with the Scottsboro defendants. Finally, he invokes the names of Lenin, Gandhi, and Sandino to ground the case in contemporaneous struggles around the world. Like the peasants and workers in Russia, the nonviolent resisters of colonialism in India, and the revolutionaries in Nicaragua, the poem implies, the Scottsboro defendants represent a conflict broader and deeper than their individual circumstances might indicate. They walk, under their sentence of death, among this company of martyrs and "fighters for the free," becoming thereby both provocation to and ground for interracial political cooperation.

Hughes first published "Scottsboro" in the December 1931 issue of *Opportunity,* at almost exactly the same time that he published "Christ in Alabama." In that context, in which only the occasional review by Sterling Brown took a particularly leftward stand, the breadth of Hughes's references and the subtle rhymes spread over the poem's short lines become its most important traits. And in "Scottsboro," Hughes trades in his Red flag for a multicolored banner. Though Lenin appears in the poem, he is hidden in the last quarter, sandwiched between two lines that name no one; he is the only figure to appear without another name either immediately before or after his. The pride of place offered Christ, as the first proper name in the list, and the juxtaposition of figures like Jeanne d'Arc and Dessalines align with the goals and methods promoted by the magazine and its parent institution, the National Urban League. "Scottsboro," then, ameliorates the dose of Communist propaganda in "Scottsboro Limited" and offers a way into the case for non-Communists who would be "fighters for the free."

Hughes more overtly and emphatically dramatizes a Communist politics in "Scottsboro Limited," which he first published in the November 1931 *New Masses.* The play, in a varying verse pattern, takes up four pages of the issue, sharing that space with several illustrations (none directly representing the play's characters) and a short poem, "Red Soldiers Singing," by David Arbanel. The play's rhetorical content—the actual speeches of its characters—lays on the Communist propaganda thickly; its broad staginess and sloganeering resemble the rhetoric of Arbanel's poem. But the play's form, drawn from experimental proletarian theater and black folk culture, quite powerfully yokes the fate of the eight black defendants with that of other workers; in its form more effectively than in its content, "Scottsboro Limited" brings black and white together under the Red flag.[31]

Hughes's stage directions establish the play's tone from the beginning. On a bare stage sits "one chair on a raised platform. No curtains or other effects needed." The drama will not be a "realistic" portrayal. Rather, the barely furnished stage, along with the rest of the theater, becomes a charged and changeable place, transformed by the characters' language and actions into a series of crucial sites across which the narrative unfolds and the case's significances shift and recombine. As the play opens, the eight black men march down the center aisle as if chained together by their right feet. Their slow and silent progress is interrupted by a white man who asks what they are doing there:

> *Man:* Now that you got the public eye, you want to show
> off, eh?
> *2nd Boy: (Seriously)* Not show off—die!
> *5th Boy: (Earnestly)* So the people can see
> What it means to be
> A poor black workman
> In this land of the free.
> ("Scottsboro Limited," 18)

The play then proceeds through the events of the "boys'" arrest and trial, with the white man portraying, in turn, the sheriff, the judge, the prison keeper, and the death house preacher. The stage transforms scene by scene as well. The "boys" sit on the platform and sway as though riding on top of a moving train, then line up beside the chair when they are arrested. When the trial begins, they stand before the judge, who sits in the chair. Small costume adjustments, like the black robe the white man dons for the trial or the overalls the white women remove to reveal cheap dresses beneath, are the only other indications of setting.

The set's spareness, the shifting settings represented by the bare stage, and the multiple parts played by one man frequently appear in the proletarian theater of such groups as the Theater Guild.[32] In

Hughes's play, these devices make of the theater a space for modeling and enacting interracial coalition. And in that space, he deploys the crucial force of poetry; when the "boys" speak their lines with lyric rhythm and rhyme, when they repeat key lines in a litanic fashion, the white man enjoins them to "[s]top talking poetry." Hughes's lines for the "boys" demonstrate that poetry is, as William Maxwell writes, "the distillation of the sensible, demotic speech of black workers; . . . only the 'Man' could want to dissociate poetic diction, black vernacular language, and a drama of black proletarian expression" (135). By the end of the play, the black "boys" have joined forces with white Communist workers, and the audience, representing the bloodthirsty mob through the earlier parts of the play, has transformed into a crowd of revolutionary workers:

> *Boys and Reds:* All hands together will furnish the might.
> *Audience:* All hands together will furnish the might.
> *Red Voices:* Rise from the dead, workers, and fight!
> *Boys:* All together, black and white,
> Up from the darkness, into the light.
> *All:* Rise, workers, and fight!
> *Audience:* Fight! Fight! Fight!
> ("Scottsboro Limited," 21)

And as the play concludes, Hughes writes in the stage directions, "Here the *Internationale* may be sung and the Red flag raised above the heads of the black and white workers together." In the play's transformative space and through the transformative media of rhythm, rhyme, and repetition, the problem of capitalist injustice unites workers of all colors under the Red flag, under the auspices of the "Internationale" and therefore the International.

When Hughes conferred with Taylor on the contents of the pamphlet early in 1932, he worried that this one-act "play in verse" might be "too red to be included" (quoted in Rampersad, *I, Too, Sing America,* 235). Taylor pressed Hughes to include it. The play's "Redness" became especially prominent at the California end of Hughes's reading tour. In Los Angeles, Hughes stayed for several days with Loren Miller, a radical member of the local John Reed Club, which had been prevented by the police from staging "Scottsboro Limited" shortly before Hughes's visit. Miller, who had little use for literature that was not directly politically engaged, urged Hughes to write a "mass chant" for Tom Mooney, the labor activist who had been jailed in 1916 for his alleged participation in the bombing of a Preparedness Day Parade in San Francisco (ibid., 236). At a mass meeting for the Scottsboro defense held on May 8, Hughes participated in a production of "Scottsboro Limited" and also led the Tom Mooney chant (ibid., 238). At this meeting, Hughes, more directly than elsewhere, linked the racist railroading of the Scottsboro defendants with the broader systemic injustice practiced on political radicals.

While we cannot re-create that meeting, in which the choral utterance of the play's lines and the poem's refrains briefly realized the interracial community Hughes demanded, we can locate the textual similarities between "Scottsboro Limited" and "Mass Chant for Tom Mooney," the means by which Hughes sought to bring about that community. The most striking device in both the play and the poem is repetition. In "Scottsboro Limited," Hughes employs an almost incantatory repetition at crucial moments, especially the trial, to highlight white fabrication of a racist "truth." After the scene is set by the white man's black robe and the introduction of the defendants, the judge turns to the "boys," who stand in a line at one side of the stage, and asks, "You raped that girl?" The first answers, "No." This question and answer are repeated seven more times, the emphatic negatives piling up what ought to be a convincing mountain of exculpatory evidence. The judge turns, though, after the last "boy" has answered "No," to the white women, who reply, "They raped us in a box car underneath the sky." The single line successfully overcomes the repeated answer of the defendants. When the "boys," together, try to point out the unfairness of their situation, the judge simply orders them to remain silent. Then he immediately begins another round of interrogation: "You had a gun." To this accusation, each "boy" again replies in the negative, this time varying the reply somewhat—"No sir," "Not one," "Nary a one," "No sir, none." Again, the judge asks, "How about it, girls," and the simple response—"They lie"—serves to refute the repeated claims of innocence ("Scottsboro Limited," 20).

Repetition, however, also fashions a united voice at the end of the play. Hughes has characters repeat each other's lines in a complex pattern that brings the "boys," the "Red Voices," and the audience together through the words each speaks:

8th Boy: With all of the workers,
           Black or white,
           We'll go forward
           Out of the night.
Boys: Out of the night.
8th Boy: Breaking down bars,
           Together.
Boys: Together.
Red Voices: Together.

.   .   .   .   .

Boys and Reds: All hands together will furnish the might.
Audience: All hands together will furnish the might.
("Scottsboro Limited," 21)

Thematically and formally, Hughes's 1930s poems on racial issues like the Scottsboro trials strongly resemble his poems on nonracially inflected left-wing political causes. As it does in "Scottsboro Limited," for example, repetition drives Hughes's "Mass Chant for Tom Mooney." In this short poem, repetition effects the revolutionary change that transforms Tom Mooney, by the poem's end, into "TOM MOONEY." Changes are wrought on a set of symbolic figures—the governor, steel bars, the prison walls, and the earth—through repeated references. In this way, "the man with the title of governor" whose speech has kept Mooney imprisoned is turned into the powerless and forgotten figure in contrast with the remembered Mooney, and the bars and walls of the prison are shaken "until the whole world falls into the hands of the workers." But the most important repetition in the poem is the repeated speaking of Mooney's name; the name acts as refrain and agent, attaining sufficient power through its repeated choral utterance to transform the world. "Today," Hughes writes, "the workers speak the name: Tom Mooney! Tom Mooney! Tom Mooney!" (*New Song,* 13). This chorus initiates the multicolored, global vibration that shakes the government's institutions, reduces its enclosing walls to "the scrap heap of time," and reconfigures the world in Mooney's name. By the end of the poem, capital letters help us imagine the volume of sound in that California hall, and the world changes each time the crowd shouts Mooney's name:

TOM MOONEY!
Schools will be named:

TOM MOONEY!
Farms will be named:
TOM MOONEY!
Dams will be named:
TOM MOONEY!
Ships will be named:
TOM MOONEY!
Factories will be named:
TOM MOONEY! (*New Song*, 14)

Strands in the intertextual web of Hughes's Scottsboro-era poetry, all of these texts — "Scottsboro Limited," "Mass Chant for Tom Mooney," and "Scottsboro" — imply readings of that web's central poem, "Christ in Alabama." Individually or in concert, these texts pull the poem in different directions through their formal and rhetorical affinities with it. Read alongside "Scottsboro Limited," "Christ in Alabama" becomes a polemic about systemic injustice in racist, capitalist American society. Its antiphonal structure replays the crucial call and response of the judge and the defendants in "Scottsboro Limited," the empowering repetition at the end of both play and poem. But the transaction carries with it some costs: the poem's engagement of the complex interconnectedness of racial and sexual oppression is obscured by the other text's preoccupation with connections between racial and economic oppression. Read with "Scottsboro," though, "Christ in Alabama" becomes an expression of one painful version of racial commingling. While "Scottsboro" forges an interracial tradition of revolution, making equal its cohort of heroes, "Christ in Alabama" reveals the violence inherent in the unequal distribution of power along racial lines. It glosses the first name in Hughes's list of "fighters for the free." The "Christ who fought alone" of one poem becomes the "Nigger Christ / On the cross of the South" in the other, an important reminder that the Christ who fought for freedom did so by dying.

The radical openness of "Christ in Alabama," which allows its articulation in a variety of positions on Scottsboro and the tangle of issues involved in the case, echoes the complex position Hughes himself occupied in American political culture. Black but not black, caught between classes, aesthetic camps, and political factions, Hughes was available for recruitment to causes and issues in various ways. An intelligent manipulator of his own subject positions, Hughes shrewdly situated himself so as to foreclose some potential meanings of the signifier "Langston Hughes" while foregrounding others. In his readings at the University of North Carolina and at black colleges in the South, Hughes carefully aligned himself with vigorously reformist groups, downplaying his involvement with the radical Left, while in California (and later in the Soviet Union), he quite actively sought to link his treatment of racial injustice to Communist critiques of capitalist injustice. "Christ in Alabama," finally, embodies the complex political work Hughes performed in his Scottsboro writings and in the dense orchestration of their contexts.

For several years following his creative outburst over the Scottsboro trials, Hughes moved more and more in radical circles. Immediately after his 1931 reading tour, he left for the Soviet Union with a group of African Americans to work on a film project, *Black and White* (Rampersad, *I, Too, Sing America*, 242). Initially quite excited by the Soviet Union, Hughes wrote "Good Morning Revolution" on the trip. But the film project soured, as Hughes learned firsthand the difficulties posed by even a proletarian bureaucracy—trouble obtaining permission to film in some places, difficulty traveling to others. He returned to the United States (by way of Korea) slightly disillusioned with that bureaucracy though still impressed by the Russian people (ibid., 274). He proposed a book on his Soviet experiences to Knopf, his publisher, but was informed that such a project would damage his career. Knopf also rejected a collection of political poems Hughes submitted. That collection, with some revisions, finally appeared as *A New Song* in 1938 under the imprint of the International Workers' Order. While he continued to do political work through his poetry, however, Hughes found the act of balancing politics and poetry more and more difficult through the heart of the decade. His patron, Noel Sullivan, grew increasingly vocal about his anticommunism, creating an awkward space in his relationship with Hughes (ibid., 337). At the same time, Hughes was not accepted as sufficiently radical by some critics on the Left (Rampersad, "Hughes and His Critics," 35–36). Once again, he found himself caught between groups and individuals with agendas he could balance only with great difficulty.

By 1937, Rampersad writes, Hughes "needed a tonic, a restorative" (*I, Too, Sing America*, 339). The civil war in Spain offered a perfect opportunity not only because a community of politically interested and engaged writers had already gathered in Madrid but also because, as Kelley points out, Spain was a setting where African Americans could "embrace both the Communists' internationalism and their own vision of Pan-Africanism simultaneously"; Spain was "the place where it all came together" ("This Ain't Ethiopia," 121). When Nancy Cunard and Pablo Neruda appealed to Hughes for a contribution to their anthology of poetry on behalf of the republic's defenders, Hughes sent "Song of Spain." He also signed (or was at least included as a signatory to) the *New Masses*' "Manifesto and Call," which dubbed Spain the first site of a "civil and international conflict that is certain to recur elsewhere" (ibid., 338). When André Malraux and Phillipe Aragon wired to urge Hughes to attend the Second International Writers' Congress in Paris (an event Hughes had previously declined to attend), he decided to go and to go on from there to Spain to see the war firsthand. Arranging with the *Baltimore Afro-American* and the *Cleveland Call and Post* to send a series of articles from Spain, Hughes left as a foreign correspondent in June 1937 (ibid., 339).

Hughes's reasons for going to Spain, his aims in publishing articles and poems on the conflict, reveal the links he perceived between racial issues and the international Left, between Spain and the United States, and between politics and poetry.[33] In his address to the Writers' Congress, Hughes indicates some of these complex linkages. Identifying himself as "both a Negro and poor," as a member of "the most oppressed group in America, the group that has known so little of American democracy," Hughes explicitly connects the treatment of blacks in the United States with international fascism: "We are the people who have long known in actual practice the meaning of the word Fascism—for the American attitude towards us has always been one of economic and social discrimination: in many states of our country, Negroes are not permitted to vote or to hold political office" ("Too Much of Race," 3). The plight of southern sharecroppers, the segregation of blacks in public facilities, the treatment of the Scottsboro defendants, race riots, and lynchings all demonstrate, Hughes argues, "Fascism in action." And these aspects of American "fascism" resemble the operation of fascism in Italy, Germany, Japan, and, now, Spain. In a rhetorically brilliant maneuver, Hughes locates the racial heart of fascism, drawing, throughout the essay, connections between the murderous policies and practices of, say, Spain and the treatment of blacks in the United States. These connections form the essay's armature as Hughes pivots on the resemblances between totalitarian regimes and his own country to mount a specifically leftist argument. He begins by arguing that "race means nothing when it can be turned to Fascist use" (3). The true significance of race becomes apparent only when we realize that "the Fascists of the world use it as a bugaboo and a terror to keep the working masses from getting together" (3). Spain is important because it is both a "workers' Spain" and a racially egalitarian society. At the end of the essay, Hughes clarifies the race/class connection and its far-reaching implications: "We represent the end of race. And the Fascists know that when there is no more race, there will be no more capitalism, and no more war, and no more money for the munition makers, because the workers of the world will have triumphed" (4). This essay's publication history is unique among Hughes's work. Delivered at the Second International Writers' Congress in Paris, then published in the *Volunteer for Liberty,* the *Crisis,* and the *Negro Worker,* the essay reaches readers primarily concerned with left-wing politics and literature, the Spanish Civil War, and issues of interest to American blacks. In both its content and its circulation, Hughes's address elucidates Spain's significance and appeals to the varied constituents of Hughes's audience.

This concatenation of racial and political motives manifests itself throughout Hughes's reportage from Spain. Rampersad writes that Hughes's merging of the *Baltimore Afro-American's* "narrowly racial . . . view" with his own "proletarianism and antifascism" yielded "excellent propaganda for the left, aimed directly at the black American world" (*I, Too, Sing America,* 351). The linkages between Jim Crow and communism appear not only in Hughes's writings but also in his actions in Spain. When Hughes arrived at the Alliance of Anti-Fascist Intellectuals in Madrid, he presented a note of introduction from Bill Lawrence, American chief commissar in Spain at the time. The note, addressed to Edwin Rolfe, serving then as Madrid's American chief commissar, introduces "Comrade Langston Hughes" and asks Rolfe to help Hughes "in whatever way possible to get necessary information" (quoted in Nelson and Hendricks, *Edwin Rolfe,* 30–31). The note reflects an awareness on the part of both Hughes and the Communist Party that, as Nelson writes, "Hughes was receiving Party cooperation in Spain and thus at the very least the Party considered him to be working on common interests" (31).

Hughes's relationship with Rolfe continued throughout his stay in Madrid. He accompanied Rolfe on his duties as commissar; arranged, with Rolfe's assistance, to give a radio talk on Federico García Lorca; and often socialized with Rolfe. In fact, one of Hughes's earliest poems on Spain, "To a Poet on His Birthday," is addressed to Rolfe. In this poem, Hughes establishes the vocabulary of images that will suffuse all of his Spain poetry, as well as the general form (long stanzas of metrically irregular lines with rhymes usually occurring in the even-numbered lines) that will come to typify his poems on Spain. Rolfe records in his diary the occasion of receiving the poem from Hughes. He writes that he ran into Hughes one day in Madrid: "Langston asked me when my birthday was, & I told him 'Today.' Whereupon he fell upon my neck and embraced me, & told me he had written a poem, but not revised it. Promised to give it me when completed" (quoted in Nelson and Hendricks, *Edwin Rolfe*, 33).

In this poem for a dedicated Communist, Hughes weaves images of poetry and war together under the same red that colored "Scottsboro Limited." In two pronounced parts, a long question followed by an equally long answer, he reinscribes that red, drawing the abstract "workers" on to fuller significance through the experience of the war. "What poems unfurl / Their flags made of blood / To flame in our sky," Hughes asks. And the answer makes clear that the Red in Spain's politics and the Red in Rolfe's poetry are also the red of the battlefield:

Listen world:
Heart's blood's the color
Of the songs that unfurl
And heart's blood's the color
Of our banners so red
And heart's blood's the color
Of the dawn that we know
Will rise from the darkness
Where yesterdays go
And heart's blood's the color
Of the red winds that blow.
(Nelson and Hendricks, *Edwin Rolfe*, 62)

The "heart's blood" necessary for life and emblematic of violent death links together the war's aims, Rolfe's poetry, and Hughes's own political and aesthetic stance toward Spain. A victory for the republic is as necessary as the heart's blood for the life of the body. Poems like Rolfe's, banners that gather the troops and birds that fly "over all the barriers of time" to record the struggle, are equally necessary. In Spain as in Scottsboro, politics and poetry are as interdependent for Hughes as blood and life.

This early poem had an audience of only one, but Hughes was soon reaching much larger audiences. Hughes began his series of weekly articles for the *Baltimore Afro-American* in the paper's October 23, 1937, issue. Perhaps not accidentally, the initiation of the series coincides with the paper's announcement of the death in Spain of Milton Herndon, brother of African American activist Angelo Herndon. Of the two items on Spain, Hughes's receives greater attention. His article on Spain tops the front page: "EXCLUSIVE!!! — From war-torn Spain, Langston Hughes, celebrated American novelist and poet, brings exclusively to AFRO-AMERICAN readers a vivid and accurate picture of the bitter struggle that is now going on. This interesting series and the accompanying photographs will appear only in the AFRO-AMERICAN" (Hughes, "Hughes Bombed in Spain," 1). Hughes's first article lives up to its headline, as the poet-cum-journalist recounts his experience of the bombardment that pounded Madrid during the fall of 1937. But the majority of the article focuses on Hughes's actions during the days before the air raid. He details his meeting and conversations with Cuban poet Nicolas Guillen, describes the city's plazas and facades, and rehearses the directions that hotel clerks gave regarding conduct during air raids. Two aspects of the preraid text stand out as significant discursive strategies of Hughes's reportage. First, Hughes spends several column inches on an account of his and Guillen's evening at the Mella Club: "We were invited to a dance that afternoon given in honor of the soldiers on leave, and here we met a number of Cubans, both colored and white, and a colored Portuguese, all taking an active part in the Spanish struggle against the fascists. And all of them finding in loyalist Spain more freedom than they had known at home. . . . In Spain, as one could see at the dance that afternoon, there is no color line, and Catalonian girls and their escorts mingled gaily with the colored guests" (3). Suggested by neither the title nor the teaser and having little to do with the bombing raid supposedly at the article's heart, Hughes's visit to the Mella Club provides an opportunity to place Spain's value up front. Hughes holds up Spain as an example of good race relations before the bombs fall and threaten to destroy it.

A second passage in the long buildup to the bombing raid evokes the remarkably normal lives of many Madrileños in spite of the war and bombardments and elicits readers' sympathy for people whose lives might seem quite like their own until explosives and incendiaries shatter them. When Hughes and Guillen return to their hotel after the dance and have dinner, they discover that the most pressing privation wrought by the war, at least for international guests of finer hotels, is the limited menu; while the dining room remains "luxurious" and the waiters continue to wear their tuxedos, Hughes writes, "there was only one fixed dinner menu, no choice of food." That said, though, the dinner is a "good dinner," with all of the expected courses present and accounted for, though "nothing elaborate." After dinner, the two writers stroll with the promenading citizens and take their coffee, "as one often does in Europe," in a sidewalk café right out of Hemingway (3).

Hughes's evocation of everyday life in Madrid, so familiar even in its minor privations, makes the bombing, when it finally happens in the last third of the article, that much more shocking. In other words, it enables Hughes to accomplish his primary aim in the piece: the re-creation of the experience of bombardment in ways that draw readers' sympathy to the Madrileños through their recognition of similarity, of shared lifestyles and values even across the Atlantic. But no sooner does Hughes begin to undress for bed than the night erupts in sirens. Just as he led readers through his relatively routine day and evening, now he recounts the confusion and fear, the utter departure from the normal, wrought by the air raid: "Suddenly all the lights went out in the hotel, but we heard people rushing down the halls and stairways in the dark. A few had flashlights with them to find the way. Some were visibly frightened. In the lobby two candles were burning, casting weird, giant-like shadows on the walls" (3). The fact that the raid does not materialize this time, that the only firing the guests hear as they huddle in the lobby is Republican anti-aircraft fire, serves to enhance rather than detract from the moment's shock and strangeness. And the night has just begun.

Sleeping soundly after returning to his room following the false alarm, Hughes is jerked awake by a nearby explosion and quickly realizes that this bombardment is for real; there is "no foolin' this time":

"The next thing I knew, the telephone was ringing violently in the dark, the siren screaming its long blood-curdling cry again, and the walls of the building shaking. BOOM! Then the dull roar of a dying vibration. And another BOOM! Through my window I saw a flash of light. I didn't stay to look again. Down the hall I went, clothes in my arms, sensing my way toward the staircase in the dark" (3). In its descriptions of the bombing and the citizens' reactions to it, Hughes's first communique to Baltimore makes good on the teaser's promise of "a vivid and accurate picture of the bitter struggle." More important, though, it humanizes the Spanish, especially the Republicans. And Hughes exploits the fact that, as Raymond Williams has argued, "to address an account to another is, explicitly or potentially, . . . to evoke or propose an active relationship to the experience being expressed" (*Marxism*, 166). The article at once shows city residents' efforts to live normally and the impossibility of living a life American readers would consider normal under the conditions of war; it renders and invites relationship. Although the article concludes with a comment about "getting used to air raids in Spain," it demonstrates through its representation of Hughes's own experience that air raids are not the sort of thing people get used to. In so doing, it grants readers a stake in what's at stake in Spain.

As "Madrid's Flowers Hoist Blooms to Meet Raining Fascist Bombs" a month later shows, everyday life is grimmer still. In text surrounding a photograph of a shell-riddled Madrid apartment house, Hughes alternates descriptions of horrific shellings and the random rain of death ("[T]here is no way of telling where the shells are going to fall—in the street or on the houses, on the east side of town or on the west side, in the suburbs or in the heart of the city") with examples of the citizenry's calm response to the situation ("[I]f the bombardment is a long one, and several guns are dropping missiles of death on the town, then people may get out of bed and seek the basement") (1). Amid the bombings, death, and general suffering, which seems to have increased or to have become more evident to Hughes in the weeks since his first article, the people of Madrid, Hughes assures his readers, "are calm, serene, even gay at times with flashes of the old gaiety for which Madrid was noted among the capitals of Europe before the war" (1).

It might seem strategically wrongheaded for a writer whose purpose is, at least in part, to elicit sympathy (and often funds) for the people undergoing the ordeal of daily bombardment to emphasize their calm, indeed, their continuing capacity for "gaiety." But by showing the Madrileños' smiling endurance, Hughes draws a stark contrast with the grim visage of Franco and his "Fascists"; by showing the Republicans remaining cheerfully and steadfastly dedicated to their embattled government's ideals, he establishes a standard that Franco, with his conscripts and his terror campaigns, cannot meet. In addition, Hughes subtly criticizes the neutral governments of Europe and the United States. In a concluding peroration, he transforms Madrid's capacity to withstand privation and bombardment into the abstraction of "Time," which he allies with such universal goods as art and freedom:

> Time is with the people of Spain. Time, and the moral consciousness of the world. The Fascists who bomb women and children, who have put to death García Lorca, Spain's greatest poet, who deliberately rained explosives on the art museum of El Prado and on the National Library with its priceless books and manuscripts, who use churches for arsenals and bring Mohammedans to battle for a "Christian ideal," and who fight for no cause at all except the forcing of the Spanish people back into economic and spiritual slavery for the sake of a handful of rich men and outworn nobles — these Fascists, Madrid feels, cannot win. (2)

Madrid endures because Madrid is right. Madrid holds out because it holds out against wrongs: destruction, privilege, closed-mindedness, and murder. And the African American readers of the *Baltimore Afro-American* can clearly see, through the lens Hughes polishes for them, their connection with Madrid's embattled citizens. Their families have been threatened, their spokespersons murdered, and their freedom, within distant memory, has been taken away by a state apparatus shielded by its own "Christian ideal."

"Hughes Bombed in Spain" and "Madrid's Flowers" put Hughes himself front and center. Through his experiences, readers experience the Spanish conflict. In his other articles, however, Hughes allots more space to stories about other blacks in Spain. By charting black soldiers' rise to command positions in the International Brigades and then placing such stories alongside accounts of the Spanish Moroccan shock troops' devastating losses in the front lines, Hughes demonstrates the opposing racial policies of the republic and its supporters on one hand and the Fascists on the other. Throughout the series, Hughes insistently explores the significance of the war for American blacks, but in "Hughes Finds Moors Being Used as Pawns by Fascists in Spain," one of his most important articles for the *Baltimore Afro-American,* he emphasizes the participation of blacks in the war in actual conflict.

In "Hughes Finds Moors Being Used as Pawns," Hughes draws the stark contrast between blacks in the International Brigades and their counterparts in Franco's army.[34] While blacks could (and did) rise to command positions in the brigades, Hughes writes, Moors served as shock troops, pressed to the front lines of offensives to absorb the highest casualties. While service in the brigades was voluntary, North Africans were forced to fight for Franco; even when not directly conscripted, they were often lured by promises of good pay and then, as Hughes has it, "paid off in worthless German marks which they were told would be good to spend when they got back to Africa" (1). Moreover, the Spanish Moroccans' participation in the war marks their return to a country they once conquered and ruled themselves. Their former status as rulers, Hughes implies, aligns the North Africans with the Ethiopians recently defeated by Italy. The "Moors" are avatars, then, for Haile Selassie's kingdom, a nation with whom African American readers deeply sympathized and whose defeat at Italy's hands provoked riots in American cities.[35] Their current status as conscripts or poorly paid, duped shock troops indicates the threat to blacks under the heel of fascism. Hughes bleakly concludes his discussion of the Spanish Moroccans by pointing out that most never live to return to Africa and try to spend the marks they have been paid. Indeed, as the war enters its second year, Hughes writes, the "Moors" "are no longer a potent force in Franco's army. Too many of them have been killed" (3).[36]

To show the contrast between Franco's and the republic's treatment of blacks, he lists the many places from which blacks have come to fight for Spain: "Within the last year, colored people from many different countries have sent men, money, and sympathy to Spain." Josephine Baker has danced to raise money for the republic, Hughes informs his readers. Paul Robeson has sung, a black band has played in the Moulin Rouge, and a large group of black writers from Africa, the West Indies, and Cuba have written and given readings for Spain. Cities all over the United States have sent black soldiers for the International Brigades and black nurses for the medical corps. More important, Hughes unites these disparate black volunteers under the shared understanding he claims for them. Not only do all of these blacks participate in order to "fight against the forces that have raped Ethiopia"; they share a broader understanding of how race and the republic's fate are intricated: "All of them [are] here because they know that if Fascism creeps across Spain, across Europe, and then across the world, there will be no place left for intelligent young Negroes at all. In fact, no decent place for any Negroes—because Fascism preaches the creed of Nordic supremacy and a world for whites alone" (1). If the republic loses to Franco and the imperial powers behind him, the world will not be a safe or comfortable place for nonwhite peoples. Fascism, Hughes writes, assumes the supremacy of white Europeans and systematically institutionalizes that supremacy through laws governing all aspects of social life. In an America already inclined to separate the races and assume the social superiority of whites, Hughes sees an analogue to the Fascists' racist codes. And the battle for Spain resonates back to the United States, for once blacks have fought together with whites for the common cause, they will refuse to return to their former social position. This, at least, is Hughes's expectation as the war rages on.

Just as important, though, "Hughes Finds Moors Being Used as Pawns" clearly articulates Hughes's aims for the reportage he is sending home: "Why had I come to Spain? To write for the colored press. I knew that Spain had once belonged to the Moors, a colored people. . . . Now the Moors have come again to Spain with the Fascist armies as cannon fodder for Franco. But on the Loyalist side there are many colored people of various nationalities in the International Brigades. I want to write about both Moors and colored people" (1). The second sentence here is crucial, for Hughes puts at the center of his Spanish mission his work for the "colored press." To help construct the kind of collective necessary for victory in Spain, the kind of collective modeled by the International Brigades themselves, Hughes must reach key constituencies, especially his black readers. By bringing home to those readers the experience of Madrid's bombardment, Hughes elicits sympathy for those who are "bombed in Spain" and attempts to mobilize that sentiment in the service of a broadly Socialist vision. At the same time, by exploring and explaining the role of blacks in Spain in the *Baltimore Afro-American,* a newspaper whose front pages were also filled with stories about Joe Louis and the Wagner Anti-Lynching Act, Hughes links American racism with international fascism and forcefully consociates international leftist politics and racial equality. In so doing, he contributes to the African American press's general aim: to raise the profile of race in the portfolio of interests at play in American attitudes toward the Spanish conflict.

The articles surrounding Hughes's pieces strengthen the connections he draws in the pieces themselves. During Hughes's months in Spain, several issues dominate the news pages of the *Baltimore Afro-American.* Articles on aspects of the Scottsboro case, now six years old, appear in almost every issue. These short pieces deal with things like the mounting costs of continued appeals and the activities of the defendants in and out of prison. Longer articles appear on the progress of the Wagner Anti-Lynching Act in the U.S. Congress and the probable appointment of Alabama senator Hugo Black to the U.S. Supreme Court. Hughes's articles on Spain, broken up over several pages and columns, physically intertwine with the coverage of these issues; Spain's significance for American blacks is thus woven into the fabric of the news. Only one issue of great interest to the paper's readers fails to connect with Spain. In the November 13 issue, coverage of boxer Joe Louis's alleged infidelity eclipses all other news; for the first time since October 23, no article by Hughes appears in the paper. The only item on Spain in the issue is a one-paragraph article about a black volunteer's anger over a mistaken report of his death.

Hughes's reportage locates him in a collective effort to link black and Red in the crucible of Spain. As Kelley points out, black newspapers like the *Baltimore Afro-American,* the *Pittsburgh Courier,* the *Atlanta Daily World,* and the *Chicago Defender* "unequivocally sided with the Spanish Republic" ("This Ain't Ethiopia," 18). The reasons for this are clear. Like many black volunteers, the editors of these newspapers saw Spain as a continuation of the Italian-Ethiopian conflict that had so enraged the African American community. More than this, though, the black press had, since before World War I, often made common cause with the American Left and, at key moments, with the international Left, including the Communist Party.[37] Black newspapers added their voices to those of Socialists and the IWW in opposition to World War I. The black press lauded the CPUSA's funding and support of the ILD, which paid for the Scottsboro defendants' appeals after their convictions. When the Popular Front Spanish Republic was attacked, black editors and writers acted on their historic sense of strategic connection with the Left.

But Hughes sought to reach other communities as well. Of the reportage Hughes published from Spain, his essay "Laughter in Madrid" reached the largest readership. Published in the *Nation* in January 1938, this article elicits the sympathies of readers for Spain's civilians as they endured Franco's bombardment. Here, as in the newspaper pieces, Hughes effectively transcends simple reportage, rhetorically establishing a relationship between the citizens of Madrid and the *Nation*'s audience by equating them and setting both against Franco's forces. The linkage between readers and represented citizens is made clear from the essay's first few sentences:

> The thing about living in Madrid these days is that you never know when a shell is going to fall or where. Any time is firing time for Franco. Imagine yourself sitting calmly in the front room of your third-floor apartment carefully polishing your eyeglasses when all of a sudden, without the least warning, a shell decides to come through the wall—paying no attention to the open window—and explodes like a thunder clap beneath the sofa. (119)

Hughes's tactical use of the second person here carries the reader from the safe vantage point of the United States to the precarious situation of every person in Madrid; any division between "them" and "us" is temporarily canceled by Hughes's "you." But "we" are not drawn into the dramatic but distant space of a battlefield. The quotidian details of this opening paragraph make it easy to comply with Hughes's direction for readers to "[i]magine yourself." Almost any reader could occupy the picture Hughes draws—sitting in an apartment, polishing eyeglasses—until the picture is violently disrupted by a shell. Madrileños, Hughes makes clear, are just like you and me.

But they (and therefore we) are not like Franco. While anyone else might restrict bombardment to military targets and to specific times, "[a]ny time is firing time for Franco." The other side, Hughes implies, invades the home with shells, disrupts domestic tasks with violence, and leaves no place safe for noncombatants. The canons of civility are replaced by the cannons with which, Hughes writes, Franco "bombard[s] the city fan-wise, sending *quince-y-medios* from one side of the town to the other" ("Laughter in Madrid," 119). More important, the enemy is driven by a system of thought deadlier than shells both for the citizens of Madrid and for the rest of the world. In a pivotal paragraph, Hughes recounts a telling anecdote:

> Not long ago, a small shell fell in the study of a bearded professor of ancient languages. Frantically, his wife and daughter came running to see if anything had happened to him. They found him standing in the center of the floor, holding the shell and shaking his head quizzically. "This little thing," he said, "this inanimate object, can't do us much damage. It's the philosophy that lies behind it, wife, the philosophy that lies behind it." (120)

In a scenario like the one Hughes opens the essay with, the shell is met with tired equanimity. Hughes's professor recognizes that the real danger is located not in the ordnance but in the social order that propelled it into the city. Such an order, clearly, is as deadly to *Nation* readers in the United States as it is to the Spanish in Madrid.

Hughes reached his largest audience with a poem he wrote on Spain months after he had returned to the United States when *Esquire* published "Air Raid: Barcelona" in October 1938. In this poem, as in his article on the bombing of Madrid, Hughes renders the human suffering of the civil war with descriptive power. While the article and the poem differ tonally, their ultimate purpose and strategies are the same; in both, Hughes strives to draw readers into the war by making both the bombings and their human costs real to readers. But while "Laughter in Madrid" humanizes the Madrileños through humor, "Air Raid: Barcelona" turns on the interplay between the senses of hearing and sight during a nocturnal bombardment of the city. The irregular rhymes throughout the poem (almost always occurring in the second and fourth lines of unmarked quatrains) emphasize the crucial role of sound in the raid. At the poem's beginning, "black smoke of sound" alerts the citizens to the approach of bombers, the siren taking on the character of a human voice distorted by disrupted sleep:

> Worse than a scream
> Tangled in the wail
> Of a nightmare dream. (*CP*, 207)

Jerked awake in the dark, citizens must depend on their hearing as they scramble for safety, stumbling half-dressed down stairs. Even the sense of sound, though, is attacked by the bombers, whose approach

Hughes characterizes as "death in the ear." In a climactic moment of the bombing, Hughes breaks from the rhyme pattern he has established to elaborate this aural death as all other sounds are overcome by the falling ordnance:

> Then the BOMBS fall!
> All other noises are nothing at all
>   When the BOMBS fall
> All other noises are suddenly still
>   When the BOMBS fall
> All other noises are deathly still
> As blood spatters the wall. (ibid.)

The repetition of the single rhyme over seven lines evokes, with the capitalized "BOMBS," the absorption of all sound into explosion after explosion. This aural death, though, is made concrete several lines later, when Hughes writes, "No other noise can be heard / As a child's life goes up / In the night like a bird." Rhyme and image link the bombs with the life they destroy; Hughes later enhances this linkage when he calls the bombers "death birds."

The actual death is a turning point in the poem, for after it, when fighters are dispatched to attack the bombers, sight replaces sound as the poem's primary sense. As a bomber goes down under fire, its flames cast orange and blue light over the scene and the night becomes "red like blood." Their work of destruction done, the bombers fly east, into the dawn. That same dawn begins to reveal to the citizens of Barcelona the damage wrought by the bombs:

> With wings like black cubes
> Against the far dawn,
> The stench of their passage
> Remains when they're gone.
> In what was a courtyard
> A child weeps alone.
>
> Men uncover bodies
> From ruins of stone. (*CP*, 208)

In a reversal of the common trope wherein the dawn brings renewal and the promise of life, Hughes illuminates the death and destruction the citizens face. What remains in the wake of the attack is the bombers' own odor. The structures of the city are reduced to ruins, to the awful absence of "what was a courtyard." The people have been similarly destroyed, reduced to the rubble of bodies or to the lonely weeping of the single child.

"Air Raid: Barcelona" effectively renders the bombing of civilian targets common in the Spanish Civil War, using such devices as imagery, repetition, and rhyme to make the destruction graphic. Moreover, Hughes appeals openly to readers' probable sympathy with "innocent" victims; children appear at three crucial moments as the emblematic victims of the bombardment. The poem seems calculated to draw on the not necessarily political sympathies of its readers in *Esquire,* pitched at almost any reader who might object to the indiscriminate murder of children under cover of darkness. William Sharpe's lithograph illustration for the poem enhances the poem's humanist appeal. The illustration, in an expressionist/realist style, depicts a woman in the foreground fleeing the destruction wrought by bombers that appear in the upper right-hand corner. Her expression clearly indicating horror, the raggedly clothed woman carries an apparently dead child in her right arm and pulls another, older child by the hand. Limp and shrouded in shadow, the older child also appears to be dead. The woman's path is obstructed by rubble, and clouds of smoke in the background indicate destruction throughout the city. Just as the illustration's style graphically renders the suffering of the Spanish, the same poetic devices that enhance the poem's presentation of terror and destruction anchor it in a mode recognizable not only as Hughes's but also as "poetic." The meter is recognizably, if irregularly, trochaic, the rhymes are frequent if not consistent, and the images and figures of speech clearly carry traditional symbolic weight.

"Air Raid: Barcelona" works as an obviously poetic representation of the war in Spain for an American audience that might not understand or care about the complicated politics behind the bombings. Shaped for and delivered to a literate but politically varied readership of a popular magazine, this poem seeks simply to attract sympathy for the victims of Franco's bombings, victims who metonymically represent the Republican side in the war. While this poem is Hughes's most obviously successful aesthetic representation of the Spanish Civil War, eliciting sympathy and perhaps funds from readers, Hughes most compellingly distills political analysis in a poem Rampersad calls "a maudlin dialect poem" (*I, Too, Sing America,* 351). In "A

Letter from Spain Addressed to Alabama," Hughes offers a sophisticated understanding of the interplay between racial politics and the war. Most important, he frames this understanding in a form particularly well suited to his aims and his audience. Hughes first published "Letter from Spain" in the *Volunteer for Liberty,* the magazine of the English-speaking International Brigades, in November 1937; while it is addressed to "a brother at home," the poem actually circulates among readers who share the speaker's situation in Spain. It works as a sort of "continuing education" for soldiers in the brigades, especially black soldiers.

Throughout the poem, the speaker, Johnny, elaborates for his correspondent the relationship between the situation of blacks on the Republican side and the plight of North Africans conscripted into Franco's army. When his unit captures a wounded Moor in battle, Johnny asks him, "What you been doin' here / Fightin' against the free?" Through an interpreter, the Spanish Moroccan soldier answers that he was forced "to join the fascist army / and come across to Spain." He adds that he fears he will never return home, at which point Johnny "look[s] across to Africa / and see[s] foundations shakin'." His confrontation with this living emblem of imperialism provokes a vision with geopolitical resonance; the foundations of the old order, shaken by a "workers' Spain" that elevates blacks to equal social status, draw the attention and defense of the world's imperial powers:

> I said, I guess that's why old England
> And I reckon Italy, too,
> Is afraid to let a workers' Spain
> Be too good to me and you. (*CP,* 201)

To cinch his point for the letter's reader, Johnny draws together the colonial powers, Franco, and, implicitly, the United States as practitioners of slavery. Empires "have slaves in Africa," and the "Moor" is enslaved by Franco (caught and forcibly deported to Spain). Johnny is rhetorically equated with the "Moor"—twice he writes that they are the same color—so he (along with his supposedly black correspondent) shares the experience of enslavement. The letter ends, though, with the linkage broken. Overwhelmed by his new comprehension of the war's significance, Johnny takes the Moor's hand. "But," he concludes, "the wounded Moor was dyin' / And he didn't understand."

Johnny closes with the customary Republican gesture, "Salud," a brief but effective reminder that the struggle remains to be resolved. As a reading of his reportage shows, this poem is part of a multigeneric front on which Hughes tried to collocate American racial politics with the agenda of the international Left. It sharpens and condenses arguments Hughes was making at the same time in prose.

An obvious departure from the form of Hughes's other Spain poetry, the form of "Letter from Spain" (and the later "Post Card from Spain Addressed to Alabama") calls out for commentary. While Rampersad holds an unqualified negative view of these "maudlin dialect poem[s]," their colloquial ballad-epistle form perfectly fits the poems' rhetorical content. The only race-inflected poems published in the *Volunteer for Liberty* during its two-year history, Hughes's "letter" and "postcard," along with his essay "Negroes in Spain," bring much-needed attention to the role of race in the conflict and the significance of the conflict for issues of race. While the paper periodically published articles on imperialism, only Hughes's work in the *Volunteer for Liberty* focused explicitly on race. The dialect in "Letter from Spain" registers Hughes's primary concern at the level of diction. Fighting in Spain empowers Johnny to speak; his experience allows him both to comprehend and to communicate the tangled relevance of race. More important, Hughes adds a level to the poems' didactic content through this formal choice. In his autobiography, *I Wonder as I Wander,* Hughes recalls that he "wrote these verses in the form of a letter from an American Negro in the Brigades to a relative in Dixie" in order to express the emotions some blacks in the brigades felt about fighting blacks on the other side, the Moors (353). But when he read these poems to a group of soldiers at the front, some "objected to the lack of correct grammar and the slightly broken English that I had used in these Letters. They said that many of their Negro comrades in arms were well educated; furthermore, I might mistakenly be aiding in perpetuating a stereotype" (378). Hughes's response makes clear the rhetorical aim of the poems' form. He concedes that many black brigadiers are educated but adds that many other brigadiers, of various racial backgrounds, are not. He compares blacks from the American South to blacks from the African North, "who had had meager, if any, opportunities for education." But most important, Hughes argues, the poems show that "even the least privileged of Americans, the Southern Negroes, were represented in the International Brigades, fighting on the side of the Spanish peasants and workers to help them preserve a government that would give peasants and workers— as were most Negroes, too—a chance at schools and the learning of grammar" (378). In the voice of an undereducated black man from the American South, Hughes demonstrates the interpenetration of imperialism, race, egalitarianism, and education; he articulates, thereby, the multiple grounds for the war's significance for American blacks.

This, at least, is Hughes's expectation as the war rages on. In "Post Card from Spain Addressed to Alabama," which he published in the *Volunteer for Liberty* in April 1938, Hughes crystallizes that expectation in the voice of Johnny, the soldier in the Lincoln Brigade:

Folks over here don't treat me
Like white folks used to do.
When I was home they treated me
Just like they treatin' you.

I don't think things'll ever
Be like that again:
I done met up with folks
Who'll fight for me
Like I'm fightin' now for Spain. (*CP*, 202)

Hughes would soon enough find out how the folks back home would treat him; by November, he had finished his commitment for the African American newspapers and prepared, however reluctantly, to leave Madrid. After a farewell party at the Hotel Victoria and brief visits to Barcelona and Paris, he sailed for the United States in January 1938.

Though he returned to the United States before the war had ended, Hughes would continue his efforts to fix and communicate the war's significance. In a lecture series set up for him by Louise Thompson, Hughes discussed Spain in the context of other global events important to blacks; the Friends of the Abraham Lincoln Brigade also engaged Hughes's services as a speaker. Most important, though, Hughes continued to explore the meanings of Spain in his poetry, even during the turbulent years of World War II and its aftermath. In 1952, he published two poems, "Hero—International Brigade" and "Tomorrow's Seed," in the Veterans of the Abraham Lincoln Brigade's collection, *The Heart of Spain*. These poems capture, in their forms as well as their thematic treatments, both a near-conventional elegiac stance toward Spain and an insistence on the continuing relevance of the conflict; the values embodied by the republic and its defenders retain a revolutionary potential.

"Tomorrow's Seed" fashions a metaphor for that dormant revolutionary potential from the buried bodies of those killed for Spain. Like Rolfe in "Epitaph," Hughes begins with death and burial.[38] The bodies lie "inert and helpless" beneath the ground, beneath "proud banners of death" that wave in the Spanish sky, their poles reaching down into the earth. But the bodies only appear passive to those for whom the conflict is over, the victors who cannot see beneath the surface. There, in the darkness underground, the bodies of the dead become "the mighty roots of liberty," the spreading tendrils of a renewed rebellion. At the grave of Arnold Reid, Edwin Rolfe imagined Reid's blood nourishing the olive trees and crops that would feed the soldiers who fought for Spain. Almost twenty years later, Hughes sees in Reid and all the other casualties of the Spanish Civil War the seeds for a "new life." He knows the crop of corpses in Spain might not flower immediately. His poem, though, joins the work of Rolfe and others in *The Heart of Spain* to tend the soil, to preserve the bodies' potential until the moment when, out of sight to the oppressors, the roots might "push upward in the dark." The poem's simple form accomplishes this task. The short lines' irregular rhymes hold out only the promise of resolution, establishing and immediately breaking a pattern of aural expectation. But at the poem's conclusion, when Hughes reads in the stars the name that will germinate a new revolution, he allows the sounds to ring with resolve and bring death and new life resoundingly together:

> Man
> Who fell in Spanish earth:
> Human seed
> For freedom's birth. (*CP*, 431)

Hughes's other contribution to the anthology makes a full circle of his Spain poetry, returning to and reprising the themes and images of his unpublished poem for Rolfe, "To a Poet on His Birthday." The earlier poem collapses the unfurling flags of poetry and the flames of war together into the controlling image of "heart's blood." As if taking off from that conflation, Hughes begins "Hero—International Brigade" by questioning it:

Blood,
Or a flag,
Or a flame
Or life itself
Are they the same:
Our dream? (*CP*, 431)

The events of the intervening years have challenged the confident as-sertions of 1937. Are there no differences between blood spilled in the war, poems written about it, and cities destroyed by it? "To a Poet" had presented poetry and war as mutually requisite; both were neces-sary. That proposition is now disputed, and to answer the challenge, Hughes must return to his experience of the war. He signals that re-turn with a narrative fragment: "I came." Through the voice of a vol-unteer killed in the war, Hughes sketches the difficulties he had to overcome in his own journey to Spain—the ocean and mountains, the opposition of governments—and re-creates the sacrifice of the volunteers in the brigades. In that sacrifice, in the very moment of the soldier's death, he finds the answer to the poem's opening ques-tion. Shot in battle, his heart cut away by bullets, the "hero" lives the confusion of Hughes's conflation:

I wondered if it were blood
Gushing there.
Or a red flame?
Or just my death
Turned into life? (431)

As he dies, the speaker realizes that "They're all the same / Our dream."

Even after the defeat of the republic and the other defeats Hughes has witnessed during the anti-Communist inquisition, "Hero—In-ternational Brigade" demonstrates that Hughes's determination to negotiate between the aesthetic and the political, the determination evident in "The Negro Artist and the Racial Mountain," remains un-conquered. Hughes finds in the political controversies and causes of the 1920s, 1930s, and 1940s both the role of race and the crucial link-ages between racial issues and other political concerns. He exploits these linkages to unite readers with varying interests and priorities in the collectives, however temporary or imagined, necessary for political intervention. Hughes infuses African American suffering with Communist ambition, making the overthrow of Jim Crow and the conquering of capitalism one and the same revolutionary project.[39] As Rampersad reminds us, Hughes performs this crucial political work as a writer. "What mattered to Hughes," Rampersad writes, "was not his political beliefs but their effect . . . on his art" (*I, Too, Sing America,* 338). Impressive at the thematic level, Hughes's achievement takes on even greater importance at the formal level. Singing the "Internationale" in the voices of nine black men and one black Christ, addressing southern racism in a modernist theatrical experiment, and exploring Spain in both lyric and dialect, Hughes continuously challenges the hegemony of bourgeois values in American culture and the dominance of white speakers in American politics. He reaches the summit of the racial mountain and from his position there calls out with simple beauty and alters the boundaries of all he surveys.[40]

3

Getting the Goofs to Listen

EZRA POUND

As we have seen, Langston Hughes and Edwin Rolfe mined the traditions at hand for cultural resources through which to fashion the communities required for social change along a variety of vectors. Few poets writing in the 1930s had more traditions at hand for such purposes than Ezra Pound, who had, in his work of the 1910s, produced versions of such poetries as the Provençal, the Chinese, the Anglo-Saxon, and the late Latin, to name only the most prominent. But in the late 1930s, when confronted by the increasing likelihood of a second European war just two decades after the devastation of the Great War (in which his friends and collaborators had fought and died for "a botched civilization"), Pound turned to the history of the American Republic and specifically to the life and writings of John Adams. Quarrying raw materials from Adams's journals and letters and subjecting those materials to the modernist alchemy of fragmentation and juxtaposition, Pound transformed the second president of the United States into a hero analogous to such figures in *The Cantos* as Confucius, Odysseus, and Sigismundo Malatesta. In this confluence of thematic content and formal operation, Pound developed a poetic intervention into contemporary history, a poetic wing in his multiple-front and single-handed effort to stop a war.

Reading Pound as a partisan political poet requires us to perform a set of destructive and constructive acts similar to those Pound himself performed in the composition of the poem. We must find the links between the cantos of a particular historical moment and Pound's political actions—textual and otherwise—at that moment. We must examine the joints and ligatures that constitute the structural bearing walls of *The Cantos*—Pound's incorporation of historical documents in the poem. In this chapter, I focus on this crucial compositional practice during the conjuncture of changing international (especially American) attitudes toward Italy in the late 1930s. Unlike his earlier use of documents (beginning in the Malatesta Cantos), Pound's incorporation of John Adams's *Works* in Cantos 62–71 directly addresses the political situation of 1938–40. The Adams Cantos simultaneously develop and retool the overarching obsessions of *The Cantos,* extending Pound's ideas of order through the Odyssean/Malatestan figure of Adams and articulating through Adams an urgent insistence on American independence from and neutrality regarding European struggles.

Recognizing the enormous difficulty and improbability of effecting political change through the unacknowledged legislation of poetry, Pound feverishly attempted more direct interventions: letters to acknowledged legislators in the U.S. Congress, numerous articles in a wide variety of periodicals, and the infamous speeches on Rome Radio. Constituents of Pound's political practice, these heretofore excluded relics must be reconnected with the fragments that constitute Pound's poetic practice of the same moment. Linked by documentary inclusion and rhetorical execution, Pound's writings of the late 1930s mount an aggressive attempt to imagine a community supportive of American neutrality in the face of an ever more certain European war.

As Michael Bernstein has argued, Pound's spatial and metonymic juxtaposition of textual fragments allows him to include in the poem "domains of experience often considered alien territory"; Pound grafts the prose of tracts, travelogues, and treatises onto the visually ordered page of his poem "without privileging either medium" (41). He demolishes generic boundaries and constructs from the wreckage what Lawrence Rainey has called a "monument of culture."[1] Following Bernstein's insights, Robert Casillo and Tim Redman, among others, have quite convincingly reconsidered the relationship between Pound's poetry and his politics, making clear the impossibility of separating them. On one hand, Casillo emphatically insists on reading Pound's poetry to find in it traces of the politics more evident in his periodical prose and in the speeches he delivered over Rome

Radio through the first half of World War II. He spells out, with critical rigor and theoretical sophistication, how Pound's fascism and anti-Semitism constitute the poem's metaphorical fabric. On the other hand, Redman explores the evolution of Pound's political thought and his relation to Italian fascism in more strictly historical ways. More recently, Michael North elaborates Pound's "political aesthetic" through a careful reading of Pound's prose alongside selected moments from *The Cantos*.

The incorporation of historical documents constitutes the single greatest poetic innovation wrought by *The Cantos*. While the spatial reading urged by critics like Jerome McGann opens our attention to the broader semiotic field of the poem, enhancing our reading at the verbal or linguistic level, only careful attention to Pound's use of historical documents sufficiently enlarges the textual field to allow us access to the poem's political potentialities. Of course, Pound is not the first or the only poet to include quotation in his work. Indeed, as Rainey has written, "quotation is a salient feature of major modernist texts" (*Ezra Pound*, 58). One has only to recall the startling pastiche of quoted material in T. S. Eliot's *Waste Land* to sense the centrality of such citation in the modernist project. More important than the fact of quotation, though, is its generic character. We might be surprised by the number and length of Eliot's quotations from metaphysical poems and Renaissance revenge tragedy, but we can fairly easily absorb these fragments as parts of the poem. They are, after all, other literary works; they share with Eliot's lines generic conventions and connotations. But when Eliot quotes a popular song, the refrain of pub closing, and a child's nursery rhyme, he begins to fray the edges of "poetry."

Pound's quotations threaten to shred that fabric altogether. Rainey argues that Pound's citation of historical documents "seems an especially intransigent form of this practice" (*Ezra Pound*, 58). Eliot only occasionally strays from the literary for his sources, but Pound's are "aggressively quotidian and anti-literary, invoking materials so alien to conventional notions of the 'poetic' as to reconstitute the boundaries of subject matter acceptable in poetic discourse" (ibid.). The place of historical documents at the heart of Pound's project requires us to read *The Cantos* in a manner McGann calls "radial." We must, in other words, keep in simultaneous view both the text at hand and the ancillary texts on which it depends. Reaching out from a crucial quotation in the poem to grasp the whole it synecdochically represents, we can resist "that spell of self-transparency which hovers over all the texts we read" (McGann, *Textual Condition,* 121). Pulling aside the text's generic curtain, disregarding admonitions to pay no attention to the man energetically working machinery behind it, we begin to see how Pound shapes his sources to fit his purposes—poetic and political.[2]

Rainey convincingly reads in Pound's adaptation of historical sources for the Malatesta Cantos an outline for "a historiographical matrix to which Pound repeatedly assimilated events from other periods," a "secret spiritual tradition" underlying and opposing the received history of Western civilization's progression from ancient Greece to the early twentieth century (*Ezra Pound,* 39). Quoting Antonio Beltramelli's account of the Tempio Malatestiana, Pound repeats a popular romantic interpretation of the fifteenth-century church (Canto 9, 238–50). But Pound integrates that tradition with his own understanding of medieval Provençal culture, juxtaposing Beltramelli with the troubadour Guillaume IX to indicate a cultural transition from the Gothic era to the early Renaissance.[3] This reconstruction of the past takes on direct significance for the present through Pound's fragmentary inclusion of references to his own moment, to the post–World War I crisis in Europe. With a single phrase —"last October"—Pound links Malatesta's inauguration of a new world in the 1450s with the end of history and the commencement of a new culture Pound had announced in the *Little Review* the previous spring.[4]

This is Pound in 1923. Still grieving for friends and opportunities lost in the world war, still threatened by poverty, still chafing under the difficulty of living by writing, and still convinced that the old world had begun to destroy itself, Pound inscribes through juxtaposed quotations a condemnation of the old world and cryptic indications of the new culture's contours. The Malatesta Cantos and the new compositional strategy they embody constitute Pound's response to the crisis that followed one world war. But Cantos 8–10 comment only obliquely, at best, on their historical context. Seventeen years later, in the crisis preceding another world war, Pound more aggressively assimilates political concerns and poetic composition. Political upheaval in Europe has drawn the long dormant attention of the United States, whose intervention Pound fears will spark global war.

The Adams Cantos of 1940 address the specific conjuncture marked by the shift in American attitudes toward Pound's European home, Italy, and by the threat of American involvement in a European war.

Throughout the 1920s and mid-1930s, or until the commencement of Italian attacks on Abyssinia in 1935, the Italian Fascist state enjoyed relative popularity in the United States, mostly because the American public largely admired Benito Mussolini. As John Diggins has written, many Americans saw the Italian dictator as a "Carlylean leader changing the course of history through sheer willpower and reason" (71). Mussolini's heroic posturing, often sympathetically reported by the American press, made him seem an admirable statesman, drawing comparisons to Lincoln, Wilson, and Stalin. An answer to communism, Mussolini was seen by the American middle-class business community as standing for "two traditional American values: rational intelligence and willpower" (ibid., 70).

Of course, the American people were not left on their own to form opinions of Mussolini; not a few journalists recorded for mass consumption glowing portraits of the dictator. William Randolph Hearst, head of the largest and most influential American newspaper chain, admired Mussolini and, in 1931, visited him in Rome. The work of the Hearst newspapers to maintain a positive American attitude toward Italy and Mussolini is evinced by a press survey, captured with other documents after World War II, in which the Italian ambassador to the United States reports that the Hearst group was "the most favorable to the regime" (quoted in John B. Carter, 436). And the Hearst papers were joined in their generally positive portrayals of the Fascist regime by the U.S. "paper of record," the *New York Times,* whose Anne O'Hare McCormick was a leading American cheerleader for Mussolini and his government.

Finally, the admiration for Mussolini by some American elected officials led the United States toward a positive stance toward Italy and the maintenance of American neutrality even after 1935, when Italian hostilities grew difficult to ignore. Breckinridge Long, the American ambassador to Italy during the early and mid-1930s was taken in by Mussolini's "quiet dignity" and "determined energy." While Long worried about Mussolini's aggressive diplomatic posture and remained unconvinced by the dictator's gestures for peace in 1934, he opposed the American embargo against Italy after the invasion of Abyssinia and advised President Franklin Roosevelt to recognize

Italian Ethiopia just before his resignation in 1936. Long's successor, William Phillips, continued to push for an American policy of recognition and amicability in relations with Italy, arguing that it was not with the Italian government as such that the United States had a quarrel but with its "spirit of aggression" (quoted in Diggins, 277–78).

But American admiration for Mussolini began to crumble when Italy invaded Abyssinia in 1935. While the early military buildup during 1934 had brought no great response from the American public, the appeals of Haille Selassie during the summer of 1935 began to generate widespread American sympathy for the underdog Abyssinians. When the Italians finally invaded in October, even the *Chicago Tribune,* which had been a supporter of Italian imperialism in East Africa, denounced Italy (October 13, 1935). A Roper poll published in the October *Fortune* found more Americans feeling less "friendly" toward Italy than toward the Soviet Union (Diggins, 282). A poll in *Fortune*'s December 1935 issue showed 47.9 percent of respondents in favor of "economic cooperation with other nations" to bring about an end to the Italian hostilities (ibid.). The announcement of the Italo-German alliance in the late 1930s dealt another series of blows to the popularity of Italy among Americans. This alliance first became known in October 1936 but was not widely attacked in the American press or in political circles because of the perception that Mussolini would work as a moderating foil to Hitler (ibid., 322; Dallek, 145). The *Anschluss,* however, wrecked that illusion. Although Mussolini's performance at the Munich peace talks in September 1938 partially resuscitated his damaged reputation among many Americans, American support for fascism had dropped by the next January from 61 percent to 54 percent (Diggins, 338). When the Italian army invaded Albania in April 1939, American sympathy for Italy plummeted more quickly still, and public opinion in favor of Mussolini, fascism, and Italy reached a nadir for the 1930s (Cannistraro, 10; Dallek, 184; Lamb, 273–79).

The increasingly apparent anti-Semitism of the Italian government finally strained Italian credibility to the breaking point. Throughout the 1920s, a vocal anti-Semitic minority had existed in the Fascist movement and the Italian Catholic Church. This minority tended to view Jews as either "exploitative capitalists" or "revolutionary socialists" and feared that the religious ties of Jewish Italians to "world Jewry" split their loyalties between nation and religion. The growth of Zionism exacerbated the latter fear until Mussolini, who had opened Italian borders to Jewish refugees from Germany earlier in the 1930s, began to worry publicly about the "malignant power of international Jewry" (Cannistraro, 29).[5] Casillo writes that "even during the years in which he derided Nazi racial theories and assumed the role of 'protector' of the Italian Jews, Mussolini denounced Zionism and 'international Jewry,' blamed many of the world's troubles on Jewish finance, linked the Jews . . . to a Masonic conspiracy . . . , and held that the Jews had led the Communist Revolution" (137).

When Jewish groups protested the Italian invasion of Ethiopia, Mussolini began an aggressive press campaign against the Jews in 1936. Finally, in July 1938, Mussolini made anti-Semitism official Fascist government policy while his ideologues wrote and published the *Manifesto of Fascist Racism*. The Fascist government forbade intermarriage between Jewish and non-Jewish Italians; removed Jews from government positions, university professorships, and bank jobs; restricted Jewish property holdings; and ordered Jewish émigrés who had entered Italy after 1919 to leave the country (Cannistraro, 28).

The change in American attitudes toward Italy and Mussolini between the mid-1930s and the decade's end can be gauged by the changing tone and tenor of the *New York Times'* coverage of Italy. As late as 1937, the *Times* approvingly reports the Fascist Council's policies for economic independence (publishing more than half a dozen articles on this topic in March alone), the government's alleged strides toward democracy (in an interview with McCormick published on February 2, 5, 1937, Mussolini declares Fascist Italy "the only true democratic regime"), and even a contest conducted by the government for an anthem celebrating the conquest of Ethiopia (March 7, 1937). When Mussolini visits Roosevelt in October, the *Times* first wonderingly reports that anti-Fascists urge the president not to receive the dictator and then positively reports the visit (and the failure of anti-Fascist agitators to stage convincing demonstrations) (October 11, 12, 1937). Two years later, the *Times* publishes a wholly different set of stories and casts these stories in a quite different tone. Roughly 500 stories on Italy's foreign relations, especially its increasingly strained relations with France and Great Britain, and on its military buildups and aggressive movements toward neighbors appear in the paper in 1939. McCormick's commentary, a mainstay of coverage in 1937, almost disappears in 1939. The majority of stories in 1939 take a negative view of Italy, fascism, and Mussolini; no article presents the regime as anything like "democratic," no article applauds the dictator's abilities to bring new self-sufficiency to Italy. And not a few articles link Italy and Germany as forces to be feared in the European tumult.

These years, 1938–40, were critical in the Gramscian sense. The Fascist hegemony constructed during the 1920s and 1930s under the pressure of international war required maintenance at all levels of civil society. More important for Pound and my discussion of him, the maintenance of one discursive sector of the hegemonic bloc in the United States, the isolationist or neutralist discourse, was necessary. The hegemonic position of that discourse had been fairly easily maintained throughout the mid-1930s by isolationist forces in Congress, including Pound's acquaintance Senator William Borah, and by public figures in the United States like Father Charles Coughlin and Charles Lindbergh (Dallek, 200). Pound evidently recognized the crumbling of that position in the late 1930s. As Pound wrote to his friend, Italian economist Odon Por, in 1938: "For five years or at least since 1933 I have been TRYING to get it into the head of yr/bloomink gerarchs that AMERICAN opinion MIGHT become dangerous, and that some steps toward keeping that jew ridden and finance cankers country OUGHT to be taken. WD/the goofs listen to papa?? They would NOT" (quoted in Redman, *Ezra Pound,* 183). Pound's writings throughout these years are a series of attempts, in poetry and prose, to get the goofs, whether Italian "gerarchs" or American rubes, to "listen to papa."

From 1937 through the first two years of the war, Pound feverishly argued—in letters, magazine articles, and the infamous radio speeches—that the United States should maintain neutrality regarding the European war. I do not contend here that Pound wholeheartedly supported the war from the Italian or Axis position; his letters show wavering support for Italy as the war broadened during the late 1930s. But Pound did develop and purvey arguments in his writings of this period, discursive moves in a war of position, designed to convince a cultural elite of the dangers of U.S. entry into war in Europe.

Pound's frantic worry during these years is most apparent in his letters to acknowledged legislators. He corresponded from Italy with U.S. officials (Congressmen George Tinkham and Jerry Voorhis and Senator Borah). When he visited the United States in April 1939,

Pound met with Secretary of Agriculture (later Vice President) Henry Wallace and tried to see Roosevelt about his concerns. In Italy, he maintained relationships with Odon Por, an economist influential in the Fascist government, and Alessandro Pavolini, the Italian minister of popular culture. After his audience with Mussolini in 1933 cemented his admiration for the dictator, Pound periodically wrote the Duce himself. Pound's letters to these official correspondents are only his most overt attempts at political influence during these years. Redman writes of the "moderate number of letters to American politicians," including an embarrassing letter to Huey Long in which Pound offers his services as a cabinet member (*Ezra Pound,* 157, 161). More typical is his letter to Senator Borah, who seemed to share Pound's dour view of the League of Nations' opposition to Italy's invasion of Abyssinia: "What is NOW wrong with the picture is the definition of Italy's activity in Abyssinia as war" (quoted in ibid., 166). This defense of Italy runs through most of Pound's letters to officials. In the same month, he wrote Secretary of State Cordell Hull: "[I]f Mussolini hasn't stopped MORE wars than all the British liars put together, I will eat my hat and breeches" (quoted in ibid.).

As conditions in Europe deteriorated through the late 1930s, Pound's letters began to address the possibility of a coming war. In these letters, Pound both assigned blame for increasing tensions and worried about the role the United States might play in a European war. Pound wrote Congressman Tinkham of Massachusetts (whom Pound encouraged to run for president in 1939) to ridicule Tinkham's apprehensions about a European war in 1939. He wrote Borah in February 1939 to applaud the senator's isolationist position: "BRAVO BORAH, My Dear Senator, KEEP AT IT. What every decent man in Europe wants is a sane Europe and NO WAR west of the Vistula. . . . Indubitably the drive for war last year was from gunbuzzards/ Rothschild implied" (quoted in Redman, *Ezra Pound,* 184). As the involvement of the United States in the war became imminent, Pound wrote Borah, Tinkham, and Voorhis, blaming the war on England and urging all three to work to keep the United States neutral. When Tinkham wrote him that Roosevelt would propel the United States into war "because it was the only thing that would save him politically," Pound began a letter-writing campaign to "keep America neutral on the grounds that the conflict was caused by 'international usury' and by England's unjustifiable attempt to embezzle mandated territories that had formerly belonged to Germany" (Carpenter, *Serious Character, 567*).[6]

But as Antonio Gramsci makes clear, the most important work of hegemony takes place in those arenas of civil society not considered "political" in the narrow or instrumental sense of the word. In Pound's cultural writings, especially those on education, we see Pound most determinedly developing and deploying the discursive strategies by which he advocates isolation. Pound takes up the position of the professor to establish and inhabit a pedagogical stance that provides him access to and purchase on discussions of education and curriculum reform; in the context of these discussions, he Americanizes fascism and lionizes Mussolini.

In these writings, John Adams becomes the discursive site through which Pound articulates American history to the struggle over American neutrality. In this deployment of Adams, Pound establishes him as an exemplar of cultural values he seeks to institutionalize in collegiate curricula. This "institution of Adams" configures what Pound calls "our National Heritage," emphasizes American independence from Europe and neutrality in European disputes, and defines American economics through a model of abundance that makes interdependence with Europe unnecessary. It also articulates Adams to anti-Semitic discourses in order to answer the American discomfort with Italy's racial policies of the late 1930s, policies that were instrumental in the plummeting of American public opinion regarding the Fascist regime. The prose deployment of Adams, finally, works as part of a strategy to construct a common sense among Pound's cultural (as opposed to officially political) audience of the need for continued American isolation and neutrality.

This strategy of forging apparent substantive links between discourses by simply connecting them syntactically is one of Pound's favorite devices in these writings. In "Reorganize Your Dead Universities," for example, Pound follows several suggestions regarding curricular reform and the use of new technology in universities with the assertion that "[t]he danger for the U.S.A. is not fascism. . . . The danger is that the U.S. will get an enormous and topheavy mass of plannings and controls from above WITHOUT either organization by guilds or any education" (*PP*, 7:319).[7] Evidently unaware that he has changed the subject, Pound follows this assurance with recommendations for the economics and history departments. Pound irritatedly comments that "the History departments could at least insist on reasonably priced reprints of the GIST of John Adams. . . . American History bulks large in the work of American University departments of history. There is no excuse for neglect of the basic ideas which initiated our nation" (320).

In an article published later in 1938 (*Hika,* October 1938), Pound again in one sentence argues that an economics class in 1938 must acquaint students with the ideas he advocates and in the next asserts that "in teaching American HISTORY the universities have not caught up with W. E. Woodward and Claude Bowers. They do NOT introduce the student sufficiently to the thought and KNOWLEDGE of John Adams" (*PP,* 7:387).

The benignity of fascism for Americans is enhanced by its appearance in an article along with suggestions for curricular reform and by the fact that it shares discursive space with academic economists and American historians, as well as former presidents. As we have seen, by 1938 American support for the Fascist Italian state and Mussolini was on the decline. This crisis required tactics different from those Pound had relied on when fascism still enjoyed something of a vogue among the American public. Pound could no longer count on a large receptive audience for overt preference for Mussolini over Roosevelt in a head-to-head comparison. He could, however, by hearkening back to early national American history, the closest thing Americans had to a heroic or mythic past, draw more subtle connections between Mussolini's state and the early American one. The essence of hegemonic strategy, after all, lies in understanding and addressing the concerns of groups whose agendas must be articulated together. Pound understood from his American correspondents that the United States was moving, under Roosevelt, toward a position more hostile to Italy, that the American public was expressing greater antipathy toward Italy. His task now was to emphasize the benign character of fascism as it related to the United States and to rekindle American sympathies for Mussolini as a heroic exemplar of American values. The imbrication of fascism with American history and the economic ideas of American presidents too long dead for the public to remember works toward that end.

As the decade nears its end and a European war comes to seem inevitable, Pound again changes tactics in his deployment of Adams and other American historical figures. After mentioning them, offering them as examples of the virtues he champions (and claims that Italy champions), Pound begins to give these figures voices of their own. He writes in 1938 a version of a complaint common in his writings of the 1930s: "Comes now 1938 and I point out to one of our most brilliant American publishers that you can get Marx, Lenin, Trotsky, and Stalin, all of them exotics, for 10 cents or a quarter a volume, and that no American can buy the best of J. Adams, Jefferson or Van Buren at any price" (*PP*, 6:108). Pound's insistence on the need for a readily accessible edition of the crucial "few hundred pages of American history" was not new; in *Jefferson and/or Mussolini* (1935), he makes the same assertion, and in a letter to Van Wyck Brooks upon Pound's election to the American Institute and Academy of Arts and Letters in 1938, Pound writes that the institute "COULD with a little gumption at least stimulate the reprint of American classics . . . the letters of Adams and Jefferson" (quoted in Carpenter, *Serious Character,* 557). That same year, he wrote to John Crowe Ransom in a similar vein: "Are you now ready for a revival of American culture considering it as something specifically grown from the nucleus of the American Founders, present in the Adams, Jefferson correspondence?" (*Letters,* 319).

One version of that nucleus that Pound composed and distributed in an educational context was his "Introductory Text Book," a pamphlet in which he collected excerpts of writings by John Adams, Thomas Jefferson, Abraham Lincoln, and the American Constitution. Pound distributed this "Text Book" to correspondents and "hawked" it on several college campuses during his American visit in 1939 (Carpenter, *Serious Character,* 565). The "Introductory Text Book" is made up of one passage each by the three presidents and one passage from the Constitution (on the power of Congress to coin money). The passages are followed by a "Note," in which Pound explains that the congressional monetary power derives from "the downright ignorance of the nature of coin, credit, and circulation." He goes on to consociate "the greatest blessing," the provision to the people of "their own paper to pay their own debts," to a famously isolationist speech given by Voorhis in Congress on June 6, 1938.

Pound did not stop at distributing the "Introductory Text Book" to correspondents and college students. He published it in the Yale student magazine, *Furioso,* in the summer of 1939, in the Japanese magazine, *VOU,* in October 1940, and at the end of "Are Universities Valid," which appeared in the *New English Weekly*'s February 1939 issue. In the article, Pound attacks endowments and the tendency of universities to tailor research to seek money, blaming the profusion of bad scholarship at American universities on "lust of profit." Answering the boast that teachers in the United States enjoy academic freedom, he guarantees that "entire freedom of teaching . . . exists in Italy," citing a conversation with an Italian college professor as proof (*PP,* 7:423).

In the April 1939 *Townsman* republication of "Introductory Text Book," Pound appends to the usual text a set of four very short essays: "Money," "The Nazi Movement in Germany," "Vocabulaire," and "Bibliography." The essay on Nazism, subtitled "Note indicating the course of that movement," constitutes a second "Text Book," this time with passages from Hitler and Nazi economist Hjalmar Schacht. Pound approvingly quotes Hitler, in German and English: "War on international finance and LOAN CAPITAL becomes the most weighty etc. in the struggle towards freedom." He concludes the "essay" with a note, writing that Hitler's final point (that a country's international position depends on its "organization and internal coherence") is also "Confucius 5th paragraph of the Great Learning" (*PP,* 7:439). The article places Hitler, as economic and political thinker, on a level with Adams, Jefferson, and Lincoln; sets Hitler's political thought and Schacht's economic thought on a par with the American Constitution; and, finally, establishes Hitler as a Confucian bringer of order. This last accomplishment, of course, repeats a tactic Pound used often in writing on Mussolini and links both dictators to the theme of order that runs throughout *The Cantos.* While Pound's attitude toward Germany was fraught with ambivalence, he works in this article to answer one major criticism of Mussolini's government (its too-solid relationship with Germany) by articulating Hitler's discourses, through the figures of Pound's "Introductory Text Book," to American virtues and Confucian wisdom.

Pound's poetic activity at the end of the 1930s consisted almost entirely of the composition of Cantos 52–71, the Chinese Cantos and the Adams Cantos. While they share some primary concerns—the creation of an ordered state, new historical developments of Pound's overarching themes—the Adams Cantos speak most directly to international events in the late 1930s; indeed, they advance precisely the same set of ideas that dominate the prose writings surveyed above. Taken entirely from the ten-volume *Works of John Adams,* this set of ten cantos comes to just under 100 pages; these cantos comprise one of the longest "decads" of Pound's poem. Edited by Adams's grandson Charles, the *Works of John Adams* consists of a biography of Adams, Adams's diary, Adams's autobiography, an account entitled "Travels and Negotiations," and, finally, his political writings, state papers, and public correspondence.

Pound composed the Adams Cantos by working through the volumes of Adams's writing in order, beginning with Charles Francis Adams's biography, then proceeding through the autobiographical material and the political and state papers.[8] This compositional method deprives the section of the chronological order and coherence of the Chinese Cantos that precede them; it is difficult to follow Adams's life in Pound's cutup version. For this reason, among others, the Adams Cantos have not been a popular part of Pound's long poem.[9] When they have received attention from critics, it has most often been negative.[10] They deserve attention, however, as part of Pound's strategy to make fascism safe for American consumption.

Of course, the ten cantos on Adams are neither the only nor the first of Pound's poetic forays into American history. Pound opens the third installment of the poem (*Eleven New Cantos,* 1934) with four cantos built around Jefferson and Adams. As Redman writes, "Pound's turn to the work of the American founders in the Middle Cantos demonstrates both a growing interest in political matters and an attempt to articulate his own American identity after so many years of expatriation" ("An Epic Is a Hypertext," 118). These cantos update Sigismundo Malatesta, the ruler-artist who forcibly creates a new world through the reconstruction of the Tempio. As the opening gesture of Canto 31 demonstrates, Jefferson is an artist figure similar to Malatesta; his medium, however, is the vast North American continent. "Tempus loquendi / Tempus tacendi," Pound writes. There is a time for speech and a time for silence, a time for action in place of words. Quoted extracts from a letter Jefferson wrote to George Washington in 1787 illustrate the sort of action Pound has in mind. Jefferson requests any information Washington might have obtained on the "navigation of Lake Erie and the Ohio"; the information will help Jefferson plan a canal project that he considers quite important for the growing nation. Jefferson's Tempio will be that nation. In place of columns and carved reliefs, he plans canals, water communication to the newly settled western country. But these physical improvements are perhaps the least of Jefferson's accomplishments. Pound repeats a line—"no slaves north of Maryland district"—to indicate the arena of Jefferson's more important work. On the foundation of the new nation's physical improvements, Jefferson (with Adams) will build a state. These American statesmen, Pound leaves no doubt, are infinitely more capable of this act of creation than their European counterparts. Jefferson writes to Washington: "I can further say with safety there is not a crowned head / in Europe whose talents or merits would entitle him / to be elected a vestryman in any American parish" (Canto 31, 154–55). The subject rhyme between the emerging American state and Malatesta's Tempio is sealed at the end of Canto 31, when Pound juxtaposes fragmentary quotations from Jefferson and Adams. Jefferson describes the collaboration between himself and other Virginians to "produce some channel of correspondence" and to take "measures circumstances of times seemed to call for." Immediately after this oblique reference to statecraft, Pound sets an even more fractured quotation from Adams: "church of St. Peter . . . human reason, human conscience, / though I believe there are such things" (156). Adams's words here, his reference to the church and his meditation on the existence of reason and conscience, link his and Jefferson's efforts to build a nation with Malatesta's heroic construction of the Tempio.[11]

In the Adams Cantos, Pound develops the heroic aspects of John Adams at much greater length. Of more importance, though, is Pound's shaping of these cantos to address, however obscurely, the increasingly tense international scene in 1939–40. The recuperation of Adams that Pound undertakes in these cantos and in his prose writings of the period is the heart of Pound's attempt to intervene in American debates over neutrality in the face of growing European tensions, to achieve a direct and narrow political effect on the question of American involvement in European intrigues. The Adams Cantos comment on contemporary political struggle from the very beginning. Canto 62 opens with a passage from the first volume of the *Works:*

"Acquit of evil intention
    or inclination to perseverance in error
to correct it with cheerfulness
    particularly as to the motives of actions
of the great nations of Europe." (341)

The canto, which moves briskly through the major events of Adams's life, ends with Pound's introduction of his hero, an introduction that makes clear the significance of Adams in this set of cantos composed in 1938–39:

But for the clearest head in the congress
1774 and thereafter
    pater patriae
the man who at certain points
    made us
at certain points
    saved us
by fairness, honesty and straight moving
ARRIBA ADAMS. (350)

Amid the tumultuous birth and painful growth of the American Republic, the clearheaded Adams brought his honesty and integrity to bear, rescuing the new country from the earlier-cited "motives of actions / of the great nations of Europe."

In Canto 65, Pound more directly speaks through Adams to the issue of American neutrality. The canto's centerpiece is Adams's voyage to Europe in 1778 as a diplomat. The American colonies have signed a treaty with France to guarantee an alliance between the two countries. Congress has sent Adams to France; his trip begins Adams's ten years of service as an American diplomat in Europe. In Canto 65, Adams's accomplishments as a diplomat take on epic proportions and constitute the heroism through which he is linked to the Odysseus of Canto 1, the Kung of Canto 13, and other of the poem's heroes. Adams's sea voyage to Europe and his travels in Europe, along with his cunning in negotiations, link him with Odysseus. His travails at sea, including storms and battles, recall those of Dionysus, related by Acoetes in Canto 2. The description of a hurricane into which Adams's ship, the *Boston,* sails serves to forge another heroic connection: "North, East by North, then North West / ane blastered bubb gan in the foresail ding / rollings" (Canto 65, 369). The line from Gavin Douglas's Scottish translation of the *Aeneid* connects Adams and Aeneas, the hero of Virgil's nationalist epic. Fleeing Troy at its fall, Aeneas must wander the Mediterranean until, landing in Europe, he conquers an old order to found a new nation. As in so many cases, Pound's brief quotation from the *Aeneid* performs a set of tasks. The connection of Adams with Aeneas, the founder of Roman civilization, indicates a connection with Mussolini, who often cited the descent from Rome as part of his Fascist state's pedigree. As much propaganda as poem, the *Aeneid* is Virgil's politically motivated justification of a structural shift in Roman government. As republic transformed under the pressure of Augustus into empire, a new order came into existence. Virgil reads and relates the legendary prehistory of Rome so that it leads inexorably to just this shift. Pound's choice of the *Aeneid* as the vehicle for his description of the hurricane signifies a similar project. As the powerful figure of Aeneas violently and single-mindedly crafts an ordered society from the chaos of Troy's fall, as a ruthless Augustus crafts an ordered autocracy from the chaos following Julius Caesar's assassination, so Adams must craft from the hurricane's directionless force an ordered ship, from the confusion of postrevolutionary America an ordered state.

Pound thus connects Adams most powerfully with other heroes in *The Cantos* as a force for order. After the storm at sea and the battle that follows (in which the *Boston* takes a British frigate, the *Martha*), Adams composes a long memorandum to the ship's captain, Tucker, suggesting improvements, many of which the captain makes (Terrell, 294; Sanders, 207). More important, one of the two poles around which Pound constructs Adams's entire journey is Adams's imposition of order on the American diplomatic mission in France, which has fallen into chaos under the corrupt leadership of Silas Deane. Once in France, Adams goes about setting the mission straight, recording that

> never was before I came here
> a letter book
> a minute book
> an account book. (Canto 65, 372)

Adams's efforts here repeat the theme of order most explicitly introduced in Canto 13:

And Kung said, and wrote on the bo leaves:
  If a man have not order within him
He cannot spread order about him;
And if a man have not order within him
His family will not act with due order;
  And if the prince have not order within him
He cannot put order in his dominions. (59)

Canto 65 proves Adams to be a Confucian bringer of order. But Confucius is not the only person with whom these actions align him. In *Jefferson and/or Mussolini,* Pound links the title figures through their dedication to order in the Confucian sense (112). Mussolini drained the Pontine marshes, modernized Italian industry, and, of course, got the trains to run on time. These actions won him the approbation of American business leaders, journalists, and politicians, along with Ezra Pound. Of course, Pound also found in Hitler another Confucian bringer of order. Adams serves as a figure here through which Pound can articulate Mussolini and Hitler to the Confucian and American virtue of order.

After Adams orders the affairs of the diplomatic mission, he must carry out his own crucial task—the negotiation of commerce treaties with France, Spain, and Holland. At the center of those negotiations lie the fishing beds off the northeastern coast of North America. These fisheries represent the natural abundance crucial for the maintenance of American independence. Adams must preserve the exclusive rights of American fishermen to the fisheries, rights threatened by the machinations of European governments and their agents. After Adams is named "head of the Board of War," Pound quotes him on the danger to fisheries:

had conversed much with gentlemen
  who conduct our cod and whale fisheries
Our seamen if once let loose on the ocean . . .
They said: wd/ruin character of our seamen etc.
"make 'em mercenary and bent wholly on plundah."
(Canto 65, 368)

A page later, in the strange passage that begins his journey, we read: "Always have been and still are spies in America (1804) / and I considered the / fisheries" (387). Adams here asserts that the fisheries are necessary "both to the commerce and naval power of this country" (Sanders, 216). The decision whether to insist on their protection in negotiations in the courts of Europe is one important enough to draw the attention of spies, to provoke intrigues by those who oppose Adams.

Similar intrigues occur throughout the canto. While Adams works to protect the rights of American fishermen to the fisheries, European diplomats, his fellow Americans in the diplomatic mission, and his enemies in Congress work to thwart him. Adams speculates that the Count de Vergennes, a French diplomat, expects easily to dupe him into revealing his instructions from Congress (Congress had sent Adams instructions to refrain from his insistence on the fisheries in negotiations for a commerce treaty). Adams records, in the volume of *Travels and Negotiations* from which Pound draws extracts for this part of the canto, that "the articles relative to the boundaries of the United States and to the fisheries were by no means agreeable to me; and I had already reasons enough to suspect, and, indeed, to believe, that the French Court, at least the Count de Vergennes, would wish me to go to the utmost extent of them in relinquishing the fisheries" (Sanders, 236). Not only must Adams deal with the intrigues of European diplomats over the fisheries. He must also overcome the machinations of one of his American colleagues, Benjamin Franklin: "Franklin intrigues manoeuvres insinuates" (377). In spite of Franklin's intrigues, Adams draws a direct connection between the fisheries and peace for the United States. He thus forcefully asserts the relationship between natural abundance and peace posited in Pound's own economic theory. In Pound's variety of social credit economics, scarcity, an artificial condition created by those in control of the money supply ("Usurers"), causes all hostilities and war. Pound's favorite example of the proper bank, the Monte dei Paschi of Siena, whose founding makes up the subject matter of Cantos 42 and 43, illustrates the importance of abundance.[12] Pound writes in a gloss on those cantos that the lesson of the Sienese bank is "the very basis of solid banking": "The CREDIT rests in ultimate on the ABUNDANCE OF NATURE, on the growing grass that can nourish the living sheep" (*Selected Prose,* 240). The fisheries can provide food and export capital for the American colonies so that the new country can remain independent of international finance, the mechanism of scarcity, and therefore remain independent of European intrigues. Pound himself emphasizes this crucial point in the canto with a bold vertical line in the margin:

> For my part though that Americans
> Had been embroiled in European wars long enough
>   easy to see that
> France and England wd/try to embroil us OBVIOUS
> that all powers of Europe will be continually at manoeuvre
> to work us into their real or imaginary balances
> of power. (Canto 65, 377)

The fisheries extracts, finally, clarify Pound's purpose in Canto 65: to articulate Adams and his actions, which represent American order, shrewdness, and independence, to the critical notion of American neutrality from European wars, a neutrality that must rest on the economic independence guaranteed by the nation's natural abundance.

One of Pound's most important rewrites in the Adams Cantos alters the politics of the early nineteenth century, smoothing over differences between Adams and Jefferson (Pound's American hero of the early 1930s and the earlier American cantos) and replacing Jefferson as Adams's antagonist with Alexander Hamilton, who symbolizes for Pound both "tricky egotism" and the faulty economics and banking policies that have brought the world again to the brink of war in 1938.[13] Adams, Pound tells us in Canto 62,

> formed own view of Hamilton's game (and his friends')
> which wd/ certainly have tangled with Europe
>
> . . . .
>
>   and as for Hamilton
> we may take it (my authority, ego scriptor cantilenae)
> that he was the Prime snot in ALL American history
>   (11th Jan. 1938, from Rapallo). (350)

For Pound, this recognition of Hamilton's unscrupulous character alone qualifies Adams for heroic stature; the canto's concluding apostrophe to Adams immediately follows this attack on Hamilton so that hating Hamilton seems to lead naturally to having "the clearest head in the congress." In the presidential and congressional politics of the United States in the 1790s, though, Jefferson and his Republicans posed as great a threat to Adams as Hamilton's forces in the Federalist Party. While Hamilton worked to turn Federalist delegates against Adams and secure the presidential nomination for his cohort, Thomas Pinckney of South Carolina, Jefferson ran as the presidential candidate of the opposing anti-Federalists. Indeed, in Pound's source, Jefferson has a harder time of it than Pound's extracts indicate. Pound accomplishes his establishment of Hamilton as the villain of these cantos through his editing, juxtaposition of edited fragments, and syntactic connections. For example, earlier in Canto 62, Pound writes:

> a new power arose, that of fund holders
> fond of rotation so that to remove
>   their abuse from me to the President. (347)

The "new power," the "fund holders," appear to be the agents modified by the predicate "fond of rotation"; they seem to be the scurrilous attackers of Adams and Washington. In Adams's *Works,* though, the "new power" refers to the "commercial and moneyed interests, which . . . at once rallied around Mr. Hamilton" (Sanders, 94). Only after reading another eight pages do we find "fond of rotation" in Pound's source; moreover, the abuse Adams reports, abuse Pound attributes to the Hamiltonians, is actually at the hands of Jeffersonian "anti-federal scribblers" (ibid., 95). The line break between "fund holders" and "fond of rotation" masks an eight-page gap and utterly alters the original meaning of Adams's text. The eight pages that separate the two phrases in Adams's text disappear in Pound's syntactic conjoining of the phrases.[14]

Hamilton's moneyed interests do not stop at attacking Adams in the canto. A few lines later, we find what appears to be Adams saying of himself, "by thought, word, never encourage a war . . . ." Pound follows this with

> horror they are in lest peace shd/ continue
> will accumulate perpetual DEBT
>   leading to yet more revolutions. (Canto 62, 348)

The syntax here appears to draw a contrast between Adams, who resolves to act so as to discourage war, and "they," evidently the Hamiltonians, who fear continued peace for economic reasons. Again, though, these lines are drawn from four pages of Adams's text. In a letter to Abigail Adams (March 27, 1794), Adams writes, "I have one comfort; that in thought, word or deed I have never encouraged war."

In another letter to Abigail written almost a month later (April 19, 1794), he writes, "You cannot imagine what horror some persons are in lest peace should continue." Pound allows "they," which has no clear antecedent, to indicate the "fund holders" who appear a few lines above, and he enhances that impression by beginning the next line with the verb phrase "will accumulate perpetual DEBT," so that those same fund holders fear peace because it will cost them. But in Adams's own writing, he himself fears perpetual debt: "I lament the introduction of taxes and expenses which will accumulate a perpetual debt and lead to future revolutions" (Sanders, 95–96).[15]

In his reconstruction of Adams's discourse, Pound constructs new significations for Adams's words. These new significations lend Adams to Pound's own political views and goals; Adams becomes the voice of peace, of American neutrality, the foil of Hamilton's banker-friendly economic policies. Hamilton, conversely, becomes the representative of economics that lead to wars and, then, the villain of the fractured narrative. Pound's editing serves an important function in the strategy by which American interests and values are articulated through American early national history to the neutrality Pound hopes to maintain.

But Pound's Adams is articulated to another of the poet's political agendas as well, and no account of partisan Pound in the 1930s would be complete without a consideration of the ways in which the Adams Cantos participate in the construction of collectivity required for this second political effect. The communities Pound envisions are frightening to contemplate, not least because they are defined precisely in opposition to a quite specific Other community. A reading of Pound's effort at community construction indicates how the most visible aspect of Pound's cultural politics—anti-Semitism—reverberates through the cantos and the cultural moment of 1940.

A famous passage in Canto 65 finds Adams at a church in Brussels:

Church music Italian style
a tapestry: number of jews stabbing the wafer
    blood gushing from it. (376)

This extract exemplifies a strain of image and allusion that runs throughout the poem—the vilification of the Jews in the contemporary world. Robert Casillo writes that Pound's original source—

Adams's description of the tapestry—seems to have no anti-Semitic intent. Pound's choice of the passage, though, along with his rendering of the word "Jews" with a lowercase "j," Casillo argues, adapts the extract to his own anti-Semitic economy (350). An examination of Pound's source shows how Pound skews the passage through his typical editing. The original passage reads: "The church music here [at the cathedral at Brussels] is in the Italian style. A picture in tapestry was hung up, of a number of Jews stabbing the wafer, the *bon Dieu,* and blood gushing in streams from the bread. This insufferable piece of pious villany [*sic*] shocked me beyond measure, but thousands were before it, on their knees, adoring" (Sanders, 239). Whereas Adams seems to stand aghast at the depiction—at this vilification of the Jews and the apparent acceptance of that depiction by the worshipers—Pound edits out all signs of his hero's response.

This is a brief moment in a long poem, and we might be content to pass over it (as we might skim long chunks of Italian, Provençal, or Greek or dismiss Chinese ideograms). But this short passage tracks back through previous cantos, even through Pound's pre-*Cantos* career. Read radially, Adams's "jews" constitute a link with earlier heroes in the poem just as surely as his sea voyage and his dedication to order do. They appear, for example, on the first page of the first canto of the newly added set (52–71) in the 1940 edition of *The Cantos.* Indeed, the opening gestures of Canto 52 render inescapable the crucial significance of "jews" not only in the new decad but in earlier sections of the poem as well. Pound begins the new section with a recap of the poem's progress so far:

> And I have told you how things were under Duke
> Leopold in Siena
> And of the true base of credit, that is
> the abundance of nature
> with the whole folk behind it. (257)

On this true base of credit depends not only Pound's poem, we soon discover, but also "peace in our time." Pound briefly crafts a pastoral scene ("Vivante in his paradise") over the next several lines and then interrupts that scene with a peasant's complaints about the cost of war. The dark cloud hanging over the whole of Cantos 52–71 looms already on the horizon. In the midst of the natural abundance that should unite "the whole folk" in peace, war threatens ruin.

If plenty is the ground for peace in Pound's scheme, poverty provides the catalyst for war. And since nature supplies what should suffice to prevent poverty, some agents must be at work to upset the natural balance. We need look no further than the next line to find those agents:

> Stinkschuld's sin drawing vengeance,
> poor yitts paying for
> Stinkschuld
> paying for a few big yitts' vendetta on goyim. (257)

The Jews who stab the Host in Canto 65's Belgian tapestry here drain the blood of European culture by provoking war. Pound's reference leaves the specific war to our imagination (or interpolation). But the particularities are irrelevant; all wars result from Stinkschuld's sin, so that, in the "present" of the poem, "we lived on through sanctions, through Stalin / Litvinoff, gold brokers made profit / rocked exchange against gold."[16] Revolution in Russia, the rise of a Communist threat in Europe, the shift to unstable, ungrounded currency that lays the groundwork for a new European war—all of these unsettling conditions result from "a few big yitts' vendetta."

But Canto 52 holds still more of interest. In the voice of Benjamin Franklin, Pound most explicitly articulates the warning he wants readers to heed: "Remarked Ben: better keep out the jews / or yr/ grandchildren will curse you" (257). Americans must follow the example of Mussolini's race policies and "keep out the jews," dealing with them as an external threat before they can constitute a domestic threat. As we shall soon see, Pound thinks the damage is already done. The Jews pose danger to America through their practice of "Stinkschuld's sin," the catalyst for all war and the heart of the monetary monkey business Pound deplores. Stinkschuld shows up after Franklin's warning:

> jews, real jews, chazims, and *neschek*
> also super-neschek or the international racket
> specialité of the Stinkschuld
> bomb-proof under their houses in Paris
> where they store aht-voiks. (257)

The "real jews" Americans must guard against are those involved in the "international racket"—finance and trade, especially in arms and currency. Governments, Pound writes, "are full of their gun-swine, bankbuzzards." These Jews foment international economic and military disturbance for their own gain. Secure in their "bomb-proof" shelters, they hoard the cultural treasures ("aht-voiks") an unstable Europe has let fall into their hands. Intent on hoarding riches, cornering markets, and creating scarcity, the Jews threaten peace throughout the world and, therefore, threaten the peace and independence of Americans.

A page flip back toward the front of the book shows that the beginning of the new decad merely echoes the end of the preceding section. These passages in Canto 52, with their concern over threats to "the abundance of nature," over the hoarding of "aht-voiks" in Parisian basements, and with their attribution of usuries to Stinkschuld, repeat and recombine images and turns of phrase from Canto 51, which concludes the 1937 *Fifth Decad of Cantos*. In Canto 51, Pound litanizes about usury, making it the agent of all corruption, all poverty, all threats to humanity. "Usury," he writes, "is against Nature's increase." Usury renders the creation of art impossible: "It destroys the craftsman, destroying craft." Indeed, usury threatens all life: "Usury kills the child in the womb." Pound creates a link between the volumes of his poem out of this malevolent force in his economic and poetic system.

But these illustrations of the corruption and deadliness of usury themselves repeat Pound's famous execration of Usura in Canto 45:

> Usura slayeth the child in the womb
> It slayeth the young man's courting
> It hath brought palsey to bed, lyeth
> between the young bride and her bridegroom
> CONTRA NATURAM
> They have brought whores for Eleusis
> Corpses are set to banquet
> at behest of Usura. (230)

In Canto 45, Pound also includes a prose definition of the usury the canto illustrates: "A charge for the use of purchasing power, levied without regard for production." "Stinkschuld's sin" is the charging of interest, the encroachment on natural abundance, human creativity, and, indeed, human life that interest effects. No longer simply the financial conquest of borrowing, interest becomes, in Pound's idiosyncratic system, the root of all evil. Usura and its acolytes sin against nature, threaten all human life and productivity. Stabbing the Host, the Jews in the tapestry bleed from bread the life it should provide. Stinkschuld's sin against nature is, perhaps more important, a sin against "the true base of credit." He threatens life and livelihood. Agents of Usura, the Jews slay the child in the womb. Pound's edited incorporation of Adams's recollection sets off waves of meaning that, reaching back through the poem, echo around and amplify the brief moment of Canto 65.

The waves reach back farther still, as one fragment's fractal pattern meshes with the radiating significance of another. Just as the tapestry's "jews" lead us back to Stinkschuld in Canto 52, the "aht-voiks" hoarded by Stinkschuld and his ilk propel us, through their accented appearance, back to Canto 35 and the cultural hell of "Mitteleuropa." Here Pound rehearses the petty preferences and predilections of a dilettantish leisure class. The canto seems to be a five-page gloss on one buried diagnostic line: "stupidity is contagious." Presenting line after line of dull conversation and deadly pretension, Pound re-creates, as the canto's centerpiece, "the tale of a perfect schnorrer":

> a peautiful chewisch poy
> wit a vo-ice dot wouldt
> meldt dh heart offa schtone
> and wit a likeing for to make ahrt-voiks. (174)

"Ahrt-voiks" link the Jewish speaker here with the rapacious money-and-munitions merchants of Canto 52. Usura threatens art and life; the man this speaker recalls dabbled in art while pursuing his real business—the implied murder of his mother and brother for their money. On these ill-gotten riches he will live magnificently and create "ahrt-voiks." And the Jew Pound turns to next, Eljen Hatvany, possesses, along with the "ideals" Pound sneeringly allows him, "a library . . . and a fine collection of paintings"—more "ahrt-voiks."

The cultural hell of Mitteleuropa points even farther back to the end of the poem's first installment, to the scatological, near-slanderous, frightening hell of Cantos 14 and 15 (1925). Hell for Pound is not simply "other people." Rather, it is, like Mitteleuropa, a "slough of unamiable liars, / bog of stupidities." In it, we find among the pus, vermin, and maggots Pound's favorite targets: "usurers squeezing crab-lice, pandars to authority" (63). In a Dantesque re-creation of *The Cantos*' opening nekuia, the poet follows his guide, Plotinus, through hell, the "last cess-pool of the universe," and discovers, in its foulest sector, the usurers, "monopolists," and "obstructors of distribution." "Cowardly inciters of violence," these servants of Usura endure punishments that simply fit their crimes. Practitioners of usury, they are "CONTRA NATURAM," doomed by Pound's poetic will to suffer in this *Canto*-nic hell the corruption they have introduced on earth. The "jews" in Canto 65 stab the wafer and shed divine blood; the "jews" in Canto 52 threaten the peace and stability of America and cause wars by hoarding natural and cultural treasures. They serve the dangerous and corrupting "usury" of Canto 51, the usury whose concrete avatar is the Usura of Canto 45. Corrupted as they corrupt, the "schnorrers" of Mitteleuropa threaten life and culture alike in their amateurish approach to "ahrt," their willingness to kill for wealth, and their "unnatural" propensity for collecting treasures and keeping them from circulation. Paradoxically both demonic and demonized, all of *The Cantos*' "jews" are prefigured in the hell of Cantos 14 and 15. Financiers wield steel wires to lash the condemned, and profiteers drink "blood sweetened with sh-t."

One final backward step remains. The fragment of Canto 65 drives us, at last, outside the hardcover of *The Cantos* and into the hot-pink-paper-covered pages of *Blast,* the 1913 magazine edited by Wyndham Lewis. In this manifesto/manifestation of prewar Vorticism, Pound's are the only poems published. The first in his selection, "Salutation the Third," contains the origin of the anti-Semitic thread we have followed through the labyrinth from its unraveling in Canto 65. In images and language he will simply elaborate and specify ten years later for Cantos 14 and 15, Pound tells off the stuffy establishment on which the Vorticists sharpen their claws:

> so you shall be also,
> You slut-bellied obstructionist,
> You sworn foe to free speech and good letters,
> You fungus, you continuous gangrene. (*Blast,* 45)

And in the poem's shift from excoriation to exhortation, Pound names the chief villains in the cultural struggle staged in "Salutation the Third":

> Let us be done with Jews and Jobbery
> Let us SPIT upon those who fawn on the
> JEWS for their money. (45)

In this, the opening gambit of his poetic celebration and demonstration of the "great English Vortex," Pound begins the vicious attack on Jews as agents of cultural and political corruption that will pervade the entirety of his work up to and, indeed, through Canto 65. Far from an isolated moment in the vastness of the Adams Cantos, the brief appearance of the "jews" in Canto 65 is a continuation of a prejudice at the heart of Pound's inescapably political poetic project. As much as Malatesta's Tempio, that church in Brussels is a luminous (and illuminating) cultural fragment.

But this moment radiates not only backward and forward along the temporal axis of *The Cantos*. The dropped stone of these three lines propels rings and waves outward into other cultural sectors of the historical moment. The Brussels church extract, as Pound edits it, sets Canto 65 in the context of other anti-Semitic discourses, and that latitudinal context makes even more powerful this extract and the longitude it indicates. Pound's writings of the late 1930s are rife with references to usury and the Jews. In "A Place for English Writers: Definition of 'Usury,'" Pound blames the lack of career possibilities for "a young writer in England unless he wishes to become either a pansy or a Communist" on the "Shylockracy" that has infected British society; he concludes that the place for English writers is Oswald Moseley's Fascist British Union (*PP,* 7:334).[17] Another article, "Infamy of Taxes," contains a passage that begins with a typical "disclaimer": "International usury is not entirely Jewish." Pound goes on, though, to argue through an image that recalls the stabbed and bleeding wafer that "the evil done by the Jewish elements in international bleeding is enough to explain hatred of Jewry ten times over" (*PP,* 7:252). And in an article on the history of *Blast,* Pound writes that "if you believe that a whole race should be punished for the sin of some of its members, I admit that the expulsion of the two million Jews in New York would not be an excessive punishment for the harm done by Jewish finance to the English race in America" (*PP,* 7:280). Pound follows this passage with an even more disturbing one. He blames the Jews themselves for anti-Semitism in an assertion that takes on added sinister resonance in the contemporaneous context of German deportation and murder of Polish and German Jews: "The Jew has brought anti-Semitism on himself by LACK OF ORGANISATION, by refusal to undertake responsibility" (PP, 7:280).[18]

In the radio speeches Pound gives in the two years after he published the Adams Cantos, his comments about the Jews become more vitriolic: "The Bolshevik anti-morale comes out of the Talmud, which is the dirtiest teaching that any race ever codified. The Talmud is the one and only begetter or the Bolshevik system. The Kike is out for all power. The Kike and the unmitigated evil that has been centered in LONDON" ("Ezra Pound Speaking," 120).

But Pound goes beyond restating or developing anti-Semitic themes of his own discourse in The Cantos. With the stock image of the Jews stabbing the wafer, he makes contact with a current of millenarian anti-Semitism that runs deeply and continuously in European culture. Casillo includes the violation of the ritually consecrated blood of Christ and the Communion wafer in his list of common anti-Semitic accusations from medieval Europe to the present, arguing that the charge is "linked to the idea of Jewish deicide" and that it is a metonymic representation of the related accusation that the Jews drink the blood of Christian children (53).[19] The unnamed speaker in the infamous forgery, the Protocols of the Elders of Zion, makes similar claims (Cohn, 32–37).[20] Pound connects with and continues a tradition in European culture more long-standing than those of legal thought or constitutions purportedly at the heart of his late-1930s project.

Perhaps more important, Pound's anti-Semitic gestures through The Cantos link up with anti-Semitic discourses in the United States during the 1930s. Robert Singerman's Antisemitic Propaganda: An Annotated Bibliography and Research Guide lists 204 openly anti-Semitic publications in the United States between 1930 and 1940. Among these are several translations of the Protocols and Hitler's Mein Kampf and the pamphlet reissue of a series of articles first published in Henry Ford's Dearborn Independent titled The International Jew. Anti-Semitic views were publicly propounded by such famous Americans as Charles Lindbergh. Lindbergh's 1941 speech denouncing the groups pressing the United States into war with Germany is a particularly chilling example. Pound forges a connection with such homegrown anti-

Semites as Ford and Lindbergh, as well as the nationally known and well-financed evangelists William Pelley and Father Charles Coughlin.[21]

While there had always been an undercurrent of anti-Semitism in American society, linked in most cases with nativism, the first decades of the twentieth century saw, as Leo Ribuffo has written, a shift "toward increasing suspicion and rejection" of Jews in the United States. More and more often, anti-Semitic articles appeared during these decades in mass-circulation newspapers and in such magazines as the *Saturday Evening Post* (Ribuffo, 8–9). Singerman suggests that the rising tide of Eastern European immigrants, many of whom were Jews, allowed racial theories of Semitic mongrelization and inferiority greater purchase in the American culture ("The Jew as Racial Alien," 108–9). The notion that Jews were "Asiatics" or "Khazars" gained credence among so many Americans that by 1933 Madison Grant, president of the New York Zoological Association, not only could write of the "tumultuous and frantic invasion" of Polish Jews into the United States and argue that these Eastern European Jews were "essentially non-European" but also could publish his book, *The Conquest of a Continent,* through Scribner's, whose imprint surely lent it greater authority than it would have gotten from Chicago's Power Press, which propounded ideas similar to Grant's.[22]

The idea of the Jew as racial alien manifested itself in American society in devices like university quotas (Synnott, 249). Educational institutions were not alone. Anti-Semitism permeated the upper echelon of the State Department during the 1930s. Among the most startling cases are Breckinridge Long and William Phillips, both of whom served as American ambassador to Italy during the decade. Anti-Semitic diplomats, some historians argue, slowed the American response to the plight of Jews in Germany before World War II and reinforced Cordell Hull's inclination against showing Jews special treatment for immigration (Kraut and Breitman, 168–69).

Perhaps more important than these examples of institutional anti-Semitism, though, were the discourses of popular figures like Coughlin and Pelley and documents like the *Protocols, The International Jew,* and *War! War! War!,* an anonymous book published in 1939 that blames the Jews for the coming war. These discourses reached broad audiences in the United States during the late 1930s, and it is with them that Pound's writings most closely ally, in spite of his own ludicrously belated characterization of his prejudice as "suburban" and shallow. The chief similarity between these discourses and Pound's writing lies in their acceptance of a theory of Jewish conspiracy for world domination, a theory that equates the Jews and the Communists and thus articulates anti-Semitism to anticommunism and American "patriotism."

Pound had certainly read the *Protocols* by the late 1930s. Barry Goldensohn writes that Pound had by then developed the "conviction that the Protocols explained the world's economic troubles as a Jewish plot" (402).[23] In a speech delivered on Rome Radio (April 30, 1942), he repeats the book's conspiracy theory and adds a wrinkle of his own: "What is the KAHAL? Why don't you examine the Talmud? Talmud said to have corrupted the Jews. Some Jews disparage it. What is really printed in the Talmud about creatin' disorder? Why did the firm, publishing firm that printed the Protocols go out of business?" (*"Ezra Pound Speaking,"* 115). But even before the war, Pound had established links with the two chief proponents of the American variety of this Jewish world-domination conspiracy theory: William Pelley and Father Charles Coughlin. Pelley, who rose to prominence as an evangelist in the late 1920s, had traveled to Siberia in 1917 and later wrote that he had learned then that a Jewish conspiracy was responsible for communism. Persuaded that Jews were inhabited by demons, Pelley "fashioned an anti-Semitic program remarkable even by the standards of fellow American bigots" (Ribuffo, 57). Upon the appointment of Adolf Hitler as chancellor of Germany, Pelley announced the founding of his Silver Legion, a Christian army to protect the United States against Satanic invasion. Pelley rehearsed in his published articles, books, and radio addresses familiar anti-Semitic accusations: the Rothschild family had subverted legitimate governments for 200 years; the Jews were responsible for the American slave trade and, under the leadership of Judah Benjamin, for Southern secession; the Jews had secured passage of the Federal Reserve Act; and Bernard Baruch, chairman of the War Industries Board, was the Jews' "uncrowned Prince" and the nation's "real master" (ibid., 59). Pelley had read both the *Protocols* and *The International Jew* and called the New Deal the "flawless" fulfillment of the conspiracy laid out in the *Protocols.*

The Silver Shirts, Pelley's paramilitary organization, promised to follow Jesus (the "outstanding Jew-baiter of his day") and to fight the Savior's "chief target, the Sanhedrin," which still led "the Jewish campaign for world conquest" (quoted in Ribuffo, 59).[24] Membership in the group peaked in 1936 at around 15,000, with the most active chapters concentrated in Asheville, North Carolina (Pelley's home), Cleveland, San Diego, Los Angeles, and Chicago. Among the membership of the group, Pelley could have counted (but never did, as far as I have been able to determine) Ezra Pound. In a letter written to Robert Summerville of the Silver Shirts in 1934, Pound applauds the Silver Shirt program and encourages some additions to it. Among these are: "That S/S should attack financial tyranny BY WHOMEVER exercised, i.e., whether by international jew or local aryan. That the plot, conscious and unconscious, manipulated by jews AND others to prevent American education from educating Americans should be exposed and FOILED" (PP, 7:35).[25]

No American anti-Semite, though, including Pelley, had a larger following in the United States during the 1930s than Father Charles Coughlin. By 1932, despite the major radio networks' refusal to carry his speeches, Coughlin was heard from Kansas City to Bangor, Maine. With a growing network of independent stations, Coughlin was, by the middle of the decade, heard weekly from coast to coast. Small contributions from listeners across the country enabled Coughlin to pay the $14,000 cost of his broadcast every week (Marcus, 37).

Because of his large following, Coughlin was perhaps more influential than any other American anti-Semite. Coughlin most clearly drew out his conspiracy theory in a series of radio talks broadcast from November 1938 to January 1939 and republished as *"Am I an Anti-Semite?"* later in 1939. Jewish Communists are anti-Christian and have persecuted Christians, while the Jewish press ("the gentlemen who control the three national radio chains") cover only the persecution of Jews in Germany, he claimed (79). Coughlin repeats the standard accusation that Jewish financiers had funded the Jewish-Communist revolution in Russia. In the United States, according to Coughlin, the Jews have worked, as the Communists have in Russia, through the schools; they have sought to eliminate Christianity from the schools so that "these public institutions will begin to contribute towards graduating a godless generation" (122). This godless generation will be susceptible to communism, and the conversion of schoolchildren to communism lurks beneath the B'nai B'rith's attempts to rid American schools of Christmas and Easter celebrations.

Pound had written to Coughlin in 1935 to praise his book, *Lectures on Social Justice,* and he writes positively of Coughlin in several of his articles of the late 1930s. He comments in 1936 that "the rightness of Senator Borah, Congressman Tinkham and the Rev. Father Coughlin in wanting to keep the U.S.A. out of European embroglios [*sic*] and swindles would, as I see it, extend—and with no delay WHATSOEVER—to abstention from the internal affairs of any and every country" (*PP,* 7:58).[26] Later in the same year, Pound adduces a Coughlin radio speech to show how Italy has suffered under undeserved sanctions from the League of Nations, sanctions forced on it by England. In an "American Notes" column, Pound writes that Coughlin has done more than Borah and Tinkham, in spite of their efforts in Congress, to convince Americans of where their best interests lie and concludes that "the worst bank pimp will be now unable to contend that Coughlin is a mere rhetorician." After the 1936 election, Pound applauds the National Union Party's effort, ludicrously comparing it to the "lone fights and desperate campaigns for the abolition of chattel slavery." Coughlin's campaign, he writes, "at least aroused tremendous fear that if *any* votes were wasted, the du Ponts, Morgans, and the bastardly Liberty League might get a look in" (*PP,* 7:108).

As revealing as Pound's explicit mentions of Coughlin are his repetitions of Coughlinesque conspiracy theories in the radio speeches. In a speech broadcast on March 6, 1942, Pound rants a shorthand version of the conspiracy theory of Coughlin involving two Jewish gangs: one in London and the other in Moscow (*"Ezra Pound Speaking,"* 54). Again, on April 30, 1942, Pound alludes to a Jewish conspiracy that caused the American Civil War and many other wars, including the present one:

> SOMETIME the Anglo Saxon may AWAKE to the fact that the Jewish kahal and secret forces concentrated or brought to focus in the unappetizin' carcass of Franklin D. Roosevelt do NOT shove Aryan or non-yittisch nations into WARS in order that those said nations may WIN wars. The non-Jew nations are shoved into wars in order to destroy themselves, to break up their structure, to destroy their social order, to destroy their populations. And no more flaming

and flagrant cause appears in history than our own American Civil War, said to be an occidental record for size of armies employed and only surpassed by the more recent triumphs of Warburgs, the wars of 1914 and the present one. (ibid., 113)[27]

The anti-Semitic moment of Canto 65, finally, reaches out not only to the poem's systematic anti-Semitism but also to an existing anti-Semitic component of American society. While Pound's aesthetic strategies and elitist positioning doom his political efforts to failure, he does seek to intervene through the Adams Cantos and his periodical prose in the political struggles of the moment. He brings to bear the weight of his own cultural capital as a well-known poet, along with the weight of American early national history and the already powerful institution of literary modernism, in his attempts to shape American foreign policy before and during World War II. More repellent, he lends that cultural capital to the small but vocal communities of anti-Semites in the United States, seeking to shape a collective will along the lines of his own political agenda that might influence the power-wielding "goofs" in the American public and government. To their credit, the "goofs" did not listen.

4

Extending the Document

MURIEL RUKEYSER

In 1929, the New Kanawha Power Company, a West Virginia subsidiary of Union Carbide, contracted the Dennis and Rinehart Company of Charlottesville, Virginia, to dig a three-and-a-quarter-mile tunnel from Gauley's Junction to Hawk's Nest, West Virginia. The tunnel, which 2,000 men worked to dig, would direct water from the nearby New River to a hydroelectric plant at Gauley's Junction. The plant would then sell the power to the Electro-Metallurgical Company, another Union Carbide subsidiary. The tunneling operation uncovered a huge deposit of extremely pure (90–99 percent) silica. The silica, useful in the electro-processing of steel, was shipped to Electro-Metallurgical's processing operation in Alloy, West Virginia. The tunnel construction was quickly transformed into a mining operation; the tunnel's width was doubled to facilitate the extraction of silica, and the faster dry-drilling method was used in order to extract the silica more quickly. According to the U.S. Bureau of Mines, silica was to be mined with hydraulic water drills, which reduced the amount of deadly silica dust raised, and miners were to wear safety masks with filters over their mouths while working. Union Carbide's insistence on drilling the tunnel dry resulted in the release of tons of silica dust (*Time* magazine compared the tunnel full of dust to a "flour bin" in which workers "died like ants") ("Silicosis," 63).[1] Moreover, the company's refusal to provide safety masks (if workers had worn the masks, they would have had to stop every hour to rinse dust from the filters) resulted in somewhere between 476 and 2,000 miners' deaths from silicosis.[2]

In a series of subsequent lawsuits, workers and their families sought compensation from Union Carbide. The company, though, attempted to conceal its complicity in the workers' deaths by bribing doctors to misdiagnose silicosis (workers were told they had pneumonia, pleurisy, or tuberculosis, and one of these diseases was given as the cause of death on death certificates) and by paying the local undertaker to bury workers secretly in a cornfield (*Congressional Record,* 10). The case was finally investigated by Congress, but the further investigation recommended by the Subcommittee of the Committee of Labor in the House of Representatives was blocked.[3] Those workers who did receive compensation were charged half their receipts by their own lawyers (*An Investigation,* 14–15).

It was a bad year all around. The stock market crash in October slammed the economic brakes on nearly a decade of postwar industrial growth and consumer confidence, ushering in the depression that would become "Great" as it stood the test of time and failed to respond to federal remedies. The depression would provoke the rapid growth of a fairly new genre, the documentary.[4] The decade prematurely born in 1929 brought to full fruition peculiarly *social* documentary, that distinctive brand of reportage that seeks not only to increase our knowledge of public facts but also to "sharpen it with feeling" (Stott, 20). Indeed, as Paula Rabinowitz has written, "anyone with even a passing interest in the [1930s] . . . [r]eferences it through the images of hungry migrants caught by the Farm Security Administration (FSA) photographers" (*They Must Be Represented,* 3–4). Unlike most earlier journalistic accounts, social documentary goes beyond simply reporting on the conditions people face; it emphasizes historical specificity and attempts to draw out the causes of those conditions in an effort to encourage social change (Stott, 21). The economic events of 1929 sent photographers and writers out to scour the country for representable stories of human suffering, stories that would make their way, within only a few years, not only onto the pages of the *New Masses* but also between the glossy covers of *Fortune* and, thereby, into the homes of middle-class readers.

Documentary culture had made its way between the hardcovers of modernist fiction as well, most prominently in John Dos Passos's

U.S.A. trilogy, whose first volume, *The 42nd Parallel,* appeared early in 1930. Alternating conventional fictional plot lines with biographies of political personalities, "Newsreel" collages of current events, and lyrical "Camera Eye" sections, Dos Passos attempted to distill the essences of "big money" and its concomitant culture in a swirl of styles as indebted to the representational vocabularies of documentary (available in such projects as Jacob Riis's *How the Other Half Lives*) as to the modernist aesthetics of fragmentation and juxtaposition. The resulting trilogy provided what Michael Denning calls "the ur-text of the Popular Front," its "charter . . . , its starting point, its founding mythology" (166–67). Dos Passos's own account of his mission in the trilogy resonates powerfully with Muriel Rukeyser's practice in *The Book of the Dead:* "[A] writer is after all only a machine for absorbing and arranging certain sequences of words out of the lives of the people around him" (*Major Nonfictional Prose,* 81).

Documentary had influenced poetry on the Left as well. This influence is best known, perhaps, in the work of Kenneth Fearing. Often mentioned as one of the "Dynamo poets" (along with Edwin Rolfe, Sol Funaroff, and Rukeyser), Fearing began to publish poems in little magazines in the late 1920s; by the mid-1930s, his work was a common feature in the *New Masses* and other left-wing magazines. His first book, *Angel Arms,* appeared in a small edition in 1929; Sol Funaroff's Dynamo Press published his next collection, *Poems,* in 1935. In his scathing satirical poems, Fearing typically juxtaposes snatches of discourse drawn from diverse registers and locations. As Walter Kalaidjian writes, Fearing "broadens proletcult verse by playfully subverting the conventional boundaries that divide the traditionally pastoral lyricism of *carpe diem* poetics from the textuality of the modern mass media" (*American Culture,* 201).

That playfulness is shaped by a thorough grounding in and imitation of (thematically and formally) the documentary culture of the photo essay and the newsreel. Fearing's "1933" is typical:

You heard the gentleman, with automatic precision, speak the
   truth.
Cheers. Triumph.
And then mechanically it followed the gentleman lied.
Deafening applause. Flashlights, cameras, microphones.
   Floral tribute. Cheers.

Down Mrs. Hogan's alley, your hand with others reaching
    among the ashes, cinders, scrapiron, garbage, you
    found the rib of sirloin wrapped in papal documents.
    Snatched it. Yours by right, the title clear.
Looked up. Saw lips twitch in the smiling head thrust from
    the museum window. "A new deal." (30)

But Fearing is not alone among left-wing poets deploying documentary conventions in the early and mid-1930s. Indeed, Kay Boyle's "Communication to Nancy Cunard," first published in Cunard's 1934 *Negro* anthology, approaches the Scottsboro case in ways that make the poem read like the script for an unshot documentary film. Boyle first sets the scene with cinematic description—"It begins in the dark on a boxcar floor, the groaning timber / Stretched from bolt to bolt above the freight-train wheels"—then plays snatches of overheard dialogue—"Christ, what they pay you don't keep body and soul together"—and finally stages whole sections of trial transcript testimony (complete with dialect renderings):

Haywood Patterson	*Victoria Price*
"So here goes an I shell try	
Faitfully an I possibly can	
Reference to myself in particularly	"I
And concerning the other boys	cain't
personal pride	remember."
And my life upto now."	
(*Collected Poems*, 66–67)	

From *Fortune* to Fearing, Bourke-White to Boyle, the codes and conventions of the documentary are a ubiquitous strand in the cultural and literary fabric of the 1930s.

In 1937, Muriel Rukeyser powerfully wove these strands—the events at Gauley Bridge and the techniques of documentary culture, especially in its literary incarnations—and a third, contemporary strand, the Communist Party's Popular Front, into a long poetic investigation of the events at and about the Hawk's Nest tunnel.[5] Rukeyser, who traveled to Gauley Bridge with her Vassar classmate and friend, photographer Nancy Naumberg, transformed the tragedy into a new political poetic in *The Book of the Dead,* the long poem sequence that would become the centerpiece of her 1938 book *U.S. 1* (Kertesz, 100).[6] She structures the sequence not on the chronology of the catastrophe but loosely on the cycle of death and rebirth in the book from which she takes her title, the Egyptian *Book of the Dead.* In its cyclic structure and the poetic strategies Rukeyser deploys throughout it, *The Book of the Dead* at once resembles and revises *The Waste Land.* The rituals of burial and their concomitant promises of rebirth set up the descent into the underworld, where Rukeyser locates redemptive and revolutionary possibilities. But this cyclic structure jostles against a documentary style and stance that seem incommensurable with its modernist tenor. A sequence of great illustrative power, presenting scenes of sheer beauty alongside stunning depictions of suffering, mingling political critique and philosophical meditation, *The Book of the Dead* sets out to imagine and construct a community of resistance to corporate power and its congressional apologists.

When *U.S. 1* was published, though, the sequence was received with either benign puzzlement or dismissal and angry rejection. Rukeyser was castigated for failure to meet the various aesthetic criteria operative among her readers. *The Book of the Dead* is too documentary, too poetic, too stridently anticapitalist, and too cravenly procapitalist all at the same time. One might argue that the sequence deserves critical attention simply for its capacity to elicit such contradictory and confrontational responses. But I argue, instead, that the sequence succeeds precisely where critics found what they saw as its aesthetic failures. Addressing a labor disaster of massive proportions, taking up the excrescences of capitalism and the paradoxically liberatory possibilities of industrial production, and seeking broad-based social change and elaborating a poetics of politicized memory that might support such change, Rukeyser addressed readers from various points on the political, philosophical, and aesthetic spectrums. Writing at the height of the Popular Front, Rukeyser develops a fragmented and many-voiced poetic similar to that at work in contemporaneous poems by liberal and leftist poets, a documentary modernism through which to train readers in a peculiarly elegiac politics.[7]

Since it shows the complexity of both the poem's address and the communities the poem sought to unify, the reception of *The Book of the Dead* is worth examining in some detail. Some shorter reviews of *U.S. 1* are cautiously positive. William Carlos Williams praises Rukeyser's "extension of the document" in the *New Republic,* comparing her handling of nonpoetic material to Ezra Pound's. Rukeyser shares with Pound, Williams writes, the understanding of "what words are for and how important it is not to twist them to make 'poetry' of them" (141). William Rose Benét, writing for the *Saturday Review,* criticizes most of the poems in *U.S. 1* for their lack of clarity and berates Rukeyser for her "peculiar intellectual aloofness from her audience." He praises *The Book of the Dead,* though, writing that Rukeyser has "handled the Gauley Bridge disaster, where so many workmen died of silicosis, with poetic quality and dramatic impressiveness" (16).

Eda Lou Walton's two-paragraph review in the *New York Times Book Review,* though, typifies the majority of the reviews. While Walton praises Rukeyser's language and diction, she attacks Rukeyser's stylistic simplification, which "has made whole groups of poems very prosaic." *The Book of the Dead,* Walton writes, "is the material for poetry, but it is not poetry. This is reporting and not the imaginative vision" (19).[8] David Wolff, in the *New Masses,* takes a similar tack.[9] Praising Rukeyser's work in the book, writing that it "deserves study and applause," Wolff focuses on her incorporation of documentary material in *The Book of the Dead.* Rukeyser discovers, he writes, the "extraordinary movement of the factual document, which proceeds almost dully, then turns and strikes at you with the abrupt violence of the event itself" (23). Her employment of the historical archive, though, also brings Wolff's only criticism. He argues that "the poet has made an error . . . in not marking off the documents clearly from the body of the poem" (23). In her attempt to assimilate her archival sources into poetic lines, Wolff writes, Rukeyser blurs the line between the two, sometimes compromising the document to wrench it into poetic lines, sometimes perverting the beat of poetry for "factual uses."

But the most critical review the sequence elicited was John Wheelwright's in the *Partisan Review.* Wheelwright's chief complaint is the failure of *The Book of the Dead* to make a "root attack upon everyday exploitation." He writes that the Gauley Bridge disaster "needs to be made memorable. But as not one line of [the poem's] thousand lines describes the wage system, a goodly number of poetry readers will say, 'We haven't the remotest idea why anyone but a dumb cluck worked there. It's a free country, isn't it?' The poem attacks the excrescences of capitalism, but not the system's inner nature" (54).

Rukeyser's "unscientific socialism," Wheelwright writes, makes her many worker portraits unconvincing, and her failure to keep her verse in the "fulcrum balance" of meter prevents any of those portraits from "striking the heart." Castigating modernist, experimental poets for their way of "making us feel stupid even before their rude erudition," Wheelwright lumps Rukeyser in with them. Her predilection for syntactic fragmentation, Wheelwright writes, "harms her work," and he finds Rukeyser's style most problematic "when it goes telegraphic and lets the subject, object, verb be taken for granted, or at any rate, omitted." He concludes his review by urging Rukeyser and other poets on the Left to "confront communication. . . . Revolutionary writing in the snob style does not reach a proper audience" (56).[10]

It is difficult, however, to see *The Book of the Dead* as snobbish. Rather, it stretches to encompass readers of all kinds, to offer them a space of recognition on the poem's textual surface. To this end, Rukeyser deploys the conventions of what William Stott calls "radical documentary reportage," a set of strategies employed by social documentarists. Radical reportage relies on case histories, descriptions of "the lives of specific individuals who represent a group of common people generally overlooked in the society," to "sabotage the general claims, the proud boasts of those in power" (172). A crucial component of these histories was the photograph, which allowed reporters to claim they were letting the images speak for themselves.[11] The Farm Security Administration, under Roy Stryker, used the photographic record most effectively throughout the decade, compiling tens of thousands of photographs to document both the suffering of rural populations (farmers and sharecroppers, especially in the South) and the effects of the Roosevelt administration's relief programs on those populations. Case histories are supplemented by what Stott calls "exposé quotation," in which a public figure is quoted verbatim in a context that ironizes the speech "to suggest something other than what the authority intended" (173). Finally, documentary emotionally enhances factual presentation by including the direct impressions of the reporter. These impressions, though proffered with restraint, serve to guide the impressions of the reader or viewer.[12] Perhaps the most famous photographic/textual documentary project of the decade was Margaret Bourke-White and Erskine Caldwell's *You Have Seen Their Faces* (1937). This book, with its combination of photographs, testimony, and reportage, is the documentary project Rukeyser's sequence seems on first examination most closely to resemble. In its self-conscious ironizing of documentary at some points, though, and its obvious indebtedness to modernist poetics, the sequence is more appropriately likened to a slightly later project, James Agee and Walker Evans's *Let Us Now Praise Famous Men*.[13]

After a camera-eye tour of the eastern seaboard (down U.S. Highway 1), a tour through space and time reminiscent of the "Powhatan's Daughter" section of Hart Crane's *The Bridge*, we find the town of Gauley Bridge (in the poem "Gauley Bridge") as if in a photograph.[14] The city appears abandoned, as if the tragedy has desolated it:

> a street of wooden walls and empty windows,
> the doors shut handless in the empty street
> and the deserted Negro standing on the corner. (*U.S. 1*, 16)

The town is doubly empty: no one moves in either the streets or the buildings, and those actions that do occur are described in terms that enhance rather than contradict the impression of emptiness. While doors shut along the street, no hands are seen to shut them. The black figure on the corner is "deserted," this standing body just another empty building. Later stanzas discover more people, more activity in the town, but these too are described so that their presence signifies greater absences. The people at the post office window are defined by their hands — "the hand of the man who withdraws, the woman who reaches her hand" — as if they are incomplete, a hand without the rest of a man, a woman in danger of losing her hand to the glass of the window (17).

Not just a ghost town, Gauley Bridge is a sort of "Everytown." "Any town," Rukeyser writes, "looks like this one-street town." A boy runs down the street with his dog, a bus stops at the station for food, posters on the movie house advertise films, the waitress at the seedy bar goes about her work, watched by "harsh night eyes." The place is nothing special, a "block of town" along the road, one town away from Alloy, a widening of the road that "flows over the bridge," a station on the railroad line. "What do you want," Rukeyser asks at the poem's conclusion, mocking the anticipated response of readers. "These people live here" (17).

Edwin Rolfe and Langston Hughes explored one way to capture collective consciousness and action in the serial interpellation of worker-readers into provisional and tactical unity. Rukeyser attempts a similar articulation of community through her representations of individual protagonists in the Gauley Bridge drama. Rukeyser is influenced in her attempt by the Popular Front aesthetic adopted by the Communist Party after the Seventh Congress of the Communist International (Comintern) in 1935. Mobilized by the consolidation of Nazi power in Germany and fascism in Italy, European Communists recognized the difference between bourgeois Fascist regimes and bourgeois democratic states and concluded that solidarity with the latter to provide collective security from the former was reasonable and within the parameters of the International. First introduced by Comintern secretary Georgi Dimitrov at the Seventh Congress, the policy shift resulted in rhetorical, organizational, and cultural changes in the American party. Antagonism to Franklin Roosevelt and the New Deal softened to the extent that the Communist Party of the United States (cpusa) actually forged alliances with progressive forces in the Roosevelt coalition. Moreover, the party joined forces with many non-Communist progressive groups and founded many others in its efforts to make common cause with liberals and Socialists on such problems as race relations and the threats posed by international and domestic fascism.[15] Finally, the Popular Front loosened aesthetic prescriptions (and proscriptions) promulgated by party publications and critics so that nonproletarian writers who espoused even liberal reforms, writers often attacked in the past, were counted as allies in the education of the masses.[16]

To claim that Rukeyser was influenced by the Popular Front raises the question of her stance toward communism and the cpusa. The question is an open one. No record exists of Rukeyser's actual membership in the cpusa or the Young Communist League, the organization's youth branch. Rukeyser's notes and diaries from the early 1930s, though, include many entries about her involvement in left-wing and Communist-affiliated organizations ranging from the John Reed Club (the cpusa's literary branch) to the International Labor Defense (ild), the party-funded organization working for new trials and appeals for the Scottsboro defendants. From 1932 to 1936, Rukeyser's sketchy diaries frequently note her attendance at ild meetings, Scottsboro-related rallies, and anti-Hitler and anti-Fascist rallies and mention the work she did, sometimes on a daily basis, for the *Daily Worker*.[17] Rukeyser traveled to Alabama to cover the Scottsboro appeals in 1933 and to Barcelona to cover the People's Olympiad, an anti-Fascist alternative to the Berlin Olympics, in 1936. She published poems in the *New Masses*, among them two excerpts from *The Book of the Dead* ("The Disease" and "The Cornfield"). But none of these activities proves party membership. Numerous writers, Communists and non-Communists, participated in similar activities and organizations during the 1930s; the times seemed, to many, to call for such activity.

According to the Federal Bureau of Investigation (FBI), though, these activities and others clearly mark Rukeyser as a Communist. Her FBI file, some fifty pages long, adduces her political work and publications, along with the testimony of anonymous informants, to prove that Rukeyser is a "concealed Communist." A 1943 memo lists numerous "Communist Party Fronts" with which she was affiliated: the American Student Union; *New Masses;* People's Radio Foundation; *Student Review;* American Continental Congress for Peace; California Labor School; National Council of American Soviet Friendship; National Council of Arts, Sciences, and Professions; World Peace Appeal; Joint Anti-Fascist Refugee Committee; Spanish Refugee Committee; China Welfare Appeal; and Abraham Lincoln Brigade. A 1952 memo recommending that a security index card be prepared on Rukeyser, thus making her an official target of surveillance and object of political suspicion, matter-of-factly marks "Communist" in the political-affiliation space.[18]

Whether or not she was a member of the party in 1937 (or later), Rukeyser certainly seems to have sympathized with the party's broad aims, and she certainly worked in her poetry to advance those aims. Nowhere is this more obvious than in *The Book of the Dead*. Rukeyser realizes Popular Front aims in the documentary-influenced monologue poems that speak to and in the voices of discrete components of the community. She attempts, in these poems, to construct an audience like that constructed by documentary, an audience, in Paula Rabinowitz's characterization, "whose position is located within history, . . . a subject of (potential) agency, an actor in history" (*They Must Be Represented*, 7–8). As in documentary, Rukeyser "foregrounds sexual, class, racial, and gender differences" within her audience, and from these differences, she "essentially remak[es] the relationship of truth to ideology by insisting on advocacy rather than objectivity" (ibid., 7). Her speakers are people with agendas.

We begin to meet these people in "Praise of the Committee." In a scene rendered as if in a black-and-white film, we enter a "dark and noisy room" where, "frozen two feet from the stove," a group of people gather to organize their response to the tunnel tragedy. Several of these, members of the Defense Committee organized to pursue suits against Union Carbide and to press Congress to investigate the tunnel tragedy, reappear later in the sequence in monologue poems of their own. As members of the committee, though, they speak not only for themselves: "Many come with them / who pack the hall, wait in the thorough dark" (*U.S. 1*, 20). These, the unnamed silicotic men who "breathe hard" and the women who are affected by their loved ones' illness, are the people whose "hands touched mastery," the people who "demand an answer" (22). In the poetic case histories that follow, Rukeyser elaborates a complex answer, delivering exposition and meditation in the distinctive voices of people in the Gauley Bridge community.

In monologues that Louis Untermeyer compares to Edgar Lee Masters's *Spoon River Anthology* (608), Rukeyser deploys the generic conventions of the social documentary—informant narrative and reportorial observation—to sabotage the claims of corporate narratives. These poems are shaped by the informant narrative common in social documentary. Stott writes that "since the aim of documentary is to make real to us another person's experience, make us see what he sees and feel what he feels, it is only sensible that the persons speak directly to us. All documentary tends to direct quotation, but documentary can be all quotation and nothing else" (191). Rukeyser constructs, through the testimony of individuals, a community of individual speakers within the poem, speakers who, differentiated by their voices, their locations in the community, and the poetic forms of their histories, provide various views of the tunnel tragedy and those responsible for it. More than this, the monologue poems provide points of access and adhesion for quite varied audiences. Like an extended version of Rolfe's serial interpellation in "These Men Are Revolution," Rukeyser's monologues hail readers of diverse backgrounds in voices something like their own. At the same time, Rukeyser both deploys and undercuts the intense sentimentality of some documentary, borrowing the pathos of her speakers' situations but laying bare the very devices with which she draws their portraits. The resulting poems establish a tension between the condescending sentiment of Caldwell and Bourke-White and conscious resistance to that sentiment, a tension Rukeyser links to a deliberately coalitional political model congruent with the Popular Front.[19]

In "Mearl Blankenship," for example, Rukeyser presents two perspectives: that of Blankenship speaking in the present and in a letter he hopes the narrator will send to the city, "maybe to a paper / if it's all right," and that of the narrator, who explicitly interprets him. These perspectives correspond to a conventionally sentimental portrayal on one hand and a highly conscious and self-referential deployment of that portrayal on the other. In the letter, we hear Mearl most clearly, the syntax and spelling indicating his class and level of education:

> Dear Sir, my name is Mearl Blankenship.
> I have Worked for the rhinehart & Dennis Co
> Many days & many nights
> & it was so dusty you couldn't hardly see the lights. (24)

Blankenship's suffering is evident—"I wake up choking, and my wife / rolls me over on my left side" (24)—and his written plea for help gives us an opportunity to see clearly the effect of tunnel work on one worker. But the means by which Rukeyser renders Blankenship's voice are precisely those that make us recoil from the captions Caldwell wrote for Bourke-White's photographs in *You Have Seen Their Faces*:

> J C Dunbar said that I was the very picture of health
> when I went to Work at that tunnel.
> I have lost eighteen lbs on the Rheinhart ground
> and expecting to loose my life
> & no settlement yet & I have sued the Co. twice
> But when the lawyers got a settlement
> they didn't want to talk to me. (25)

The misspellings and incorrect punctuation comprise a textualized dialect representation of Blankenship's speech. His class position and lack of education are typographically exposed not only for sympathy but, potentially, for a stance of superiority, for parody, for ridicule.[20] Blankenship's "letter" in the poem is really his, not a fabrication; Rukeyser quoted it verbatim and kept it for reference when she worked on the poem. Yet she runs the risk of condescension in using it as she does. As Stott, Rabinowitz, and others have argued, documentary works by deploying documents in a highly selective and tactically framed manner while appearing simply to adduce them.

However problematic, the self-representation of Mearl's suffering is compelling on its own, but Rukeyser splices it with the narrator's description both to broaden its significance and to show the hand that draws the portrait. When the narrative voice interrupts Blankenship's letter, Mearl and the surrounding scene (river and rocks) are intertwined:

> He stood against the rock
> facing the river
> grey river grey face
> the rock mottled behind him
> like X-ray plate enlarged
> diffuse and stony
> his face against the stone. (25)

The scene is Mearl himself writ large. The river is the color of his face, and the rock against which he stands is transformed into an enlarged X ray of Mearl's own lungs. The adjective Rukeyser uses to describe the rock, "mottled," appears at several points in the poem to describe a silicotic lung. A metonymy for the region itself, Mearl, in this monologue, effectively performs the "case history" function in Rukeyser's poetic documentary. Through his testimony and his carefully constructed representation, the figure of this individual worker provokes the collective response necessary to encourage social change. Repeated and recombined throughout the sequence, the documentary conventions Rukeyser borrows here provide the ground and the guide for readers to think through the cluster of problems the Gauley Bridge disaster dramatically embodies for American society. And the conventions simultaneously refer to themselves so that the object of our sympathy is already ironized, already placed within critical quotation marks, already recognized as a construction; our sympathy itself, therefore, is bracketed by Rukeyser's complex eliciting of it.

Others whom we hear in the monologues seem representative types, opening out to groups of people like them. In these sections, Rukeyser effectively adds to the documentary strategy of the case study the associative resources of poetic form, letting the speech of individuals represent larger groups. In so doing, she speaks *to* various audiences by speaking *as* them, in language marked somehow as their own. She is, of course, not alone in this effort. Many poets on the Left experimented with dialect and vernacular verse forms to demonstrate solidarity with blacks and others, with varying levels of success and with the consistent corollary drawback of at least apparent condescension. Rukeyser's most obvious attempt at this speaking-for/to-by-speaking-as occurs in the voice of "George Robinson" (Rukeyser's spelling; the person on whom the character is based was named George Robison), who stands overtly for blacks who worked in the tunnel and contracted silicosis and, by extension, for all working-class blacks who might read this sequence.[21]

David Kadlec, in "X-Ray Testimonials in Muriel Rukeyser," reads Rukeyser's representation of George Robinson against the congressional testimony of "a silicotic bench driller named George Robison" in order to uncover the racial (and potentially racist) unconscious in Rukeyser's poem and in 1930s "radical alliances" more generally (24, 26). Kadlec's argument is ingenious, and his close reading not only of the poem but also of the medical discourse surrounding the X ray photograph as a new diagnostic tool provides considerable force for his claim that "Rukeyser restored a universalizing whiteness to the blackened workers that Robison had summoned before the congressional committee" (26). Of course, Rukeyser's purpose throughout *The Book of the Dead* is to call into being a community united across such lines of demarcation as race and gender, a community united by the fact of death (generally but also, and more important, the fact of the deaths of *these* workers in *this* industrial disaster) and by the possibility of resurrection and revolution through a politicized memory. That Rukeyser fails to follow Robison's lead in his congressional testimony and blacken the community rather than whiten it might indicate, as Kadlec argues, a sacrifice of racial interests to class interests, but the form Rukeyser adopts in "George Robinson: Blues" complicates this judgment for it demonstrates that Rukeyser sets about her alleged restoration of a universalizing whiteness by taking on a voice marked by its poetic form as black.

In "George Robinson: Blues," Rukeyser joins in a widespread practice among poets on the American Left. Drawn to "the Negro question" and matters of segregation, prejudice, and interracial violence by their personal convictions as well as by the CPUSA's attention, these writers sought both to make common cause with blacks and to speak authoritatively on what might be considered "black" issues (issues they saw in terms of social justice more broadly). Kay Boyle's "Communication to Nancy Cunard" undertakes just such a mission through its juxtaposition of quoted testimony and lyrical description. Sol Funaroff, the editor of *Dynamo* magazine and the Dynamo poetry series, wrote a series of "Negro Songs" for a musical (*Scufflin' Along*); these are sympathetic borrowings or parodies of blues and dialect folk songs that articulate working-class political issues through the prism of race. At their most successful, as in Funaroff's "Goin Mah Own Road," these poems reject white capitalist values and draw together the concerns and attitudes of black and white workers:

Ah wukked mah time and ovahtime
Ah wukked mah time and too much time
When ah quit wuk
Ah hadn't a dime.

Goin mah own road
Goin mah own road
Goin to wuk foh mahse'f

Ah tol the boss to go to hell
Ah kicked his ass, you go to hell
Me an mah kind don need you. (8)

"Me an mah kind" here works to unite the black workers in whose voice Funaroff tries to speak and the white workers whom he biographically represents (and whose voice controls much of his other poetry). In some of the "Negro Songs," though, Funaroff courts a condescension as unpalatable as Caldwell's:

No time fo learnin,
No time fo sights,
No time fo shufflin
to fast tunes at nights. (19)

Other poets attempt to prevent this condescension by avoiding dialect, speaking, in Genevieve Taggard's words, "To the Negro People" in a voice only gesturally their own. Taggard's poem (written in 1939 and 1941) imaginatively absorbs the pains and aspirations of blacks in forms drawn but now quite distant from spirituals and blues:

> The Gulf dances level
> Sapphire blue near his elbow, where his bones
> Sleep in the dust of song, where we lift up our voices
> Crying with the dark man when we cry
> My way's cloudy. (51)

Here the speaker inhabits the (attenuated) voice of the black people while simultaneously noting, in the text itself, her difference; there is no need to lift one's voice "with the dark man" when one *is* the dark man, and the poem foregrounds its own practice of trying to be one with its object through the borrowing of cultural forms.

"George Robinson: Blues" steers a sort of middle ground between the alternatives marked by Funaroff and Taggard. Rukeyser eschews dialect but still manages to make explicit this speaker's representative status in the poem's form. Like the poem's title, the three-line stanzas of Robinson's monologue, while longer and less metrically regular than blues lines, echo blues forms in their rhythm, repetition, and rhyme:

> Gauley Bridge is a good town for Negroes, they let us stand
>   around they let us stand
> around on the sidewalks if we're black or brown.
> Vanetta's over the trestle, and that's our town. (33)

The typical *aab* structure of the blues stanza is evident, though attenuated, in Rukeyser's stanzas.[22] While the first two lines in the standard blues stanza are repeated with only slight variation, Rukeyser continues in the second line the thought begun in the first. The third line, with its characteristic medial caesura, completes the thought. We might more easily see the stanza's connection to blues form if we relineate it thus:

> Gauley Bridge is a good town for Negroes, they let us stand
>   around
> they let us stand around on the sidewalks if we're black or
>   brown.
> Vanetta's over the trestle, and that's our town.

Loosened for Rukeyser's purposes, the single-rhyme, three-line blues stanzas structuring Robinson's monologue record the experience of black tunnel workers, neglected by company doctors, dying in the tunnel camps, forced off the crews when visibly sick and unable to work, and buried by their own community in a makeshift graveyard. Robinson voices facts about the tunnel work that have become refrains through their insistent repetition in previous poems—the workers are forced to return to the tunnel after dynamite blasts have raised clouds of silica dust, their drinking water is contaminated by the dust, and the workers are covered with the dust. For Robinson, though, the dust (and the death it brings) lead to a bleak equality:

> As dark as I am, when I came out at morning after the tunnel at
>   night,
> with a white man, nobody could have told which man was
>   white.
> The dust had covered us both, and the dust was white. (34)

Like the common end that awaits people of all races, the silica dust of Gauley Bridge elides racial difference. All are the same in death or in work that ends in death; all, then, should join against these circumstances. In theme and form, "George Robinson: Blues" calls out to black readers to recognize their common stake in overcoming common oppression. The poem, especially in the context of the sequence as a whole, with its later invocation of the spirit of martyred abolitionist John Brown, participates in what Michael Denning has called the Popular Front's "pan-ethnic Americanism" (131).

Blankenship and Robinson were crucial from the earliest stages of Rukeyser's work. In a letter she wrote Rukeyser soon after their return from Gauley Bridge, Nancy Naumberg mentions these two by name (along with Vivian Jones, the subject of another poem in the sequence) as she advises Rukeyser on the writing of a piece about the tunnel tragedy:

> Stress, through the stories of Blankenship, Miller etc the necessity of a thorough investigation in order to indict the Co., its lawyers and doctors and undertaker, how the company cheated these menout [*sic*] of their lives. . . . How when Jones and Robinson testified, they were taken off work relief, and only put back because

of Congressional pressure. Stress the importance of silica rock—
use Robinson's testimony for silica dust stories.[23]

With Mrs. Jones, the speaker of "Absalom," these two are the most
important speakers in the sequence. Their poems lay out the facts of
the case (along with "Philippa Allen," "The Face of the Dam: Vivian
Jones," and "Absalom"), and they make compellingly clear the human
costs. They do the work Naumberg urges, the work of showing "how
the company cheated these men" (and women).

But not all of the testimony in Rukeyser's documentary comes
from the Gauley Bridge community itself. Two poems late in the se-
quence focus on the congressional investigation of the tunnel project,
bringing into play the voices of individual congressmen and the pub-
lic institution itself. In "The Disease: After-Effects," Rukeyser pre-
sents a congressman from Montana, a lonely crusader for corporate
reform that might ensure that no similar tragedy would occur in the
future. Like a newsreel (which Rukeyser mentions in the text), this
poem locates us through a brief montage in "the life of a Congress-
man" and, more concretely still, "on the floor of the House." There,
before the crowded galleries, the congressman from Montana pro-
poses "a bill to prevent industrial silicosis." This representative of the
people has a personal stake in the prevention of the disease; his father,
he tells the assembled representatives, had contracted it. The con-
gressman's monologue repeats on a new discursive plane the gener-
alizing move of earlier poems, the linkage of individual suffering,
through imagery and figurative language, with a broader population
and project. The speaker takes advantage of his experiential authority
to make clear the disease's impact on the national community:

> Widespread in trade, widespread in space!
> Butte, Montana; Joplin, Missouri; the New York tunnels,
> the Catskill Aqueduct. In over thirty States.
> A disease worse than consumption.
>
> Only eleven States have laws.
> There are today one million potential victims.
> 500,000 Americans have silicosis now.
> These are the proportions of a war. (60)

We have come quite a distance from the small towns of West Virginia,
from the relatively small numbers of workers in the Gauley Bridge

tunnel. The congressman speaks to and for the nation as a whole. "All our meaning," Rukeyser writes, "lies on this / signature: power on a hill / centered in its committee" (60–61).

But even here, amid the trappings of power on the national stage of the congressional floor, the "gentleman from Montana" testifies in a manner quite similar to that of Blankenship or Robinson, a manner marked by personal voice and individual memory:

> I'm a child, I'm leaning from the bedroom window,
> clipping the rose that climbs upon the wall,
> the tea roses, and the red roses,
> one for a wound, another for disease,
> remembrance for strikers. I was five, going on six,
> my father on strike at the Anaconda mine;
> they broke the Socialist mayor we had in Butte,
> the sheriff (friendly), found their judge. Strike-broke.
> Shot father. He died: wounds and his disease.
> My father had silicosis. (59–60)

Like other speakers in the monologues, the congressman is authorized by his personal experience, here the recollection of childhood and the death of his father. And his testimony shares the symbolic vocabulary of the other case history poems in the sequence; whereas Rukeyser reads the rock in "Mearl Blankenship," finding in it Mearl's silicotic lung writ large, she makes of the roses the congressman recalls symbols of antiworker violence and industrial illness. The red blooms evoke, in the congressman's memory, the bleeding bullet wound and the debilitating lung disease, both factors in his father's death. Like Mearl's rock, these roses are a "remembrance," further testimony that enhances and enlarges the congressman's individual experience. The significance and relevance of that experience are poignantly rendered in the dramatically flat concluding moment of this testimony: "My father had silicosis." Returning from memory and its symbolic resonance, the congressman concludes in the matter-of-fact register of testimony. In this highly charged context, the simple fact cinches the case.

Rukeyser's deployment of the conventions of social documentary at key moments in the sequence is fairly straightforward. Case histories of individuals and groups are presented through narrative, description, testimony, or a combination of these. The "portraits" are allowed to stand as authentic documents, to "speak for themselves" through the pictorial and testimonial codes readers would recognize from the omnipresent documentary culture of the 1930s. Of course, these poems are not unmediated testimony; like the documentary projects they resemble, the poems are careful constructions, artful selections and combinations of significant detail. In their poetic staging of familiar documentary scenes alone, these poems are striking accomplishments. But Rukeyser is not content merely to adapt poetry to perform the critical function of social documentary. To simply repeat in verse the mechanisms of documentary serves no productive purpose; indeed, it would doom Rukeyser to replicate the class-based voyeurism and sentiment to which documentary is so often heir.[24] Rather, as her "Note" at the end of *U.S. 1* makes clear, she also wants to "extend the document" through the compositional practices and aesthetic expectations of modernist poetry.[25] To this end, she takes a page from such manuals of modernist poetic practice as Pound's *Cantos* and Eliot's *Waste Land,* dramatically editing a source document (the published report of the hearings of the House Committee of Labor's investigating subcommittee) not only to make it poetry but also to make it say what she needs it to say. Presiding over a strange marriage between Stott's "exposé quotation" and Pound's "luminous detail,"[26] Rukeyser destabilizes powerful institutional voices in more clearly modernist poems like "The Dam"; juxtaposing fragments and styles, she both lays out the complex problem posed by Gauley Bridge and, through radical bricolage, limns the possible solutions. In "Absalom," Rukeyser shores up and empowers the culturally disadvantaged female speaker as a site of revolutionary and redemptive potential.

Rukeyser's poetic extension of the document situates her in the literary battles over the relationship of poetry to history, battles also joined by Ezra Pound, perhaps nowhere more clearly than in his famous characterization of *The Cantos* as "a poem including history." This phrase would come to have quite literal significance for Pound, beginning in Canto 8, would incorporate increasingly large swatches of historical documents into the poem's textual fabric.[27] But in the contrast between Rukeyser's incorporation of historical documents and Pound's, we find a difference in the range of cultural-political valences of this crucial compositional practice. Whereas Pound exerts his editorial control over his sources in an all-encompassing remaking of the world, Rukeyser focuses her attention on the specific institutions at fault for contemporary human suffering. Whereas Pound imagines an artistic paradiso, Rukeyser takes the first step on the long march through the industrial purgatorio of America.

Rukeyser's work with historical documents quite directly addresses and challenges the world from which those documents are drawn. Male speakers who bear a great deal of institutional power — doctors, congressmen, Union Carbide corporate representatives — do not fare well under Rukeyser's editing hand. For example, the cutting and splicing together of excerpts from the congressional testimony of several doctors in the poem "The Doctors" destabilizes the authoritative voice of the local physician, Dr. L. R. Harless, and, through him, the institutional authority of the medical profession.

The testimony of Dr. Emory R. Hayhurst, a consultant to the U.S. Public Health Service and the Bureau of Mines with twenty years' experience "in occupational diseases," opens and closes the section, and Hayhurst's is the only voice Rukeyser does not aggressively undercut. In fact, Rukeyser strengthens Hayhurst as a speaker by summarizing his education and credentials at the beginning of the section. Hayhurst receives this treatment because his testimony contains forceful statements about the contractors' culpability in the Gauley Bridge tunnel silicosis deaths; in fact, Rukeyser's editing makes Hayhurst's condemnation of the contractors more forceful than it actually was. Whereas Hayhurst hedges in his trial testimony, Rukeyser includes only his critical comments. Testimony is made to fit Rukeyser's poetic and political agendas.

The poem opens with Hayhurst's list of qualifications, condensed into sentence fragments for brevity. But just as important as what Rukeyser cuts for concision and poetic fragmentation is what she adds to Hayhurst's critical language. The list of qualifications is followed by a comment about the tunnel situation:

Danger begins at 25%
here was pure danger
Dept. of Mines
came in, was kept away. (37)

This comment *is* Hayhurst's, but it is drawn from the testimony of Senator Rush Dew Holt of West Virginia, who reads it into the congressional record as part of a letter from an unnamed correspondent who spoke with Hayhurst more than a year after his examinations in Gauley Bridge; testimony at two removes, the passage appears forty pages after the body of Hayhurst's trial testimony in the hearings. Rukeyser here cuts and pastes a stringent and poetic critique from a large block of lukewarm testimonial prose. We return, in the next lines, to that earlier portion of Hayhurst's testimony:

> Miner's phthisis, fibroid phthisis,
> grinder's rot, potter's rot,
> whatever it used to be called,
> these men did not need to die. (38)

While the first three lines here come from Hayhurst's testimony in the civil suit, the fourth and most critical line is again drawn from Holt's testimony, in which Hayhurst is quoted through two textual mediations. Rukeyser's editing in these two cases strengthens a sympathetic speaker by condensing and focusing his speech. The "good doctor" is a construction of documentary editing. At the same time, Rukeyser's editing undercuts Dr. L. R. Harless's discursive authority. Harless is introduced by Hayhurst in an excerpt from his trial testimony. The doctor we have come to trust through Rukeyser's presentation of his speech presents the doctor we will be led to distrust. Hayhurst's mention of Harless is followed by a fairly lengthy quotation: "We talked to Dr. L. R. Harless, who had handled many of the cases, more than any other doctor there. At first Dr. Harless did not like to talk about the matter. He said he had been subjected to so much publicity. It appeared that the doctor thought he had been involved in too many of the court cases; but finally he opened up and told us about the matter" (38). The passage seems to be Hayhurst's elaboration of his simple mention of Harless, and that impression is strengthened by the thematic continuity between the two passages; Harless is an agent of revelation in both, showing Hayhurst Cecil Jones's lungs in the first and "open[ing] up" to talk about the silicosis cases in the second. The quotation is drawn, though, from the testimony of Gilbert Love, a Pennsylvania journalist who had traveled to West Virginia to cover the story for the *Pittsburgh Press* and the Scripps-Howard service. The next long quotation is also drawn from Love's testimony; it is Love's response to a congressman's query about whether Harless thought the silicosis outbreak "was a very serious thing in that section of the country": "Yes, he did. I would say that Dr. Harless has probably become very self-conscious about this matter. I cannot say that he has retracted what he told me, but possibly he had been thrust into the limelight so much that he is more conservative now than when the matter was simply something of local interest" (38). Again, we can hear in this passage the voice of a doctor hesitant to criticize a colleague; the qualifications and justifications sound like the professional courtesy one doctor would extend to another. We have been led to hear the language in this way by the suppression of the name of the new speaker (Love), by the continuities that join these passages to Hayhurst's testimony, and by the title of the section ("The Doctors"), which predisposes us to attribute all of the section's language to doctors. Rukeyser's editing has worked quite well.

Rukeyser further subverts Harless's authority by letting us see that his testimony is in the form of a letter; absent from the proceedings and thus exempt from the scrutiny of the congressmen, Harless lacks the authority lent by "presence." Most important, though, Rukeyser edits Harless's letter to further dissipate his authority as a speaker. Harless's carefully worded claim that the "situation at Gauley Bridge, W. Va., has been grossly exaggerated by statements appearing in certain newspapers and by wild rumors current in this section" is condensed to a two-word phrase — "Situation exaggerated" — whose indeterminate agency seems to implicate the congressmen themselves. When Harless says that only 13 people had died from silicosis and 139 "had some lung damage," both the basis of his claims (the medical examination of a specific and limited set of subjects) and the concurrence of Hayhurst in the results of the examinations are effaced. Of the seven paragraphs of Harless's letter, only the last two appear in anything like their original form. The first five paragraphs, or about two-thirds of the letter, are reduced to ten short lines in the poem. Rukeyser quotes the last two paragraphs at length. In these, Harless contradicts his earlier assertion that there were "only a few cases," writing that he "warned many [workers] of the dust hazard" and that "many of the men continued at this work and later brought suit." Finally, he charges that many people "took advantage of this situation and made out of it nothing less than a racket" (39).

Rukeyser's practice in "The Doctors" hides beneath the poem's documentary codes; her purpose in the poem is best served by obscuring her own editing hand, by subordinating the "poetic" to the depiction of the doctors' disagreements. Other poems, though, find Rukeyser just as aggressively subordinating document to the disciplined disjunction of modernist verse. In "The Dam," for example, Rukeyser exploits the poetic resources of fragmentation and syntactic dissolution in a powerful hymn to water's natural force and, at the same time, deploys the juxtaposition of varied discursive fragments to effect a damning cultural critique.

"All power is saved," the poem begins, "having no end." In the verse paragraph that follows, Rukeyser poetically evokes and enacts the illimitable energy of falling water; the grammatical constructions of her poetic celebration resist syntactic order, blurring distinctions between subject and object:

> Water celebrates, yielding continually
> sheeted and fast in its overfall
> slips down the rock, evades the pillars
> building its colonnades, repairs
> in stream and standing wave
> retains its seaward green
> broken by falling rock; falling, the water sheet
> spouts, and the mind dances, excess of white.
> White brilliant function of the land's disease. (54)

How are we to parse this sentence (or these sentences—the fragment making up the last line seems an appositive defining "white" at the end of the long sentence)? After the independent clause that begins the sentence, where do we pause, how do we fashion the phrasal elements into coherent units? Should we read the sentence as "Water celebrates, yielding continually, sheeted and fast in its overfall[;] [it] slips . . ." or as "Water celebrates, yielding continually[;] sheeted and fast in its overfall, [it] slips . . ."? In either case, the addition of a semicolon to mark a new independent clause and the addition of a pronoun to provide a subject for that clause seem necessary. And how do we read the end of the sentence? Does "excess of white" describe the dance of the mind or the spout of the water sheet? Both? Neither? The fragment that ends the paragraph seems to define the "excess of white" and, in turn, the waterfall, but its lack of a subject leaves it indeterminate. We can guess at a relationship between the land's disease and the water's celebration, but we cannot posit a grammatical relationship between them.

Rukeyser also blurs the subject/object relationship by deferring predication. In the third verse paragraph, for example, the piling up of participles prevents sentence completion:

> Many-spanned, lighted, the crest leans under
> concrete arches and the channelled hills,
> turns in the gorge toward its release;
> kinetic and controlled; the sluice
> urging the hollow, the thunder,
> the major climax
> > energy
> total and open watercourse
> praising the spillway, fiery glaze,
> crackle of light, cleanest velocity
> flooding, the moulded force. (54)

The second clause begins with a construction roughly parallel to the first: an introductory adjective phrase followed by the subject and verb. While the first clause's present-tense verb forms a proper predicate, the second clause's present participles ("urging," "praising," "flooding") do not, and the sentence remains a fragment. The lack of predication here renders the relationships between the subject ("the sluice") and the series of nouns and noun phrases throughout the rest of the clause indeterminate.

In these passages, water (as subject) diffuses into an uncontainable proliferation of significance just as water (as image and metaphor) diffuses into uncontainable energy. Through her polysemous juxtaposing of fragments, Rukeyser releases surpluses of meaning the poem cannot contain; she overcomes the spatial limitations of the poem and the containment implicit in its title by yoking the thematic anarchy of water to the rhetorical anarchy of language. She also stages the continuous struggle between stasis and ecstasy, enclosure and explosion, for only in tension with the forces that would block it is water's potential energy realized. Fragments drawn from physics, law, and finance jostle against each other in a field of mutual interruption and destabilization. After feverishly celebrating the power of water for two pages, Rukeyser dramatically shifts registers to view the same scene from the vantage offered by applied physics:

How many feet of whirlpools?
What is a year in terms of falling water?
Cylinders; kilowatts; capacities.
Continuity: $\Sigma Q = 0$
Equations for falling water. (56)

We have jumped from the aesthetic contemplation of the waterfall to a scientific and instrumental analysis of it. More important, we have shifted from the discourse of poetic contemplation, in which water and power are related through metaphoric condensation and parallel description, to the discourse of electrical engineering, in which the two are related through the laws of physics. The discourse of electrical engineering is itself interrupted by the discourse of finance in a reference ("balance-sheet" [56]) whose significance becomes apparent only later in the poem and by a return to the poetic portrait of power as the agent in a series of statements drawn from earlier in the sequence.

But the poetic portrait is again interrupted several lines later, when congressional testimony appears. These passages introduce legal discourse ("Mr. Griswold: 'A corporation is a body without a soul'"), but they also introduce the popular cultural discourse of news accounts and gangster films:

> Mr. Dunn. When they were caught at it they resorted to
> the methods employed by gunmen, ordinary machine-
> gun racketeers. They cowardly tried to buy out the people
> who had the information on them.
> Mr. Marcantonio. I agree that a racket has been practised. (57)

The congressional testimony is followed by assertions whose diction marks them as poetic: "The dam is safe . . . the dam is the father of the tunnel." But three lines later, we come upon the most dramatic discursive interruption, the stock quotation showing Union Carbide's net profits for one day. The ticker tape appearance of the quotation, unlike the other interruptions, actually alters the physical space of the page; finance intrudes on the textual space of poetry. The stock quote shows the bottom line, the economic fact that renders all else—human suffering, legal wrangling, even water's energetic flowing—momentarily meaningless: Union Carbide stock rises in value, up three points in the day's trading. The bit of ticker tape mocks the "mastery" touched by tunnel workers and stands as a graphic illustration of Griswold's charge—"A corporation is a body without a soul." Moreover, the stock quote, set off from the surrounding text by solid horizontal lines, literally embodies blockage. It cuts the page in half.

Lifted from the business page of a newspaper, the quote here stands in a relationship of mutual challenge with the poetic lines that surround it. But in the poem's concluding moment, this textual bit of capitalist culture and the discourse of finance is ultimately absorbed. Its blockage lasts only a moment and then is overcome by the very natural force on which it is, itself, based—the water flowing through the dam's channels, converting its kinetic energy into electric power. This power finally triumphs:

> This is a perfect fluid, having no age nor hours,
> surviving scarless, unaltered, loving rest,
> willing to run forever to find its peace
>
> in equal seas in currents of still glass. (57)

In "The Doctors," Rukeyser edits the congressional subcommittee's published hearings to subvert the institutional authority of individual doctors and of the medical profession, and in "The Dam," she more overtly deploys fragmentation and juxtaposition to destabilize other powerful institutions and discourses. In other poems, though, Rukeyser edits to strengthen the discursive authority of a sympathetic speaker. This is nowhere more apparent than in the crucial poem "Absalom," where Rukeyser melds the testimony, spread over forty pages of congressional hearings, of three different speakers—social worker Philippa Allen; the poem's speaker, Mrs. Jones; and her husband, Charles Jones—into the single speaking voice of Mrs. Jones. In so doing, she collects and focuses the dispersed story of Mrs. Jones and her family, strengthening the voice of the poem's most important single speaker.

Walter Kalaidjian finds in "Absalom" the strongest evidence for the sequence as a feminist intervention into the popular imaginary (*American Culture*, 172–73). I cannot quite concur. The poem does position a female speaker as its most powerful agent, but it does so in a way that draws on what Denning has called "the sentimental maternalism of Popular Front representations of women" (137). Rukeyser's development of a "Mother Earth" in the figure of Mrs. Jones (and,

in the sequence's concluding poem, a Carthaginian stone that signi-
fies woman) places her amid the array of left-wing discourses in the
first half of the century that tactically deployed such images. Rukeyser
envisions "nature"—the earth and the river—as the site of the trans-
formative and ultimately uncontrollable "power." She takes that posi-
tion, though, with some crucial differences from other women writ-
ing on the issues of nature and motherhood. Writers like Rebecca
Pitts and Mary Inman negotiate a difficult rhetorical course to resist
the linkage between the natural process of childbearing and the op-
pression of women and, at the same time, to naturalize the rights of
women to control their own bodies.[28] Rukeyser, however, says little
about the dangers of linking nature and women through mother-
hood. Rather than being a marker for the sequence's feminism, the
portrait of Mrs. Jones in "Absalom" seems a symptom of what Rabino-
witz describes as the Left's lack of an "aesthetic and political culture
of feminism" (*Labor and Desire*, 137).[29]

The poem is, indeed, a crucial one, but not, I would argue, because
it advances the sequence's "feminist" aims. Rather, the importance of
"Absalom" derives from the way it models and invites participation
in a politics not only dynamic but also elegiac. It constitutes a crucial
node in the sequence because it is the point at which documentary
and modernism meet to mount a critically unmasking and ritually
remembering political life. Mrs. Jones lives in Gamoca, near Gauley
Bridge; her husband and three sons have all contracted silicosis. The
focus of the poem is on the third son, Shirley, who dies of the disease
but brings about the silicosis scandal when he urges his mother to
"have them open me up and / see if that dust killed me" (27). Shirley's
wish leads to the discovery of the cause of the workers' deaths, but the
poem most importantly explores Mrs. Jones's own struggle to tran-
scend the limits placed on her by poverty and suffering and to find in
her circumstances some measure of power. The mother's testimony
takes us again over ground covered by the sequence's earlier exposi-
tory passages; she explains that her husband and sons had worked in a
coal mine and had been convinced by a power company foreman to
come to work at the tunnel for better money. After eighteen months,
Shirley "came home one evening with a shortness of breath." From
the beginning of her son's illness, Mrs. Jones takes action, begging
money for X rays and pleading with the company doctor to take her

son's case for half of any compensation she might get. Her work results in legal action: "The case of my son was the first of the line of lawsuits." The suits, though, bring only meager compensation, for which she has to hitchhike eighteen miles.[30] With three sons dead and a husband dying, Mrs. Jones is left scraping to get by on $2.00 a week.

Defeated by the disease, the doctors, and the duplicity of lawyers and corporations, Mrs. Jones has one last recourse—her testimony; her only power is to speak, to fulfill her resolution: "I shall give a mouth to my son." Her matter-of-fact tone throughout the testimony makes more harrowing her descriptions of suffering—of carrying Shirley "from his bed to the table, / from his bed to the porch, in my arms" and of her three sons' deaths:

> The oldest son was twenty-three.
> The next son was twenty-one.
> The youngest son was eighteen. (29)

Like Mearl Blankenship and George Robinson, Mrs. Jones appears to be a simple citizen stoically suffering through this tragedy. Her diction is plain, her recollections starkly and unsentimentally delivered. Readers familiar with the documentary culture of the period would recognize in Mrs. Jones, in her understated determination and her flat tone, the strong and stoic mother figure represented over and over again in the work of Bourke-White and Caldwell or, perhaps most famously, that of Dorothea Lange.[31] But, of course, Mrs. Jones's appearance here is a carefully crafted illusion. The first twelve lines of "Absalom," for example, are taken from Philippa Allen's testimony (Subcommittee of the Committee of Labor, *An Investigation*, 6). Rukeyser makes only minor changes to Allen's version, reversing the order in which Mrs. Jones's three sons are listed, for example, and omitting Allen's explicit claim that Shirley was his mother's favorite son. In the middle of the section, though, Rukeyser seamlessly weaves together material from Allen and material from several separated passages in Mrs. Jones's testimony. A graphic representation shows this more clearly than an explanation. In this excerpt, the roman text marks material from Mrs. Jones's testimony, the italic text marks material from Allen's testimony, and the bold text marks invented language:

When they took sick, *right at the start,* I saw a doctor.
I tried to get Dr. Harless to X-ray the boys.
He was the only man I had any confidence in,
the company doctor in the Kopper's mine,
but he would not see Shirley.
He did not know where his money was coming from.
I promised him half if he'd work to get compensation,
but even then he would not do anything.
I went on the road and begged *the X-ray* money,
the Charleston hospital made the **lung pictures**,
he took **the case** *after the* **pictures** *were made.*
And two or three doctors said the same thing. (28)

The compression Rukeyser achieves by jumping back and forth between speakers and by switching the order of statements renders Mrs. Jones's recollections more powerful and poignant; the impact of the material is enhanced when Rukeyser brings it together and into focus.

Later in the poem, Rukeyser manipulates the text of the hearings to shift to her female speaker a power she lacks (and male speakers have) in the congressional testimony, the power to name. In the hearings, Charles Jones, testifying after his wife, lists the men he knows who have died:

Shirley was the first to die, then Cecil died, and then Jeffrey died, and then Oren, and then Raymond Johnson, and then Clev. Anders, Oscar Anders, Frank Dickinson, Frank Lynch, Henry Palf, Mr. Wall, who was assistant superintendent, Mr. Pitch, a foreman. . . . There was a slim fellow who carried steel with my boys. His name was Darnell, I believe. (Subcommittee of the Committee of Labor, *An Investigation,* 43)

Rukeyser puts her edited version of this list in the mouth of Mrs. Jones:

There was Shirley, and Cecil, Jeffrey and Oren,
Raymond Johnson, Clev and Oscar Anders,
Frank Lynch, Henry Palf, Mr. Pitch, a foreman;
a slim fellow who carried steel with my boys,
his name was Darnell, I believe. (29)

Mrs. Jones, through Rukeyser's editing, becomes the speaker who names the dead, reading them into the record; she has the power to preserve their memory through the act of naming them. In the Egyptian myth system from which Rukeyser borrows her poem's structure, Mrs. Jones takes on the role of Thoth, the Egyptian scribe god. Naming the dead, she exercises the power to give them new life. She also attains, by calling this roll, a vantage point that commands the entire valley, shifting from the names of the men to the names of the towns they came from, broadening her scope to show how "the whole valley is witness." Mrs. Jones's compelling final resolution ("I shall give a mouth to my son") rests, at least in part, on the power she exhibits in these lines, a power she attains only through Rukeyser's manipulation of the congressional text, her careful work to "extend the document."

Rukeyser's editing strengthens the agency Mrs. Jones attains through her actions. While her husband grows sicker and cannot work, Mrs. Jones files lawsuits, hitchhikes the eighteen miles to town for the meager compensation checks, and holds the family together on $2 per week. When her sons become ill, she takes them to the doctor, begs money for X rays, and convinces the doctor to take the case. When Shirley cannot move about, she carries him from his bed to the table and the porch. Mrs. Jones's agency appears even in the grammatical structure of her speech, which differs from the structure of Mearl Blankenship's in the preceding section. Blankenship repeatedly follows references to his own actions with references to what others have done or might do for him. He wakes up coughing, but his wife turns him over; he has written a letter but asks the narrator to send it; he has sued the company but asks if his audience can do anything for him. Blankenship, of course, is dying, and Rukeyser's construction of his speech and writing quite poignantly shows that he is not master of his own fate. Mrs. Jones, though, exercises greater control over hers. Her sentences persistently begin with "I" and a verb: "I first discovered," "I saw the dust," "I would carry him," "I tried," "I promised," "I went on the road and begged," "I hitchhike." This pattern culminates in the poem's concluding resolution: "I shall give a mouth to my son."

This resolution is a key to the lived politics Rukeyser evolves and models in the sequence. Just as water creates usable power only in tension with that which would block it, memory becomes power only in the speaking of it, the dynamic repetition of speech and action against forces that would silence and repress. Rukeyser elevates Mrs. Jones, through her suffering and her power to speak and memorialize, to a mythic stature that makes her central to the sequence as a whole. Mrs. Jones's testimony is interrupted at several points by sets of italicized lines that seem to be spoken by a different voice. Set off from Mrs. Jones's voice not only by typography but also by diction, rhythm, and content, the italicized lines add a mythic dimension to "Absalom." But the mythic does not exclude this mother; rather, Rukeyser takes Mrs. Jones up into the realm these lines create. The same grammatical structure that characterizes Mrs. Jones's speech organizes the elevated rhetoric of the italicized lines:

> *I have gained mastery over my heart*
> *I have gained mastery over my two hands*
> *I have gained mastery over the waters*
> *I have gained mastery over the river.*
>
> . . . .
>
> *I open out a way*
> *I come forth by day*
> *I force a way through*
> *I shall journey over the earth.* (29)

The grammatical similarity between Mrs. Jones's monologue and the italicized lines allows us to read the lyrical interruptions not only as a "mythic discourse" that supplements Mrs. Jones's "plainspoken idiom," as Walter Kalaidjian writes (*American Culture,* 173), but also as a version of Mrs. Jones's own rhetoric, an elevated variant of her own maternal agency.[32] The lines transform the mother's localized and limited agency into a broader and uncontained power. The collocation of mother and tunnel brings a measure of new power to Mrs. Jones, elevating her from mother to the Mother who is able to proclaim, after her youngest son's death, "*I have gained mastery.*" Rukeyser's strategic editing and startling juxtaposition of the documentary and the poetic fashion in Mrs. Jones a powerful female figure who bridges the all-too-earthly realm of tunnels, silica, and workers and the seemingly supernatural realm of waters, rivers, and air. Like the phoenix, she rises from the wreckage of her family to fly and to speak. And in so doing, she embodies the Eliotic structure that exists in tension with the sequence's documentary style.

As we have seen, Rukeyser sometimes retains the representational authority and political purchase of documentary by playing the codes in fairly conventional ways. In other poems, she blends documentary depiction and modernist fragmentation to heighten poetic intensity, enhance thematic cruxes, and lay bare the discursive devices underpinning powerful institutions. But the last half of the sequence is shaped less by documentary imperatives than by the cycles of life, death, and rebirth activated by the sequence's title (and the ancient text to which it alludes). This shift from workers' testimonials to wasteland terrors begins in "The Cornfield," which marks both the spatial and thematic center of *The Book of the Dead*. Rukeyser has, by this point, sketched and populated the community of Gauley Bridge. She has activated the pictorial and testimonial codes of documentary representation to bring readers through the experience of silicosis-stricken tunnel workers. Now she brings to the foreground the cyclic structure of the Egyptian *Book of the Dead,* alluding to and revising that most prominent "book of the dead" in modernist poetry, *The Waste Land.* Rukeyser effects thematic and formal shifts to limn the mythological and revolutionary possibilities the Gauley Bridge tragedy evokes. From death, we move to the underworld through a series of meditations on power and its obstacles to a final resolution that locates revolutionary possibility in communal memory.

This progression begins with a return to the poem's opening trope: "these are the roads you take." Now, though, the roads lead to the cornfield where H. C. White, the local mortician, has buried workers who have died of silicosis:

> Buried, five at a time,
> pine boxes, Rinehart & Dennis paid him $55
> a head for burying these men in plain pine boxes. (42)

White becomes a wealthy man by transporting corpses in his car, "knees broken into angles, / head clamped ahead," and secretly burying workers so quickly that, in one instance, a woman arriving three hours after her husband's death is too late to dress the corpse. To obscure the company's responsibility for workers' deaths, White alters the causes of their deaths:

> tells about Negroes who got wet at work,
> shot craps, drank and took cold, pneumonia, died.
> Shows the sworn papers. Swear by the corn.
> Pneumonia, pneumonia, pleurisy, t.b. (42)

"Here is the cornfield," Rukeyser writes, ". . . the planted home." Invoking the opening gestures of Eliot's poem—the worm's-eye view of the first lines and the sprouting corpse—Rukeyser taps into the poem's structural principle, the death and resurrection of the vegetative god.[33] We journey on the roads Rukeyser lays out in her poem to a land laid waste, the "audacious landscape" of a "commercial field, its hill of glass" a "blinded field of white / murdering snow" (47). We witness the planting of corpses. We travel with the dead to underworlds real and metaphorical, and we emerge in the poem's final sections to the possibility of renewal and redemption. In that possibility, Rukeyser's poem revises Eliot's. While Eliot evades history, retreating into abstruse literary allusion even at the rare moments when he addresses contemporary political events, Rukeyser embraces and enters history, locating both her wasteland and the way out of it in historical specificity and action.

In the death/rebirth structure of *The Book of the Dead*, "The Cornfield" marks the poem's lowest moment, the burial of the dead. At the same time, though, "The Cornfield" bears with its crop of corpses the potential for a ripening harvest. The nameless dead buried here share the bleak equality George Robinson sees in the white dust that coats workers so completely they cannot be distinguished by the color of their skin. Most are buried without markers; only a few graves are marked with "wood stakes . . . scratched and named (pencil or nail)" (44). The dead here are, Rukeyser writes, "all the anonymous." They refuse, however, to be silent. These dead men are "Abel America, calling from under the corn / Earth, uncover my blood," and their cries resonate with the revolutionary potential hidden within the leveling power of death: "Does Mellon's ghost walk, povertied at last, / walking in furrows of corn, still sowing, / do apparitions come?" (44). Andrew Mellon, the figure of capitalist exploitation, sows the cornfield with corpses. Brought to a poverty of his own by death, the robber baron sows his own figurative destruction, for the corpses planted here, Rukeyser intimates, will begin to sprout, will bloom this year: "Sowing is over, harvest is coming ripe" (44).

"Alloy," following "The Cornfield," surveys the wasteland, the landscape dominated by the fatal industrial glass, a "Crystalline hill," a field of "white murdering snow." Like the infertile and unyielding land of Eliot's poem, Rukeyser's countryside is rendered lifeless and life threatening. But she locates the cause for this condition in the historical actualities of Alloy, West Virginia. Alloy is the nearby town where the mined silica was sent for use in the electro-processing of steel, the town where furnaces transform the deadly glass of the silica dust into the benign "perfected metal":

> Here the severe flame speaks from the brick throat,
> electric furnaces produce this precious, this clean,
> annealing the crystals, fusing at last alloys. (47)

The smoke rising from these furnaces is weaker than the silica dust. Not "white enough, not so barbaric," the "roaring flowers" of smoke are "less poison" than the dust. While the smoke will rise and dissipate, the dust, blown by the wind, maintains its lethal character, finally "rising over the mills, / crystallized." It turns tree-covered hills to monuments of glass, destroying their capacity to sustain life. And perhaps more important, the crystal snow renders meaning-making myths impotent as well. In a closing figure that calls to mind Benjamin's angel of history, Rukeyser envisions the dust rising over the "fierce corrosion disintegrated angel on these hills."[34] The dust that strengthens and tempers steel for technology's purposes lacerates the hills as it blows from the "field of glass." Deadly for the people who bring it to the surface, the dust disintegrates even the unearthly and powerful figure of the angel.

After presenting this scene of the scarred surface of the wasteland, Rukeyser describes a descent into the underworld in "Power." A mysticism, latent in earlier poems in the sequence, becomes manifest here. The poem opens with an evocative description of the landscape around the New Kanawha power plant, the river, cliffs, and gorge. Illuminated by the sun, these sights elicit a physical reaction from the observer—"the entire body watches the scene with love" (49).[35] As if to establish a standard to which the descent can be contrasted, Rukeyser describes "a brilliant / day when love sees the sun behind its man / and the disguised marvel under familiar skin." The skin of the lover becomes, in the next stanza, the "powerhouse stand[ing] skin-white . . . over the rapids." Here the descent begins. The power plant occupies the space "between water and flame," between the falls and the electricity that will be generated and distributed (49). Rukeyser also locates the plant in the metaphorical space between water and flame, the earth beneath which the dead reside. "Power" shows Rukeyser in one of her most powerful modes, holding in suspension contradictory or even opposite possibilities, giving the sense of a "between" where forces at odds might come together.[36]

"This is the road to take when you think of your country," she writes, linking the plant to the repetition of that phrase in "The Cornfield," where the road leads to the unmarked graves of workers. Here, as in "The Cornfield," we arrive at a place that is "terminal." At that place, we meet Vivian Jones, the engineer who has his own poem earlier in the sequence. Like the tutelary figures leading epic heroes on their journeys in the underworld, Jones guides us into the depths of the plant, the underworld of Rukeyser's poem. Jones welcomes the poem's speaker to the plant with pride, describing his wish for "the men who work here to be happy." Indeed, the plant is beautiful. Rukeyser describes it in terms strikingly similar to those she used to describe the natural scene outside; adjectives like "brilliant," "green," and "light" recur, both the plant and the gorge are called landscapes, and both are characterized as "design[s]." At the plant's upper level, in fact, the sun shines in gaily, "laughing on steel." This impression does not last. The line breaks after "the gay, the tall sun," holding us suspended until the next line begins—"given away." We are moving from the light into the darkness. In terms that recall the X ray of a diseased lung shown in Congress and the stone against which Mearl Blankenship stands, Rukeyser begins the descent with reminders of the human costs the power plant has extracted from the community: "mottled; snow comes in clouds; / the iron steps go down as roads go down." The repetition of the poem's refrain phrase here links the power plant to the poem's opening journey down the east coast to Gauley Bridge. The road to take when you think of your country ultimately leads to the underworld. Other rhetorical figures in "Power" strengthen the connection between the nation and this underworld by recalling or anticipating the use of similar figures in connection with the congressional investigation. The galleries of the House of Representatives, for example, mentioned in "The Disease: Aftereffects," appear here as the "empty galleries" of the plant's second circle. Jones, in fact, alludes to congressmen's comparison of the plant to "the Black Hole of Calcutta," wondering "how they ever got to Congress." These figures, in conjunction with Rukeyser's repeated imperatives to "descend" and "go down," make the descent in "Power" a common one, a descent the nation makes into the underworld, a descent all readers are compelled to make.

At the end of the journey, of course, we find death. Rukeyser establishes the expectation of this discovery by scattering death and tomb imagery along the descent. The second circle, for example, is a "world of inner shade," the description evoking the appearance of the shades of the dead to Odysseus, Aeneas, and Dante. The final five lines of the poem bring us to the death waiting at the bottom of the plant:

> Down the reverberate channels of the hills
> the suns declare midnight, go down, cannot ascend,
> no ladder back; see this, your eyes can ride through steel,
> this is the river of Death, diversion of power,
> the root of the tower and the tunnel's core,
> this is the end. (51)

But this death is not the end. As we have seen, "The Dam" figures the defeat of all such ends: "All power is saved, having no end." And in the last two lines of the sequence's penultimate poem, the precursor of war memorialized on a monument in Gauley Bridge rises from the dead to usher in the final resolution:

> dead John Brown's body walking from a tunnel
> to break the armored and concluded mind. (65)

The figure of John Brown represents not only the region's history but also an existing discourse that Rukeyser's sequence joins—a literary and historical evocation of John Brown carried on by figures as diverse as Robert Penn Warren and Michael Gold. The high-water mark of this effort is, of course, Stephen Vincent Benét's *John Brown's Body,* the long poem that won the Pulitzer Prize in 1928. Benét's poem was enormously popular, sparking both sympathetic recirculations like Robert Delaney's *John Brown's Song,* a choral poem for mixed voices and orchestra that sets extracts from Benét's work to music, and more motivated retellings like Warren's biography of Brown and Gold's 1923 *Life of John Brown.*[37] While Rukeyser's politics at this point approach Gold's and her use of Brown in the poem is shaped by those politics, Benét's version exercises much greater influence over Rukeyser's voicing of Brown here and elsewhere than any other version. In fact, the themes announced at the end of "West Virginia," the most historical poem of the sequence, and the themes of the sequence as a whole clearly resemble themes on which Benét plays in Brown's voice:

> *"There is a song in my bones. There is a song*
> *In my white bones."*

> I hear no song. I hear
> Only the blunt seeds growing secretly
> In the dark entrails of the prepared earth,
> The rustle of the cricket under the leaf,
> The creaking of the cold wheel of the stars.

> . . . .

> I hear no song. I only hear the roar
> of the Spring freshets, and the gushing voice
> Of mountain brooks that overflow their banks. (Benét, 59)[38]

The figure of John Brown carries great importance for Rukeyser. Two years after the publication of *The Book of the Dead* in *U.S. 1,* she published *The Soul and Body of John Brown,* in which she more fully developed Brown's significance. In that poem, Rukeyser takes Brown through a seasonal progression much like that in *The Book of the Dead,* from "October's fruition-fire" through the winter, the spring, and finally "summernoon," when the sun reaches its zenith. The poem's movement through the seasonal cycle develops the characterization of Brown as a messianic figure, a characterization that begins with the poem's epigraph from the Book of Joel—"Multitudes, multitudes in the valley of decision" (1).[39] A martyr who, as Louise Kertesz writes, "took upon himself the guilt of the age" (204), Brown rises in the spring and gathers "the winter invalids," bringing their frustrated dreams to consciousness and new life. But Brown's rising is neither mystical nor meek. Rather, the executed body of the militant abolitionist, the "fanatic beacon of fierceness," molders in the grave until the depression-era mistreatment of workers beckons him and sparks his violent resurrection. Only when "the cities of horror are down," only when the workers "stand in the factory, deal out identical / gestures of reaching," only when all other resources have been tried and exhausted, does Brown arise. And when he rises, it is not as an individual body but as a revolutionary mass. Identified throughout the poem with the stylized tree from which he was hung, Brown is dispersed in death:

A tall tree, prophet, fallen,
your arms in their flesh laid on the mountains, all
your branches in the scattered valleys down.
Your boughs lie broken in the channels of the land,
dim anniversaries are written on many clouds. (5)

But when the workers finally beckon, this dispersal enables a mass res-
urrection. The tree, Brown's body, has "become the land," and from
that land it grows again, "demanding life / deep in the prophet's eyes,
a wish to be again / threatened alive, in agonies of decision / part of
the nation of a frantic sun" (6).

The roads we have followed through *The Book of the Dead* bring us
twice to John Brown. Early in the poem, in Rukeyser's initial survey
of the West Virginia terrain, we find the monument to this heroic
precursor's execution, and in the final lines of the poem's next-to-last
section, we confront the risen John Brown, walking from the tun-
nel as if to lead a new movement of rebellion. Brown's progress is
a miniature version of the poem's progression through struggle and
death, through an underworld where powerful forces of nature and
humanity are blocked by capital, to a resurrection that brings together
the cycles of the natural world, the mystical vision of rebirth, and the
key to a revolution that will overcome the forces that have blocked
these powers up to now.

In the sequence's concluding (and title) poem, "The Book of the
Dead," Rukeyser throws over the worn ritual repetition of Western
mythologies, replacing it with a life-from-death powerful in its his-
torical specificity. To do so, she draws on the prosody and imagery of
her greatest American visionary forebear, Walt Whitman. Like the
leaves of grass that grow as hair from the buried dead in Whitman's
"Song of Myself," the dead of Gauley Bridge are "planted in our flesh"
(68), and in them lies the potential for revolutionary redemption.[40]
"The Book of the Dead" brings the martyrs of this poem up from the
underworld in a resurrection that indicates the potential for renewal
of the industrial wasteland. "These roads take you into your own
country," the section begins, repeating the refrain from the poem's
opening and from the central "Cornfield" section, and in the coun-
try to which these roads lead, we discover "a landscape mirrored in
these men" (66). The image of the mirror here brings not only the

workers of the tunnel but also the poem's readers into a relationship of identity (or inverted identity) with the landscape. We must confront ourselves in this landscape, in these men; we must follow the poem's road "past all [our] influences . . . all evasion's wishes" (66). And in recognizing ourselves in these men, we confront a set of forbidden knowledges, taboo words and visions. We confront not the cryptic utterances of the distant thunder but, instead, the word that "must never be said," the resignation to and acceptance of death as an ultimate obstacle. Our confrontation with the tunnel workers and their fate forces us to recognize in them our age's Fisher Kings, to see how "these men fight off our dying" by taking upon themselves what Kertesz calls, in her discussion of John Brown, the guilt of the age, by martyring themselves. "What two things shall never be seen?" she asks, answering immediately, "They: what we did. Enemy: what we mean" (66). The responsibility for the martyrdom of the tunnel workers ultimately rests not only with Union Carbide and its contractors in West Virginia but also with the people of the nation, who never saw what was happening in Gauley Bridge, who never came to understand their own complicity in the corporate abuse.

Our confrontation of the spectacle of death in Gauley Bridge leads beyond these recognitions to a more important one, the first step to a spiritual revolution that will prevent similar tragedies in the future. "What three things can never be done?" the poet asks in her final question, and the shift in tone marked by her verb choice ("can" rather than the earlier "must" or "shall") indicates that these are things we cannot allow ourselves to do, not things we are prevented by others from doing. These are the things that can never be done if we are to overcome the obstacles that would block revolutionary change as they blocked the lungs of the workers, the compensation of their families, and the investigation of the corporation's abuses. We can never "Forget. Keep silent. Stand alone" (66). We can never allow the community of opposition to fragment, the powerful glass of rushing water to crystallize into the lethal glass of silica dust. The reward for such actions will always be "the hills of glass, the fatal brilliant plain" (66).

"The Cornfield" bore a promise that the corpses sown there would one day yield a harvest. The nature of that harvest is made clear in the second part of "The Book of the Dead." We live in a "ritual world / [that] carries its history in familiar eyes," preserving a dead past in aestheticized "half-memories"—"the shimmering names, / the spear, the castle, and the rose" (69). Our confrontation with the tunnel's dead forces us to realize that the corpses of the cornfield are "planted in our flesh" and from this ground they might sprout. Attention to the occurrences in Gauley Bridge and the surrounding valley brings knowledge of "the illness," and the real history of complete and stubborn memories is "forced up, and our times confirm us all." The valley, with all of its planted dead, "is given to us like a glory." Amid this wreckage held and studied for its significance, Rukeyser finds an alternative to Eliot's mythic fragments: "the Carthaginian stone meaning a tall woman / [who] carries in her hands the book and cradled dove" (69). Like Mrs. Jones a female figure of redemption, this stone strikes us awake and makes us put into play the skills we have learned for confronting, the art we have developed for seeing the world.

The vision we achieve when we confront the workers who are "our strength," a vision illuminated by the miners' lighted helmets and the radium workers' luminous lips, allows us to see both the positive and the negative aspects of our "myths of identity." In achieving this vision, we have realized the promise borne in the unattributed lines of "Absalom":

I open out a way, they have covered my sky with crystal
I come forth by day, I am born a second time,
I force a way through, and I know the gate
I shall journey over the earth among the living.

The myths that identify the nation with its technological advances create, as they stand over the land, a crystal shell over the sky. This shell is broken, though, by the figurative rising of the workers from their graves, from the tunnel. The vision they enable becomes their rebirth in the consciousness of the living. In this way, Mrs. Jones is finally able to "give a mouth to [her] son."

Rukeyser concludes the poem in the imperative mode. We, too, must "carry abroad the urgent need . . . to extend the voice, to speak this meaning." As Rukeyser writes in The Life of Poetry, "[I]n time of the crises of the spirit, we are aware of all our need, our need for each other and our need for ourselves. We call up, with all the strength of summoning we have, our fullness" (i). The way out of the wasteland lies through the remembering of the dead and the summoning, through that memory, of "our fullness." As the poem's closing gestures make clear, that fullness, in turn, requires intellectual rigor as well as the emotions concomitant with memory; we must learn to hold in mind the "mastery, discovery at one hand, and at the other . . . [the] fanatic cruel legend." This way, through the point between the seas, between water and flame, between ignorance and exploitation, lies power. "These roads will take you into your own country," and the mapping of the roads, the repetition of the names, completes the transformation of the corpses planted in the cornfield, making of them "seeds of unending love."

Conclusion

THE AGE DEMANDED

If the alternative narrative of modern American poetry that informs this book begins with the trial and execution of Sacco and Vanzetti, it seems appropriate to turn, in this conclusion, to poems about another politically inflected execution, that of Ethel and Julius Rosenberg in 1953. As Rebecca Walkowitz writes, "[T]he trial of the Rosenbergs on charges of 'Atomic Spying' and 'stealing the secrets of the Atomic bomb' galvanized America, provoking public debates on all sides" (Garber and Walkowitz, 2). Whether or not the couple were involved in espionage (and most evidence now seems to indicate that Julius Rosenberg was), the case as it was conducted through the trials and executions was, in the words of Karl E. Klare, "a massive, brutal act of political terrorism carried out by the government in order, among other things, to frighten the Left of the early 1950s into submission" (276).[1] But the apparent symmetry offered by Sacco and Vanzetti in the 1920s and the Rosenbergs in the 1950s masks a deeper asymmetry, for the American climate twenty-six years after Sacco and Vanzetti died in the Massachusetts electric chair afforded much less discursive space for protest, and the vocal community of opposition to the Rosenbergs' electrocution was smaller and narrower than that which raised its collective voice in 1927. The poetry surrounding the Sing Sing death house attempts the same cultural work as that collected in *America Arraigned!,* but while the strategies are similar, the absence of a sustaining left-wing literary culture (or activist political literary culture more generally) renders the poetry less powerful and moving than that which arraigned America for the murders of Sacco and Vanzetti.[2]

The most prominent poetic speaker in support of the Rosenbergs, or the poetic speaker given the most prominent space in which to speak, was Ethel Rosenberg herself, whose poem "If We Die" appeared on the cover of *Masses and Mainstream*'s July 1953 issue. Dated "Ossining, NY / January 24, 1953," the poem addresses the couple's two young sons and figures the Rosenbergs' politics (if not the espionage of which they were accused) as "the faith we kept / for you, my sons, for you." Rosenberg urges her sons to look beyond the accusations that doom her and her husband and to focus instead on what their deaths will accomplish. She imagines a full-blown martyrdom for Julius and herself, a sacrifice that will enable all she values and hopes for finally to come to be:

> Earth shall smile, my sons, shall smile
> and green above our resting place,
> the killing end, the world rejoice
> in brotherhood and peace.

Rosenberg's voice is joined, in this issue, by that of poet Ettore Rella, whose "To the Rosenbergs" expresses this sense of valuable martyrdom at greater length, in anaphoric lines drawn from Whitman and the work of poets like Sol Funaroff and Kenneth Fearing and in Christ imagery identical to that which appears throughout *America Arraigned!* "[Y]ou are alive alive alive," Rella writes:

> and the killers will peer into tomorrow
> and they will see that you are still there
> and they will wish to their abandoned Christ
> that they could find a way to destroy you. (3)

These notes are struck more loudly still in poems published after the execution. W. E. B. Du Bois, in "The Rosenbergs," begins with an invocation that not only sees the Rosenbergs as crucified Christ figures but also calls upon God to visit the same fate upon "us," the people who, through the state, perpetrated this act:

> Crucify us, Vengeance of God
> As we crucify two more Jews,

Hammer home the nails, thick through our skulls,
Crush down the thorns,
Rain red the bloody sweat
Thick and heavy, warm and wet. (10)

And Martha Millett, in "In Memoriam," more pointedly villainizes
the American people when she links the Rosenbergs not only to
Christ but also to the Jews murdered in the Holocaust:

For no blood must be spilled on the Sabbath.
(Did Jesus, the Nazarene, know that
As the sun sank over Golgotha;
Did our six million brothers and sisters
And their little ones know?) (30)

The Christ and crucifixion imagery recurs in poems about this
execution, but we also find other images, other figures, we ought to
recognize from the political poetry of the 1930s. Millett, in her poem,
envisions the Rosenbergs' death nurturing a political struggle, a com-
munity of resistance, in much the same way that Edwin Rolfe imag-
ined Arnold Reid's death feeding the Spanish Republic in "Epitaph":

Courage poured into us,
You, lovers, before whom
The earth bows with burden of tenderness,
Like breasts too full with milk,
Poured yourselves into our veins, to be our life. (29)

Millett later elaborates a choral "we," a collective subject pieced to-
gether through serial acts of interpellation, just as Rolfe and Langston
Hughes did in their 1930s poems:

We are an avalanche of tears.
We, from the tall, the topmost Andes,
In strongholds built against the "conquerors";
We from the new villages and looms of China
Avenging rape, dishonor, ruinous yesterdays;
We in the swamp-homes of freedom
On ocean-circled islands,
And in the seething capitals of Europe;
We from Africa, stupendous against our chains;

We with your song of freedom on our lips
We in American places where the crime
Was done. (30)

Similarly, J. Brandreth, in his "Epitaph," sees the dead much as
Rukeyser saw the dead in "The Cornfield" and "The Book of the
Dead": as seeds prepared to sprout if only nurtured by the memory
of "we" who are left behind. A. B. Magil takes a more Poundian tack,
juxtaposing the Rosenbergs with mythical and religious fragments
to grant them heroic stature, to collapse the present into history. Du
Bois, as Hughes did with the Scottsboro "boys," sketches a tradition
of martyrs, a pantheon of political sufferers, and inserts the Rosen-
bergs into it. In the work of these various poets, known and un-
known alike, we see continually deployed the very devices and values
through which the political poets at the center of this study attempted
to articulate their politics.

But the political pressures summarized in Rolfe's injunction to
himself—"write as if you lived in an occupied country"—forced most
partisan poetry underground. The age demanded well-wrought urns.
American poetry in the first generation after World War II retreated
from the barricades and, briefly at least, from the grand experimen-
talism of modernism. The beautiful changes, as Richard Wilbur at
once stated and demonstrated in his much-lauded book of that name.
In the wake of an apparently exhausted experimental impulse, the
densely personal lyric rose again to prominence in literary and edu-
cational institutions. Indeed, the dominant poetic mode in the de-
cade after World War II might best be characterized by Wilbur's ac-
ceptance of the "New Formalist" appellation: "I will accept the label
provided it be understood that to try to revive the force of rhyme
and other formal devices, by reconciling them with the experimen-
tal gains of the past several decades, is itself sufficiently experimen-
tal" (quoted in J. Breslin, 25). Robert Lowell's *Lord Weary's Castle* won
the Pulitzer Prize in 1947, consolidating the retrenchment Wilbur
describes. The late 1940s also saw the publication of Howard Neme-
rov's *Image and the Law,* and the first books of Adrienne Rich (*A
Change of World*) and W. S. Merwin (*A Mask for Janus*) appeared in the
Yale Younger Poets series in 1951 and 1952, respectively. All of these
poets' early work is characterized by metrical complexity, metaphori-
cal richness, verbal precision, and a mastery of intricate verse forms.

The age demanded a retreat from the barricades of the 1930s, a retreat institutionalized in the spread of New Critical pedagogy in the postwar university and in the rationales for awarding Pound the Bollingen Prize for the *Pisan Cantos* in 1948. Typical of the latter is Archibald MacLeish's justification. Staging a debate between Mr. Saturday (of the *Saturday Evening Post,* no doubt) and Mr. Bollingen (representative of the Library of Congress's committee and MacLeish's own mouthpiece), MacLeish summarizes the attacks on Pound. Mr. Saturday charges that the *Pisan Cantos* should be denied the award: "Because of the fascism. Because of the anti-Semitism. Because of the sneers at decency and the applause for murder. Because of the opinions of Mr. Pound as the poem spells his opinions out" (13). Mr. Bollingen counters by arguing that poetry is not like other statements, that it is "an instrument of knowledge of a certain kind—knowledge about our lives—intuitive knowledge of the kind neither reason nor science is able to supply" (43). MacLeish concludes that poetry can be judged only on its merits as poetry, without regard for the opinions expressed in it: "[J]ustification, to be valid, must be found in the art. In the same way your condemnation of the poem because of its opinions must be a condemnation of the poem *as a poem*" (36; emphasis in original). "[P]oetry makes nothing happen" with a vengeance. Pound's "poem including history" ends up being "about" nothing; its content must be left aside as we judge the poem—in the Bollingen committee's formulation—only by criteria consistent with "the validity of that objective perception of value on which any society must rest" (Barrett, 344). The age demanded a method, a critical narrative, and provided both in the New Critics' treatment of modern poetry, a treatment Michael Bérubé has characterized as "the passage from modernism to New Criticism, from formal experimentation to ossified critical dogma" (*Marginal Forces,* 190).

The literary turn from politics accompanies, and seems almost a cultural wing of, a broad depoliticizing of American society during the shift from world war to Cold War. In 1947, when Lowell won the Pulitzer, President Harry Truman handed down Executive Order 9835, which instituted a political test for government employment; Communists, Fascists, and any others tainted by association with proscribed political groups were prohibited from working for the U.S. government. In 1948, the year Pound's *Pisan Cantos* were published in the United States, Richard Nixon grandstanded before the House of Representatives' Committee on Un-American Activities (HUAC) and brought the case of Alger Hiss to public prominence, and by the next year, Joseph McCarthy's open congressional hearings were under way. Many writers repudiated their Communist pasts. Clifford Odets named other writers before the HUAC, John Dos Passos wrote and published virulently anti-Communist articles, and the once-Communist *Partisan Review* disavowed even the Trotskyism its editors had embraced during the anti-Stalinist late 1930s and zealously pursued the anti-Communist line. Other writers, though, persevered in their dedication to politically committed literature even during this, the "time of the toad."³

The age demanded loyalty to the United States, disavowal of earlier political commitments, paranoid vigilance in defense of limited freedom, and poems whose tightly crafted forms enclosed (or closed out) history. This could not, and did not, last. As James Breslin's *From Modern to Contemporary* makes inescapably clear, the postwar lyric retrenchment was ultimately a dead-end. The beautiful changes, and within a decade of the war, the trademark styles of early Lowell, Wilbur, and the other New Formalists lost their cultural dominance. Beat, Black Mountain, Deep Image, New York school, and confessional poetries crowded the American scene. Experimentalism returned with a vengeance.⁴

This is not, of course, to say that politics was absent from American poetry in the 1950s. For all of its alleged tranquillity, the decade was rife with political turmoil, and that turmoil made its mediated way into much of the 1950s' most important poetry. While fewer poets than during the 1930s wrote the openly partisan sort of work with which this book has been largely concerned, politics bubbled up precisely in the poetries that broke out of the New Formalist crucible of the postwar decade. The programmatic open form promulgated in Black Mountain and Deep Image poetries bore political associations with Whitmanesque democracy; free verse was intricated with freedom.

Even the New Formalism against which other poetic movements of the 1950s tended to define themselves carried within it a sometimes urgent political charge. While canonized, almost from the beginning of his career, for his well-wrought urns, for his poetry's conformity to then-dominant New Critical tastes and expectations, Robert Lowell also aimed his poems at shifting the popular imaginary on issues ranging from American military involvements to electoral politics to racial conflicts. While the mode of political participation changed over the course of Lowell's career, from the jeremiad stance and tone of *Lord Weary's Castle* to the self-doubting and self-dramatizing of *Life Studies* and the critical self-implication of *For the Union Dead* and *History,* Lowell remained committed not only to personal political action (he was imprisoned for his conscientious objection to World War II, and during the Vietnam War, he refused a White House invitation and joined the March on the Pentagon) but also to a political role for poetry.[5]

But while the age demanded and canonized first the taut verbal surfaces of Wilbur and Nemerov and later the various poetries that developed in reaction against that formal polish, other writers who published in *Mainstream, California Quarterly,* and the few other outlets they could find continued to give the age what Pound, thirty years before, had called "an image of its accelerated grimace." In spite of widespread cultural and institutional pressure to make nothing happen, poets persisted in exploiting the resources of their chosen medium to criticize, memorialize, and mobilize.

Thomas McGrath became, during the 1950s, the strongest voice of postwar partisan political poetry and the single most frequent poetic contributor to *Masses and Mainstream,* inheritor of the *New Masses* and one of the very few homes for explicitly political poetry during the inquisition. In ballad stanzas, rhymed quatrains, and modernist free verse, McGrath insistently attacks postwar American society, political oppression, and the common sense of Joseph McCarthy and James McCarran. At times, in fact, McGrath seems to carry out Rolfe's own project, to share, to extend and refine, the elder poet's vision.[6]

In "The Year the Spots Fell Off the Dice," for example, McGrath imagines the blighted present and/or the dystopic future in figural terms quite similar to Rolfe's in "A Poem to Delight My Friends Who Laugh at Science Fiction." The speaker looks back on this devastated year as if he has survived it, and from its opening lines, the poem locates the year's evils in the culture's economic base:

That year the spots fell off the dice
And ten dollar bills were stricken by blight.
In the gilt mantraps of circumstance,

Old fashioned heroes learned to dance
With the iron whore of compromise. (65)

Capitalism's gamble fails in this vision, but that failure brings no revo-
lution, no classless society. Instead, those who might bring about
positive change themselves capitulate, seduced by commerce in its
glittering guises. The worst aspects of this doomed year, McGrath
implies, follow precisely the failure to take advantage of the system's
failure, to press the advantage posed by money's blight. This tacti-
cal blunder holds consequences for every type of human endeavor;
literature "[sinks] under the page," religion goes unnoticed, and intel-
lectuals try in vain to find "the word that would not sink" (65). At
fault, then, are not capitalists themselves, though McGrath suggests
the year's catastrophes began with "Money's crazy priests" marrying
"Murder and innocence." Instead, the blame lies with meliorists, re-
formers, compromisers: "Angel-wise above / The liberal conscience
cried 'love, love' / And turned its eye away" (66). Hidden in the sur-
realist imagery, McGrath's poem, like Rolfe's, bears a pointed and spe-
cific social critique, implies and quietly urges a political resolution.

But McGrath is not always so subtle in his satire. Sometimes the
gloves come off entirely, and he attacks the state and its policies di-
rectly in a voice that shakes in anger and drips venom. Even in these
poems, though, McGrath allies his message with the literary tradition.
Indeed, the best of his viciously antistate poems have as their fulcrum
the U.S. government's betrayal of ideals at the heart of that tradition.
"The Isles of Greece," provoked by American covert participation in
fighting between Greek Communists and anti-Communists, figures
American evils as willed and violent blindness to the meanings of
classic texts on which American society itself is supposedly based:

Here Plato's questionable state
To savants of the C.I.A.
Is redder than the Soviets.
Its archetypal imagery,

Half underground, half in the clear,
Excites the cop in Nixon's brain;
Insolvent Socrates becomes
A vagrant proletarian

And therefore shootable. (72)

Adapting, as Rolfe does and as political poets for hundreds of years have done, the four-stress line and chiming rhyme of quatrains to his agenda, McGrath relentlessly exposes the American government's grotesque misreading of Athenian democracy in this "unclassic war" and attributes to this misprision the darkness that blots out all human history, the strain of history that stains humanity's highest accomplishments "as dark as blood, / And darker than the wine-dark sea" (73).

Although he was the most frequent and accomplished of the political poets active during this most difficult decade, McGrath was by no means the only one. *Masses and Mainstream* alone published a large number of poets in its monthly issues. Many of these, of course, remain unknown: Eve Merriam, Charles Humboldt, John Fontany, Martha Millett, Jean Jenkins, Shirle Chapper. Others are better known for other work, literary or political: Walter Lowenfels, Alvah Bessie, Dalton Trumbo, V. J. Jerome, W. E. B. Du Bois. But *Masses and Mainstream* also published poems by Mike Gold, Meridel LeSueur, Alfred Kreymborg, and Langston Hughes during the 1950s, as well as work by non-American but very well known and intensely political poets like Paul Eluard and Pablo Neruda.

But few magazines during the early and mid-1950s published poetry overtly critical of the U.S. government, and even those few shied away from especially vigorous partisan poetry; the *Nation* demurred about publishing Rolfe's "Ballad of the Noble Intentions," and *California Quarterly* backed out of publishing his "Little Ballad for Americans — 1954" (Nelson, "Lyric Politics," 45). The four poets at this study's center suffer the decade's quietude in different ways, but each is affected: Hughes revises his earlier career and is persecuted by right-wing racists, Pound produces ever more recondite fragments from St. Elizabeth's Hospital, and Rukeyser takes a long hiatus from poetry altogether. And in 1954, under pressure to testify before the HUAC, Rolfe dies.

The year of Rolfe's death, the year after the execution of the Rosenbergs, might be seen as a logical interment date for the partisan poetry that was so much more possible in the 1930s. Rumblings could be heard, however, from a variety of sites in the historical and literary landscapes. The Supreme Court unanimously struck down the "separate but equal" standard that had historically sanctioned race-based segregation in public education and accommodations in the

Brown v. Board of Education case. Tensions immediately arose between African Americans impatient for the long-denied noon promised by the dawn of Reconstruction and the post–Civil War constitutional amendments and white Americans intent on maintaining racist systems of segregation; the nascent civil rights movement was fueled and fed by this judicial victory. Across the globe, at Dien Bien Phu, the French army, bent on maintaining a colonial regime in Vietnam but exhausted after seven years of war, was defeated by Vietnamese nationalists. The stage was set for American military involvement in what would become the nation's longest war and its first unqualified military defeat and for the movements that would rise to challenge America's role in the war. As the Old Left saw its end in McCarthyism and Cold War, a New Left would begin to find its voice in resistance to the war in Vietnam. And as the year ended in San Francisco, a howl could be heard protesting American materialism and militarism, American society's conformist expectations and horrific willingness to sacrifice its youth. A newly open and aggressive, newly partisan poetry raised its voice:

> I saw the best minds of my generation destroyed by madness,
>   starving hysterical naked,
> dragging themselves through the negro streets at dawn looking
>   for an angry fix. (Ginsberg, 126)

Allen Ginsberg diagnosed a set of social problems in "Howl" and set about, with his beatific vision and his Whitmanesque long line, imagining a community of the mad who would take arms against "Moloch! Solitude! Filth! Ugliness! Ashcans and unobtainable dollars!" (131). In a continuous and building gesture of connection, a repeated act of union signified in the anaphoric "I'm with you in Rockland" addressed, in the poem's final section, to his fellow former mental patient Carl Solomon, Ginsberg not only imagines that community but articulates its program by rearticulating to his vision precisely the defining traits of Moloch's America:

> I'm with you in Rockland
>   where we wake up electrified out of the coma by our own souls'
>   airplanes roaring over the roof they've come to drop angelic
>   bombs the hospital illuminates itself   imaginary walls collapse
>   O skinny legions run outside   O starry-spangled shock of

mercy the eternal war is here   O victory forget your under-
wear we're free. (133)

Poets continue to write poems of protest. They continue to exploit
the resources of the medium, the weight of a long tradition, and the
enduring cultural weight accorded poetry (even by those who do
not read it) in the service of activist agendas. In closed lyric forms,
in verses based on musical idioms, in experimental, highly theorized
avant-garde forms, poets criticize, remember, and exhort. Some such
poets are among our greatest: Adrienne Rich, Michael S. Harper,
Susan Howe, Carolyn Forché.[7] Others are not yet so widely known,
and others still will never achieve such a poetic reputation. Indeed,
many political poets write few poems, driven only by the needs of
a specific moment, by the call of a crisis that impels them to textual
action; when the moment passes, their poetic vocation passes with it
and they disappear. These various kinds of poets—the near-canonical,
the not-yet-known, and the all-but-invisible—offer alike their his-
tories, passions, and expertise to intervene in the culture's political
understanding. When they do, they allow us to see that the strategies
deployed by Edwin Rolfe and Muriel Rukeyser, by Langston Hughes
and Ezra Pound, are still among those most commonly put into play
by political poets. They give voice to silent suffering. They provide
images and vocabularies with which we might, ourselves, try to re-
solve the intractable divisions and demands with which we are beset.
We mistake poetry's importance to us if we neglect this work, if we
forget its past and foreclose its present possibilities. And, more im-
portant, we miss the opportunities such work affords us to find new
ways to make something happen.

NOTES

INTRODUCTION

1. For biographical information on Pound, see Carpenter, *Serious Character.*
2. Biographical information on Rolfe here is taken from Nelson and Hendricks, *Edwin Rolfe,* 8–10.
3. *First Love and Other Poems* was published by Rolfe himself through the Larry Edmunds Bookstore.
4. The publication of Rolfe's *Collected Poems* (1993) and of a selection of his poems in *Triquarterly* (1994) and in the Heath *Anthology of American Literature* (1998) has begun to put this story, and, more important, Rolfe's poetry, back into circulation.
5. For a treatment of Auden's developing attitude toward the relationship between politics and poetry over the course of the 1930s, see Hynes. On the mechanics of Auden's poetry's political instability via shifting pronominal structures, see Fowler, 91–95. See also Sharpe.
6. Peter Collier's essay on Auden and "the poetry of protest" finds in "Spain," typically cited as Auden's most clearly political poem, "Auden's most precise commitment to a political future" (42), but Robert Sullivan's reading of "Spain" as "a moral fable of Auden and his contemporaries . . . [and] a figurative denouement of 'the truly strong man' participating in the building of the 'Just City'" (234–35) is far more convincing in light of Auden's purposely (and perfectly respectable) noncommittal status throughout his poetry of the 1930s. Earlier readers most often interpret "Spain" along lines closer to Sullivan's. Edgell Rickword encapsulates the poem as "[t]oday the struggle, tomorrow the poetry and fun" (quoted in ibid., 237), and Stephen Spender writes that Auden expresses in the poem "an attitude which for a few weeks or months he had felt intellectually forced to adopt, but which he never truly felt" (30).
7. For a theoretically sophisticated critique of New Critical attacks on "sentimentality" and a compelling demonstration of the powerful uses to which women writers put the sentimental, see Clark.
8. Murphy's book nuances the *Partisan Review* interpretation, in which all proletarian literature and criticism is "leftist," and foregrounds the important fact that Rahv, Phillips, and others in the *Partisan Review* circle had themselves written "leftist" criticism during the early 1930s. While Rahv and

Phillips, then, lambaste Mike Gold, Granville Hicks, and other proletarian critics for leftism, they fail to recognize the antileftist writings of Joseph Freeman, for example, who published critiques of leftism in the *Daily Worker* as early as 1933, as well as important changes in the thought of critics like Gold, who by 1933 was also questioning his earlier positions on proletarian literature and criticism (Murphy, 133). At the same time, the orthodox *Partisan Review* account overlooks writings by Rahv from the early 1930s, in which he argues that writers on the Left should only selectively place themselves in positive relation to the literary tradition. Rahv writes in 1932, for example, that from the "symbolists and the romantics . . . the proletarian writers can learn little" (quoted in ibid., 151).

9. For a discussion of the cultural logic of agrarian "squirearchy" and its imbrication with New Criticism, see Kalaidjian, "Marketing Modern Poetry." Kalaidjian examines Ransom's, Owsley's, and Tate's contributions to the agrarian manifesto, *I'll Take My Stand,* in which these positions are articulated (306–7).

10. On the rise of political criticism as concomitant with the rise of "theory" in American literary studies, see Graff, *Professing Literature,* esp. chaps. 14, 15. See also Cain, *Crisis in Criticism.* The political decoding of literary texts that Graff and Cain point out can be found in Robert Scholes's *Textual Power,* a textbook that equates critical reading with attention to the ideological function of a literary text's semiotic codes.

11. The work of Julia Kristeva, especially her development of a conceptual vocabulary for the analysis of *écriture féminine,* has been cited often as of central importance in politicizing both the study of women's writing and literary studies more broadly, but of course, the political community of feminists inside and outside the academy as a whole has been broadly influential. On feminist criticism, see Showalter. In studies of modernism and modern poetry, feminism has had a profound impact both on the poets studied and on the ways in which critics and students approach them. See especially Gilbert and Gubar, *War of the Words* and *Sexchanges;* Juhasz; and Montefiore.

12. Marcus Graham published these poets' work together in his 1929 *Anthology of Revolutionary Poetry.* Nelson writes that "it does not matter what intentions these poets may have had for their work. History has taken these poems up and given them new meanings" (*Repression and Recovery,* 149).

13. My definition here is broader than Van Wienen's formulation that political poems are "poems written on behalf of or purposely used by political organizations to promote their agendas" (231). I find more useful his slightly more flexible definition that political poetry is "poetry engaged in a specific set of political struggles, which took place at a particular historical juncture and had definite winners and losers" (231).

14. Of course, Freeman's chronology is polemically skewed: the Sacco and Vanzetti case did not have the galvanic effect he claims for it until after the 1922 publication of *The Waste Land.* The point, however, is a valid one. Cases like

that of Sacco and Vanzetti, and issues like those in play in the case, did dominate the attention of left-wing political writers during the 1920s, perhaps even to the exclusion of so prominent a poem as Eliot's.

15. For an examination of *Poetry* and its editorial decisions, including a brief discussion of political poetry in the magazine, see Marek.

16. See Gramsci, 325–28. Gramsci's discussions of the role of intellectuals in articulating the interests of subaltern classes to the priorities of the ruling bloc (348–53) and of the Roman Catholic Church in maintaining hegemonic structures (331–33) are especially helpful in understanding how the institutions of civil society work to resolve in the minds of historical subjects the contradictions out of which their political disquiet arises.

17. The theory of aesthetic function is best articulated by Czech theorist Jan Mukarovsky. Briefly, as Peter Steiner writes, "[T]he aesthetic function was seen as present in all activities pursuing practical goals, and practical functions were present in those pursuing aesthetic goals. Thus art is not hermetically sealed from non-art; the two always interpenetrate and overlap" (quoted in Mukarovsky, xvii). For an elaboration of this insight, see Mukarovsky, chap. 3.

18. For a solid biographical treatment of this incident and of Duchamp's further use of ready-mades to challenge dominant definitions of art and the aesthetic, see Tomkins. For a more analytical and fully theorized discussion of Duchamp and his significance in modern art and in contemporary thinking about art versus nonart, see Weiss.

19. This conception of the poem as "act" rather than object does not, of course, result only from recent textual and/or critical theory. As Roger Gilbert has shown, the definition of poetry as action arises among modern poets themselves and is explicitly stated by Frost, Stevens, Pound, and Williams, among others (12).

20. I take this phrase, of course, from Benedict Anderson's *Imagined Communities*. While the context of Anderson's analysis of nationalism grants the term its specific meaning, I would argue that the efforts of poets participating in hegemonic struggles through civil society, efforts aimed at drawing together through language subjects with disparate agendas and widely diverging needs and desires, aim to yield a body similar to the nation as Anderson defines it—collective, limited, and, most crucial, imagined.

21. For an illuminating discussion of the process by which Eliot won the Dial Award and secured publication of *The Waste Land* from Horace Liveright, see Rainey, "Price of Modernism."

22. My quotations of Rolfe's poems here and in Chapter 1 are from his *Collected Poems* (hereinafter abbreviated *CP*). When a poem's appearance in a previous publication affects the interpretation or is important to my argument, I will also cite that publication.

23. On these magazines' popularity and influence on the American poetry scene around the turn of the century, see Perkins, 84–89, and Lentricchia, 47–61.

24. On the place of poetry in American education in the early twentieth century, see Van Wienen, 9.

25. See Stevenson and Nye, as well as Van Wienen, 2–11.

26. Van Wienen provides the similar example of Angela Morgan's Detroit performance of "Battle Cry of the Mothers," a near-sonnet she wrote in opposition to World War I. Appearing in a Greek costume and reciting "with great eloquence and feeling," Morgan appealed through her poem's form and through sartorial citation to the values articulated to poetry by the practice of school recitations (67).

27. Wordsworth, of course, has much more polemical and hortatory moments in some of his other sonnets, especially "To the Men of Kent, October, 1803":

> Vanguard of Liberty, ye men of Kent,
> Ye children of a Soil that doth advance
> Her haughty brow against the coast of France,
> Now is the time to prove your hardiment! (179)

28. Much scholarly ink has been spilled over Wordsworth's political poetry, especially since the advent of New Historicist critical modes. For discussions that seek to revise the conventional chronology of Wordsworth's political development in poetry, see Chandler; Levinson; and McGann, *Romantic Ideology.* For a challenge to these accounts, see Grob. On later nineteenth-century political poets and their use of the sonnet form, see Maidment and Scheckner.

29. For an exemplary discussion of such informal but important networks of circulation, see Nelson, "Politics and Labor."

30. See also Kalaidjian's discussion of Kenneth Fearing's transpersonal poetics (*American Culture,* 199–210).

CHAPTER ONE

1. Rolfe here echoes and elaborates a position he first publicly articulated two years before. Substituting for Mike Gold in Gold's *Daily Worker* column on October 13, 1933, Rolfe writes that revolutionary poetry suffers from the efforts of poets to maintain "a rigid isolation of themselves as human beings from their writings." These poets, seeking to import wholesale the discourse of politics without first giving life to that discourse through their own experience, force the politics into the poetry. Their artificially created work, Rolfe concludes, "may contain all the correct slogans, all the perfectly phrased correct ideas on the subject, and yet remain lifeless, stilted, false."

2. See Murphy, chap. 5. Specifically, Murphy takes up the emergence of such critiques in a discussion of the *New Masses* and the *Daily Worker,* showing Gold's shift from his earlier "proletcult" position to a recognition of the need for "a long apprenticeship in technique" for writers on the Left and ex-

amining the expansions of this recognition by Freeman and Rolfe (122–23). On the "workers' schools" that served to provide writers, including Rolfe, this apprenticeship, see Kalaidjian, *American Culture*, 44–46.

3. Indeed, according to Murphy, "form" and "technique" become the bywords of Gold's and Freeman's criticism (as well as that of Granville Hicks). Gold writes in 1933 that "it is extremely important to strive after form" and, later that year, that proletarian writers must "strive to learn the technique of writing" (quoted in Murphy, 122–23). Freeman writes in November 1933 that "[w]e, by no means, want to praise books that show intentions may be good, but whose execution is poor" and that such books are "not only bad art, but bad propaganda" (quoted in ibid., 123).

4. On the *Daily Worker*, see Buhle et al., *Encyclopedia of the American Left*, 178–82.

5. See Nelson, *Repression and Recovery*, 135–40, 295.

6. Most songs included in the IWW songbook are set to popular and recognizable tunes, from the nineteenth-century "Battle Hymn of the Republic" to contemporaneous Tin Pan Alley songs. See ibid., 136. For a thorough and compelling discussion of the IWW's use of poetry, especially in the songbook, see Furey, 85–133. On choral forms and mass recitation more broadly, see Kalaidjian, *American Culture*, 53–55.

7. For a sympathetically critical reading of "Credo" as exemplary of proletarian theoretical complexity, see Kalaidjian, *American Culture*, 56–57.

8. Histories of the Spanish Civil War are numerous. My account is informed by several, especially Jackson and Thomas.

9. On the American and European responses to the Spanish Civil War, see Jackson, 256–60, 354–56. See also Pike. On the formation of the International Brigades, see Carroll; Landis; and Rosenstone.

10. Nickson's illustrations appear in *CP*, 127, 146, 159, 172, and in Rolfe, *First Love and Other Poems*, 8, 34, 52, 70.

11. Descriptions of the bombardment and its effects recur throughout the literature of the Spanish Civil War. Of the first air raid on Madrid, Regulo Martinez recalls, "There were civilian casualties, a young girl holding a doll was among the dead" (quoted in Fraser, 175). I discuss Langston Hughes's reports from Madrid during the bombardment in Chapter 2. A number of letters collected in Nelson and Hendricks, *Madrid, 1937*, detail the experience of civilians and combatants during the bombing, including a letter Rolfe wrote to his wife Mary on August 3, 1937:

> What I've written is merely tentative; I'm still feeling around for a core for the poem. The completed four pages describe a bombardment of Madrid which occurred last night, beginning at 12:15. Most of us went to the roof of our building where we watched the flashes on the horizon and, closer by, the answering fire of our own artillery. Two German comrades, both officers, were standing next to me on the roof; and they had a very heated argument about the number of cannon in operation.

One said six: the other insisted seven. I am still not certain how many heavy artillery pieces participated. All I know is that the shells fell on the city for more than 2 ½ hours. (289)

12. See Alpert, 81–90, and Jackson, 390–94. For discussions of these actions focused on the involvement of the International Brigades, see Brome, 186–200, and Rolfe, *Lincoln Battalion*, 107–39.
13. Rolfe describes his actions in *Lincoln Battalion*, 111–12. Battalion commander Robert Merriman's note ordering Rolfe to assemble the troops and the convoy is in the Rolfe Archive at the University of Illinois at Urbana-Champaign and is reproduced in Nelson and Hendricks, *Edwin Rolfe*, 26.
14. The fourth and fifth parts of "City of Anguish" were first published in *Romancero de los voluntarios de la libertad* (Madrid: Ediciones del Comisario de Las Brigadas Internacionales, 1937), 81–82.
15. *New Republic*, July 19, 1939, 300.
16. Founded in 1914, the *New Republic* was one of the dominant liberal magazines in the United States by 1920; its circulation after only seven years in existence was around 40,000. By the 1930s, the magazine was pro-Roosevelt but cautious in its positions on international affairs; it supported American neutrality in Spain, often took a hard isolationist stance, and only in 1941 began to support American involvement in European antifascism. See Nourie and Nourie, 301–4.
17. See Jackson, 398–400, and Alpert, 151–58, for a more general treatment of Teruel. Rolfe's discussion of the battle focuses almost entirely on the role of the International Brigades.
18. On this retreat, see Jackson, 400; Alpert, 93; and Brome, 224.
19. For discussions of the Ebro offensive, see Jackson, 454–56, and Rolfe, *Lincoln Battalion*, 258–93.
20. For further discussion of Reid and his relationship with Rolfe, see Nelson and Hendricks, *Edwin Rolfe*, 12.
21. "Postscript to a War," *CP*, 160; "Survival Is of the Essence," *CP*, 164.
22. *Volunteer for Liberty*, January 3, 1938, 9.
23. *New Republic*, May 25, 1938, 65.
24. As Nelson writes, the name of this city had become "a rallying cry and an incantation" in a number of poems; "[t]he poems echoed one another across time and space and national or political difference, rang changes on the suffering and courage of the Madrileños, and established, in print, in voice, in dream and nightmare the point of articulation of an antifascist politics for its time" ("Lyric Politics," 42).
25. Nelson recounts the poem's circulation and reception and quotes Hemingway's appreciative letter to Rolfe ("Lyric Politics," 43–44).
26. For further information on Unamuno, see Rudd, whose *Lone Heretic* is the lone scholarly biography of Unamuno in English. For a complete recounting of Unamuno's speech, see Thomas, 502–3, and Jackson, 300–301. Rudd's

account is much more detailed in its treatment of the consequences of the speech for Unamuno himself (301–3).

27. Barcia, whom Rolfe met in exile, translated "Elegia" into Spanish (*CP*, 298).

28. Claiming that "what we believe to be the motives of our conduct are usually but the pretexts for it" (261), Unamuno argues that a true faith abides in the transcendence of easy belief: "Those who believe that they believe in God, but without any passion in their heart, without anguish of mind, without uncertainty, without doubt, without an element of despair even in their consolation, believe only in the God-idea, not in God Himself" (193).

29. See also Jackson, 300–301, and Rudd, 300–301.

30. Nelson recounts the anecdote in his introduction to Rolfe's *Collected Poems:*

> When a train full of American volunteers was scheduled to leave Spain, Rolfe and the correspondent Vincent Sheean were among others there at Puigcerda to see them off. As it happened, the train arrived and left early, and it was well it did, for at the scheduled arrival two squadrons of Franco's planes flew over and bombed the station heavily. They thus missed their intended target, and that group of internationals left safely. Shortly thereafter, Sheean saw one swan on a nearby lake and remarked the contrast to Rolfe. ("Lyric Politics," 37)

31. On the liquidation of the POUM and the struggles between partners in the Republican coalition (and the international supporters of the Republic), see Jackson, 370–73. For an autobiographical and anecdotal account, see Orwell.

32. McWilliams's *Witch Hunt* (1950) is an early reportorial account. For scholarly treatments, see Buckingham; Caute; and Schrecker. Red-baiting activities actually predate even the formation of the Dies Committee in 1938. While the Palmer Raids and the Red Scare of 1919 are the most famous instances of prewar anti-Communist activity, the Federal Bureau of Investigation and a series of congressional committees worked throughout the 1920s and 1930s to discredit the Communist Party of the United States, to criminalize activity in Communist-affiliated organizations, and to propagandize against communism (O'Reilly, 13–20; Buckingham, 31–45). The deeper historical roots of twentieth-century American anticommunism are ably traced by M. J. Heale, who locates them in the 1830s.

33. See Buckingham, esp. 41–43. Even during the depth of the depression, the special committee of the U.S. House of Representatives chaired by Hamilton Fish submitted a report that linked, as Buckingham writes, "communists, blacks, aliens, and advocates of free love to the Kremlin" (42).

34. See O'Reilly, 36, and Buckingham, 45–48. Heale briefly discusses the Dies Committee (24–25); Schrecker's treatment of Dies and his committee is quite thorough (91–113).

35. O'Reilly attributes the willingness of Hoover to cooperate with the difficult and unpredictable Dies to their shared opposition to New Deal policies. Hoover, seeing that Dies was motivated by the drive to discredit the New

Deal, offered the committee access to selected bureau information and conducted surveillance under the auspices of the committee. Opposition to the New Deal also drew conservative Democrats and some Republicans to support the formation of the committee, though, ironically, it was the support of House members (such as Dickstein) who saw the committee as a means to combat anti-Semitic and pro-Nazi groups on the Right that helped the committee strengthen its position (36–37).

36. See also Buckingham, 47–48.

37. While my focus here is on actual government activities against Communists, we should remember that the anti-Communist propaganda war was waged as viciously in other sectors of society as it was in the federal and state governments. Steinberg details the anti-Communist activities of labor unions, the Catholic Church, and non-Communist liberals to show the extragovernmental front of this propaganda war (20–21).

38. Vincent Brome recounts the troubles these men faced in the military because of their status as "premature antifascists" (245–47). Schrecker summarizes the treatment as follows:

> [Veterans] would go through basic training and then, at the last moment, when the other members of their units were shipped overseas, they would be held behind and put through yet another training program. They were, in the Army's bizarre terminology, "premature antifascists," subjected to harassment by military intelligence officers and, in many cases, sent to special camps where they were treated almost like prisoners of war. (105)

Peter Carroll's discussion of the VALB's travails in the late 1930s and 1940s is comprehensive (esp. 244–75). Nelson and Hendricks provide details of Rolfe's own military experience (*Edwin Rolfe*, 40–46).

39. The biographical information here and below is taken from Nelson and Hendricks, *Edwin Rolfe*, 44–60.

40. Quoted in ibid., 53.

41. On the McCarran Act, see Buckingham, 73–74, and Schrecker, 250–75.

42. Rolfe, unpublished manuscript, n.d.

43. Ibid.

44. Rolfe, unpublished manuscript, December 1947.

45. Rolfe, unpublished manuscript, September 1947.

46. Holograph note at bottom of third page, unpublished manuscript, n.d.

47. The poem also circulates, and performs similar elegiac and preservative work, in two early-1950s commemorative documents: Alvah Bessie's *Heart of Spain* anthology (1952), in which it follows Genevieve Taggard's "Andalucia" in the section titled "'Madrid Will Be the Tomb of Fascism,'" and Rolfe's own *Lincoln Battalion,* in which the poem appears as a frontispiece, a lyrical distillation of the history that follows it.

48. For a modern recounting of the story of the children of Lir, see Heaney, 37–49.

CHAPTER TWO

1. In her important and insightful essay, "Making Poetry Pay," Karen Jackson Ford puts it slightly less sympathetically: "Hughes eked out a living writing poetry because he had the good sense to understand that the poem could be 'used' in many ways—that is, it could be commodified. . . . Langston Hughes was a relentless marketer of his own poetry, successful because he recognized that promoting his poetry involved handling both the product and the consumer" (276). While I agree that Hughes was a canny marketer and self-promoter, I would add that he engaged in these activities, at least at key moments in his career, not (or not only) out of self-interest but in the interest of a political agenda in which he deeply believed and for which he worked quite hard.

2. In *Hegemony and Socialist Strategy,* Laclau and Mouffe describe political space as the sum of multiple and fragmentary fields of political struggle. These fields are constituted equally discursively, partaking in the transformation from "relations of subordination" to "relations of oppression," and therefore impossible to privilege one over another (107–8).

3. Classifying Hughes as a black poet, as a member of the Harlem Renaissance, achieves some important successes: Hughes's work, along with that of other Renaissance writers, receives the critical attention it deserves, and African American literary expression is valorized by the academy. Such classification, though, allows us to forget much of Hughes's most explicitly political work. But as Nelson writes: "Not to link Hughes with other socially conscious poets amounts to maintaining, by way of the discourse of literary history, the same racial and cultural divisions and antagonisms . . . that the capitalist class in America promoted to prevent the working class from organizing effectively" (*Repression and Recovery,* 180).

4. The story of Samson's destruction of the temple appears in Judges 16:23–30.

5. James Smethurst rightly points out that this passage is an example of the African American voice that frequently "erupts from within the address of the 'hard-boiled' speaker" that is typical of Hughes's 1930s left-wing poems (110); what seems more important, though, is the subordination of "Negroes" to the broader, class-based coalition the poem constructs through its serial address. While African Americans are certainly present as invitees into the coalition and as speaking subjects marked by their vernacular, their position here testifies to Hughes's political purposes in the poem.

6. See, for example, the famous Art Young illustration in the December 1913 issue of *The Masses.* Along the top, Young writes in capital letters, "He stirreth up the people," and beneath the picture of a tough-looking Jesus appears the caption: "Jesus Christ The Workingman of Nazareth Will Speak At Brotherhood Hall—subject—The Rights of Labor." Poems, too, tap into this attempt at rearticulation. Sarah N. Cleghorn's "Comrade Jesus," which appeared in *The Masses* in April 1914, for example, concludes:

Ah, let no Local him refuse;
Comrade Jesus hath paid his dues.
Whatever other be debarred,
Comrade Jesus hath his red card.

7. The poem's last line reads slightly differently in the *New Masses,* where the "EL" of the telephone number is spelled out as "El Dorado." The pun on the "El" (elevated train) is present in that initial publication, then, but is followed by the abbreviation's reference to the mythical City of Gold, an irony that would not have been lost on Hughes's readers.

8. See also Kalaidjian, *American Culture,* 97–101, and Maxwell, 132–41.

9. Cullen's long poem, the title poem of his 1929 volume, *The Black Christ,* explicitly treats the theme, and the cover illustration by Charles Cullen graphically connects the crucified figure with the lynched black man (see Nelson, *Repression and Recovery,* 94–95). But the trope's roots extend more deeply into the African American past to works like Frances E. W. Harper's *Iola Leroy* (1892) and anonymous spirituals dating to the early nineteenth century.

10. "Signifyin(g)," as Henry Louis Gates Jr. writes, is the rhetorical strategy of ironic or parodic repetition. For fuller definitions, see Gates, 68–88.

11. During his 1931 reading tour through the South, Hughes had grown frustrated with the silence of black community leaders, college administrators, and others on the Scottsboro case. In "Cowards from the Colleges," which he published in the *Crisis* in 1934, Hughes recalls the infuriating quietism of these leaders:

> I was amazed to find at many Negro schools and colleges a year after the arrest and conviction of the Scottsboro boys, that a great many teachers and students knew nothing of it, or if they did the official attitude would be, "Why bring that up?" I asked at Tuskegee, only a few hours from Scottsboro, who from there had been to the trial. Not a soul had been so far as I could discover. And with demonstrations in every capital in the civilized world for the freedom of the Scottsboro boys, so far as I know not one Alabama Negro school until now has held even a protest meeting. (227)

12. Later versions of the poem do not include the italics and alter the lineation. The alternation of typefaces in the poem's original publications (in *Contempo* and the *Scottsboro Limited* pamphlet) is a reminder of the need to read poems like "Christ in Alabama" where and as they first appeared. When William Maxwell, in *New Negro, Old Left,* reads the poem as "the final text in the *Scottsboro Limited* collection," he quotes the typeface and lineation of later versions, not the *Scottsboro Limited* version he is discussing (140–41). His reading is therefore based not on the poem in the publication at issue in his discussion but on the poem in one of the later publications that have become standard.

13. For a comparison of these early versions of the poem with the later ver-

sions (in *Panther and the Lash* and *Collected Poems*), in which the italicized lines are printed in roman type, the stanzas are divided by colons instead of dashes, and the final stanza is broken into five lines instead of four, and for a discussion of the significance of the differences in terms of Hughes's self-promotion, see Ford, "Making Poetry Pay," 280.

14. See, for example, a number of the songs collected in Dudley Randall's *The Black Poets* and in Henry Louis Gates Jr. and Nellie McKay, eds., *The Norton Anthology of African American Literature;* see also the entries on work songs and spirituals in William Andrews, Frances Smith Foster, and Trudier Harris, eds., *The Oxford Companion to African American Literature.*

15. In a famous quotation that Hughes himself later repeated, a Chapel Hill politician griped that "[i]t's bad enough to call Christ a bastard, but to call Him a nigger—that's too much" (quoted in Hughes, *I Wonder*, 46). The *Southern Textile Bulletin* called Hughes's writings "insulting and blasphemous," and the *Daily Tarheel*, the University of North Carolina's student newspaper, reported the next spring that 300 people had signed a protest to the governor in which Hughes was characterized as one of the "angels of darkness" (quoted in Rampersad, *I, Too, Sing America*, 225).

16. Of course, the conversation between the two essays is one that neither Steffens nor Hughes, both of whose works were solicited by *Contempo*, planned; by positioning the essays on the same page, the editors provide readers with the opportunity to activate the two essays, along with the poem and illustration, in a dialogic reading.

17. Hughes repeatedly refers to nine defendants in this essay, though only eight were awaiting execution; Roy Wright, thirteen at the time of the crime, was convicted but not sentenced to death.

18. Hughes seems, in this essay, to contradict his statements in "The Negro Artist," but in the earlier essay, Hughes does not resist the Americanness of blacks. Indeed, throughout his career, Hughes worked to convince white readers to grant blacks the full benefits of citizenship, to recognize that blacks were as American as whites. What Hughes resists in "The Negro Artist" is the tendency among some black writers (especially a barely disguised Countee Cullen) to give up the cultural specificities of blackness in an effort to achieve a bland, white "American standardization."

19. The *Contempo* front page strengthens a reading of "Christ in Alabama" proffered by William Maxwell, who argues that the poem "describes an interracial triangle founded on the systematic sexual use of black women by white men, a triangle whose sheer southern pervasiveness was dimmed by the debate over lynching" (141). But Hughes's essay, positioned next to the poem, complicates Maxwell's characterization of "the poem's silence on Scottsboro's Two White Women" (141). While the poem, taken in isolation or read outside this initial publication, says nothing explicitly about the two women, its juxtaposition with the essay speaks volumes.

20. In a brief (and problematic) gesture, Hughes writes the corruption of southern mores onto other bodies as well. Characterizing "Dixie justice" as "blind

and syphilitic," Hughes implies that southern gentlemen themselves cannot escape the costs of their entertainment. At the end of the essay, Hughes joins in the general attack that defenders of the Scottsboro "boys" made on their accusers, Victoria Price and Ruby Bates: "Dear Lord, I never knew until now that white ladies (the same color as Southern gentlemen) travelled in freight trains. . . . Did you world? . . . And who ever heard of raping a prostitute?" ("Southern Gentlemen," 1). Hughes's eloquent critique of southern gender dynamics (for example, his indictment of mill owners for paying their women employees so little that they were forced into prostitution) is compromised by this attack, for Hughes performs here on the women the same rhetorical equation of social position with guilt that the Alabama justice system performed on the defendants.

21. Arnold Rampersad details the poverty of Mary Langston (Hughes's grandmother) in Lawrence, writing that the family often rented out rooms or vacated the house and lived with friends in order to rent out the entire house and that family members often relied on charity and Langston's resourcefulness to survive (*I, Too, Sing America,* 13–16). Moreover, the examples of Lewis Leary, Hughes's grandmother's first husband, who had been killed at Harpers Ferry as a member of John Brown's band, and his great-uncle John Langston, the only black representative from Virginia in Congress after Reconstruction, were often recited to Hughes by his grandmother. He was pressed by this background to see himself as somehow separate from, and destined for a fate different from, the working class.

22. George Cunningham attributes Hughes's spiritual and literal wanderings in the early 1920s to the difficult marginal class position he occupied:

> Hughes was heir to the black abolitionist's tradition of cultural and political assimilation and a tradition of bourgeois economic nationalism, while his childhood experiences were closer to that of the poor black migrants from the South. His marginal position between two visions of life was a source of alienation for Hughes, and he began the twenties spiritually cast adrift from the two significant groups that defined alternative versions of black culture. (iii)

23. Hughes's difficulties negotiating the class differences within his own family are, perhaps, nowhere more apparent than in his short stay with relatives in Washington, D.C., in 1924–25. Hughes embarrassed his prosperous relatives by taking jobs in restaurants and laundries and by telling stories of his odd jobs and travels. In *The Big Sea,* he recalls that "my cousins introduced me as just back from Europe, but they didn't say I came by chipping decks on a freight ship—which seemed to me an essential explanation" (203). After repeated humiliation by these relatives (especially directed at his mother), Hughes moved with his mother and half-brother to a one-room apartment (Rampersad, *I, Too, Sing America,* 100–101).

24. Hughes was evicted from his Harlem apartment in 1941 when tenants to whom he had sublet it fell behind on the rent and Hughes was unable to

make it up (Rampersad, *I, Too, Sing America*, 392). At the same time, Hughes, broke after poor sales of *The Big Sea*, poor returns from his spring 1940 reading tour, and the repeated rejection of a children's book he had written with Arna Bontemps, was forced to rely on financial help from friends in California, where he was living.

25. Hazel Carby writes that Hurston "chose to represent black people as the rural folk; the folk were represented as being both the source of Afro-American cultural and linguistic forms and the means for its continued existence" (10). We can see Hughes drawing on folk culture in a similar manner, bringing blues and the conditions of urban blacks together in a way that complicates both.

26. The conflict over sexuality and racial responsibility among Harlem Renaissance writers is complex and intense. Briefly, Fauset herself might best exemplify the worries about sexuality with respect to racial responsibility. Her novels repeatedly figure black women's sexual repression as the key to developing a morality that sets the new black middle class above the working class. At the same time, Nella Larsen's *Quicksand,* with its openly sexual heroine, explores the connections between sex, race, and power in both rural and urban settings. Carby writes that Larsen "condemns the ways in which female sexuality is confined and compromised as the object of male desire" (11). Hughes's work seems closer to Larsen's on this point, and their work together challenges the rather conservative position taken by Fauset, Cullen, and, to a lesser extent, Locke.

27. On all aspects of Garveyism and its career in the 1920s and 1930s, see Tony Martin's fine study, *Race First: The Ideological and Organizational Struggles of Marcus Garvey and the Universal Negro Improvement Association.*

28. See Mark Naison's exhaustive *Communists in Harlem during the Depression,* as well as Philip Foner's briefer but forceful account in *American Socialism and Black Americans: From the Age of Jackson to World War II.*

29. Hughes's political positions and participation during this period are well described by Michael Denning (217–18), who argues for Hughes's "importance as a model and emblem of proletarian writing" (217). See also Smethurst, 93–95, and Maxwell, 133–34.

30. In some versions of *Scottsboro Limited,* a different illustration accompanies "Christ in Alabama." Instead of the crucified black man and the mourning woman, Taylor depicts the eight defendants immobilized, cruciform, against a grid of prison bars. The Beinecke Library at Yale University has copies of both versions.

31. Smethurst argues that the play's subsumption of "folk" into "class" seems to conflict with the CPUSA's "Black Belt" thesis since it at once fails to distinguish between northern and southern blacks and to register the distinctive "national" characteristics the defendants, as southern blacks, should bear (105). But the play's broader movement, which unites people across races through the medium of class, fits perfectly well within the CPUSA's aims. More than this, the play is one of many texts in which we see borne out

both William Maxwell's claim that "U.S. literary communism took scant dictation from Moscow" (5) and Robin D. G. Kelley's argument that African American writers were often able to play fast and loose with party positions because the party's tendency to "place virtually everything black people did under the rubric of 'folk'" insulated black writers' works from ideological scrutiny (*Race Rebels*, 116).

32. Hughes himself had been briefly involved in plans to organize a workers' theater group, the Suitcase Theater. While he had been named in the September 1931 *New Masses* as one of the directors of the proposed group, along with Jacob Burck, Paul Peters, and Whittaker Chambers, the project never materialized. Hughes had, of course, worked in more mainstream theatrical projects, from the revue *O Blues!* to the folk opera he planned with Zora Neale Hurston, both unfinished, to the play, *Mule Bone,* over which Hughes and Hurston and Wallace Thurman broke off their friendship (Rampersad, *I, Too, Sing America,* 134–35, 184–85).

33. It is thus surprising, and unfortunate, that James Smethurst's chapter on Hughes's 1930s poetry makes no mention of his writing on the Spanish Civil War. Robert Shulman gives similarly scant treatment of Hughes's writing on Spain; he briefly discusses "Madrid—1937" in his chapter on Hughes (291–93).

34. The article heralds a booklet Hughes planned to publish, in which, Rampersad writes, "he would include portraits of individual blacks on both sides of the fighting" (*I, Too, Sing America,* 351). The booklet was never published.

35. William R. Scott describes the role of the black press in informing African Americans about the conflict and, in some cases, prefiguring left-wing newspapers' more direct participation in the hostilities through their editorial call for volunteers to join the war and defend the beleaguered nation (128). In the booklet he planned to publish on Spain, Hughes intended to include a chapter explicitly comparing Spain and Ethiopia, both victims of international fascism (Rampersad, *I, Too, Sing America,* 351).

36. In "Negroes in Spain," a short essay Hughes wrote for the *Volunteer for Liberty,* Hughes further elaborates his description of the Moors' plight. He recounts a meeting with a wounded Moorish boy who explains how he came to Spain:

> Then I learned from this child that Franco had brought Moorish women into Spain as well as men—women to wash and cook for the troops.
> "What happened to your mother," I said.
> The child closed his eyes. "She was killed at Brunete," he answered slowly.
> Thus the Moors die in Spain, men, women and children, victims of Fascism, fighting not for freedom—but against freedom—under a banner that holds only terror and segregation for all the darker peoples of the earth. (106)

37. On the black press and its relationship with the Left, see Washburn, esp. chap. 2. Works on individual editors of African American newspapers also include information on the "black-Red" nexus as it manifested itself in the black press. See, for example, Buni and Ottley.

38. See *CP*, 142. For my discussion of "Epitaph," see Chapter 1.

39. Amaranjit Singh writes, "Hughes's work is of a piece in recognizing the inseparableness of race and class in African-American life and literature" (38).

40. For a strong discussion of Hughes's "aesthetic of simplicity," see Ford, "Do Right to Write Right." Ford argues that "utter simplicity is the only adequate response to a dislocated life in an urban ghetto in a racist country." Characterizing Hughes's work as powerful in its formal simplicity, Ford concludes that Hughes is willing to "forgo the complexities of 'great poetry' in order to express something that is 'of great importance'" (454). While I would not characterize much of Hughes's poetry as rhetorically or formally simple and while surface simplicity often hides deeper complexity, Ford's conclusion is convincing.

CHAPTER THREE

1. Focusing on the Malatesta Cantos (8–10), Rainey in *Ezra Pound* painstakingly illustrates Pound's compositional practice of editing and juxtaposing historical documents to show how Pound built his version of Malatesta's Tempio, how he made *The Cantos* a similar monument.

2. The practice of editing, even rewriting, source material is not in itself wrong. As I argue in Chapter 4, Muriel Rukeyser edits at least as aggressively as Pound does, and I find that one of her work's strengths. My criticism of Pound's strategies in this chapter relates to the political motives and goals of his compositional strategies, not to the strategies themselves. For a strong discussion of Pound's drama of interpretation and its relationship to his politics, specifically to fascism, see Rainey, "'All I Want You to Do.'" Rainey argues that the "complex of hermeneutical motifs—experience, faith, action" that Pound develops in the Malatesta Cantos "was fundamental to Pound's understanding of literature and its social functions, and it furnished the framework in which he assimilated his emerging interest in fascism and Mussolini during the period 1925–1935" (88).

3. See Rainey's discussion of Pound's composition of this section in *Ezra Pound*, 37–50.

4. Pound announced the end of the Christian era and the beginning of the Pound era in the "Little Review Calendar," published in the magazine's spring 1922 issue. See also Pound's note to the calendar, published in the same issue.

5. See also Morgan, 160–63.

6. Later discussion of American anti-Semitic discourses makes clear that Pound here echoes the sentiments of isolationist anti-Semites, who blamed

a Jewish-Communist-British conspiracy for World War II and for dragging the United States into the hostilities.

7. *Ezra Pound's Poetry and Prose Contributions to Periodicals* is abbreviated *PP* throughout.

8. For a very thorough discussion of the composition of the Adams Cantos, including tables summarizing the precise distribution of the source material through the ten cantos, see Cantrell and Swinson, 82–83.

9. Only one of the ten cantos is included in the *Selected Cantos* that Pound himself edited in 1966, and it is reproduced as a one-and-a-half-page fragment (Canto 62). The whole set of cantos has received much less critical and scholarly attention than other parts of the poem. Books that treat the whole poem devote few pages to the Adams Cantos: George Dekker gives them four pages in *Sailing after Knowledge* (1963), while Clark Emery, in *Ideas into Action* (1958), gives them one. Even newer studies grant them scant space and attention. Robert Casillo mentions them only six times in *The Genealogy of Demons* (1988), half of these in notes. Studies of Pound's entire career, such as Hugh Kenner's *Pound Era* (1971), also give them short shrift. Albert Gelpi, in his long essay on Pound in *A Coherent Splendor* (1987), mentions only that the multivolume *Works* was one of Pound's many sources in the poem. Even books that are explicitly and predominantly concerned with Pound's relation to America and American history and culture often neglect the Adams Cantos. Wendy Stallard Flory's 1989 *American Ezra Pound* cites only one of the Adams Cantos (Canto 62) and refers to Adams himself only a few times.

10. The attention the Adams Cantos did receive throughout the first generation of Pound criticism was generally negative. Dekker admits difficulty harmonizing the Adams Cantos with the rest of the poem and concludes his short discussion of these cantos with the pronouncement that the set of cantos fails on every front (186). Daniel Pearlman, in his 1969 *Barb of Time,* discusses the Adams Cantos as "a continuation of the dynastic theme of the Chinese cantos," but he goes on to argue that Pound treats Adams "in excessive detail and at disproportionate length, so that after the Chinese cantos the Adams section figures as an anticlimactic bulge which even the relatively open form of the *Cantos* can ill assimilate" and that "the general failure of these cantos to achieve poetic intensity is hardly disputable" (232–33). Even Kenner, who also considers the Adams Cantos an extension and development of the dynastic theme of the Chinese Cantos in an American context, concludes that these cantos are decidedly "uncanorous" (432).

11. For a discussion of how the American Cantos (31–33, on Jefferson and Adams, and 37, drawn from Martin Van Buren's life) chart "Pound's voyage . . . [f]rom a dead president-philosophe to a live tyrant [Mussolini]," see Redman, "An Epic Is a Hypertext." Significantly, Redman finds in Canto 33 "evidence of a decisive change in sympathy and focus of thought," if not an outright conversion to fascism (124).

12. These cantos follow immediately upon Canto 41's nomination of Musso-

lini as a solution to the problems of government corruption treated in the preceding ten cantos; these three cantos (41–43), then, form a triptych demonstrating right action at the individual and institutional levels.

13. Cantrell and Swinson discuss the shift in Pound's American tradition from Jefferson to Adams (93–95), as do Carpenter (*Serious Character,* 572) and Dasenbrock (518).

14. Peter Nicholls discusses this passage in his *Ezra Pound: Politics, Economics, and Writing.*

15. On the deliberate imprecision of Pound's grammatical constructions, the ambiguity of his syntax, and the deliberate vagueness of his broadly suggestive appositions, see Goldensohn, 406.

16. "Stinkschuld," of course, is Pound's pseudonym for the Rothschild family.

17. See "Rothschild Arrested," *PP,* 7:327; "Usury," *PP,* 7:424; and "Anti-Semitism," *PP,* 6:56, for other examples.

18. This blaming of the Jews for their own oppression is remarkably similar to comments made by Father Coughlin. While Pound had read Coughlin, his attitude here is a frightening index of the commonality of such attitudes among Americans in the late 1930s.

19. Casillo argues further that the most important similarity between Pound's anti-Semitism and that of medieval European societies is "that both involve an essentially corporate concept of society," and he makes a convincing case for the theory that the anti-Semitism of fascism grew out of Fascist corporatism.

20. The *Protocols* were partially reprinted in Fry's *Waters Flowing Eastward,* and Casillo speculates that Pound had read this version of the forgery. For a history of the several manifestations of the *Protocols,* see Cohn, 65–76.

21. Ford's newspaper, the *Dearborn Independent,* ran a series of articles, republished as *The International Jew: The World's Foremost Problem,* which appeared immediately after the republication of the *Protocols.* Ford lent the prestige of his name to the effort to distribute the book (Cohn, 159–60).

22. For the names of more such publishers, see Singerman, *Antisemitic Propaganda.*

23. To read *The International Jew* on the influence of Jewish financiers on North American commercial practices and European wars is certainly quite like reading Pound on these subjects. In a 1936 article in the *British-Italian Bulletin,* Pound blames the nineteenth-century disruption of Europe on the Rothschild family, which had amassed its wealth during the American Revolution by providing Hessian mercenaries to the British. This denunciation reads as a paraphrase of a chapter in volume 4 of *The International Jew* entitled "The Jewish Associates of Benedict Arnold."

24. Like many of his contemporary anti-Semites (including Madison Grant and the compiler of *The International Jew*), Pelley denied that Jesus had been Jewish, claiming instead that he had descended from emigrant Gauls.

25. "Ezra Pound, Silvershirt," *New Masses,* March 17, 1936, 15–16.

26. "A Civilizing Force on the Move: The Bank Reform," *British-Italian Bulletin,*

May 23, 1936, 3. The country whose internal affairs Pound seeks to protect is Italy.

27. See also June 19, 1943 (*"Ezra Pound Speaking,"* 344–46) and June 29, 1943 (356–58).

CHAPTER FOUR

1. For other contemporary media treatments of events in Gauley Bridge, see "Silicosis," *Newsweek,* January 25, 1936, 33–34, and "Silicosis Village," *Nation,* February 5, 1936, 162. See also Marcantonio.

2. Most of this information can be gleaned from Rukeyser's *Book of the Dead* itself. I have corroborated Rukeyser's version of events by consulting Sub-committee of the Committee of Labor, *An Investigation Relating to Health Conditions of Workers Employed in the Construction and Maintenance of Public Utilities,* a report on hearings held to determine whether a full-scale investigation into the Gauley Bridge affair should be undertaken by agencies of the federal government. See also Cherniack.

3. For a full account of the investigation, see *Congressional Record,* 74th Congress, 2d sess., vol. 80, pt. 5, April 1–21, 1936, 4752–53.

4. F. Jack Hurley's *Portrait of a Decade* provides an introduction to photography's centrality in the documentary reportage of the depression. William Stott's *Documentary Expression and Thirties America* is still the best survey of radical reportage and social documentary techniques. Paula Rabinowitz, in *They Must Be Represented,* brings a heightened critical sophistication to the topic and more effectively contextualizes and reads the documentary projects that Stott describes. For a strong account of women's reportage that focuses on the work of Meridel LeSueur and Tillie Olsen, see Coiner.

5. Once a well-known poet, not only on the Left but in American letters more generally, Rukeyser won the Yale Younger Poets prize for her first book, *Theory of Flight,* and was generally highly regarded through the mid-1940s. After a hiatus from poetry, she rose again to prominence in the wake of feminist activism inside and outside the academy (though she resisted efforts to categorize her as a feminist). Typical of efforts to recover Rukeyser as a feminist is Rachel Blau DuPlessis's "Critique of Consciousness and Myth." With her inclusion in several important anthologies of American poetry and American literature in the last decade and with the publication of a "selected poems" volume (*Out of Silence,* edited by Kate Daniels) and *A Muriel Rukeyser Reader,* edited by Jan Heller Levi, Rukeyser's work has once again begun to receive the critical attention it deserves. Much of that attention has focused on her later career; for exemplary essays, see Rich and Ware.

Recent scholarship has brought renewed attention to Rukeyser's earlier work, especially *The Book of the Dead.* David Kadlec's "X-Ray Testimonials," for example, examines the racial politics of Rukeyser's handling of the congressional hearings, especially those involving African American tunnel worker George Robison. In a new collection of essays and poems in tribute to Rukeyser, *"How Shall We Tell Each Other of the Poet?,"* three readings of *The Book of the Dead* appear: John Lowney's "Truths of Outrage, Truths of Possibility," Stephanie Hartman's "All Systems Go," and Shoshana Wechsler's "Ma(t)ter of Fact and Vision." Robert Shulman writes on the sequence in his 2000 book, *The Power of Political Art.* Each of these intersects with my own discussion of Rukeyser. Lowney, for example, reads *The Book of the Dead* against the horizon of the Popular Front, while Wechsler reads it as a complement to Pound's Adams and Dynastic Cantos of the late 1930s. While any or all of these might have referred to my work on Rukeyser, either my essay "Documentary Modernism as Popular Front Poetic: Muriel Rukeyser's *Book of the Dead,"* *Modern Language Quarterly* 60 (1999): 59–84, or my 1995 University of Illinois dissertation, none do. The important thing to which all of these essays, along with my own work, testify is a moment of scholarly convergence upon Rukeyser's vitally important poem sequence, a convergence Rukeyser's admirers, among whom I count myself, can only welcome.

6. According to Rukeyser's journal and letters, Naumberg was also present at meetings of the John Reed Club and the International Labor Defense that Rukeyser attended between 1932 and 1936 (Rukeyser Papers).

7. My analysis, then, diverges from Kate Daniels's reading of *The Book of the Dead* and Rukeyser's other 1930s poetry. Writing that Rukeyser "knowingly flung herself headfirst into the literary quarrels of the 1930s by publishing . . . poems that were simultaneously tied to the apolitical and highly aesthetic tradition of high modernism and to a self-conscious left-wing political identity derived from Marxist theory," Daniels argues that Rukeyser was consciously attempting to provoke her critics (250). On Rukeyser's reception and the difficulties posed by her hard-to-categorize work for critics both in the 1930s and now, see Flynn.

8. Morton Dauwen Zabel (in *Southern Review*) and Willard Maas (in *Poetry*) fault Rukeyser for abandoning what Zabel calls "personal intensity of pathos" (600) and what Maas simply calls lyricism and for the sequence's accumulation of journalistic detail.

9. David Wolff was the pseudonym of Communist writer Ben Maddow.

10. Wheelwright's review seems a retort to ideas Rukeyser initially advanced in her *New Masses* review of Wheelwright's *Rock and Shell;* there, Rukeyser had argued that writers like Wheelwright, whose work was attacked as "eccentric" and "confusing," were "laying a base of literary activity and revolutionary creation which must be realized as one of the important fronts of the growing cultural movement" ("With Leftward Glances," 28).

11. Of course, the photographs do not really "speak for themselves." While Margaret Bourke-White argued that photography was more effective because it was more mechanical than writing ("The shutter opens and closes and the only rays that come in to be registered come directly from the object in front"), her practice demonstrated her awareness of photographs' posed and constructed representation. See, for example, her recollection of an episode

that occurred in the home of a black woman while she was working on *You Have Seen Their Faces* (*Portrait*, 126–27). Some photographers, like Walker Evans and Ben Shahn, were fully aware that it was photography's *appearance* of objectivity, not an elusive real objectivity, that made it so effective for political purposes. See Stott, 32, and Hurley, 46–50.

12. Often, the documentary gives the impressions only of its subjects, with the reporter remaining in the background (except, of course, as editor of the subjects' testimony). Perhaps the best examples of this are two books produced by the Federal Writers' Project: *These Are Our Lives* and *Lay My Burden Down*. But the material even in such oral histories is shaped in support of a polemical agenda.

13. Agee and Evans evince a critical stance toward *You Have Seen Their Faces,* most biting in their inclusion of an article about Bourke-White in the book's appendix but also in their separation of text and pictures and their strenuous attempts to avoid Caldwell's and Bourke-White's sentimental representations. For a reading of *Let Us Now Praise Famous Men* against Caldwell and Bourke-White, see Rabinowitz, *They Must Be Represented,* chaps. 2, 3. I would argue that Rukeyser participates in the same attempt at revising documentary that Agee and Evans undertake.

14. Rukeyser's emphasis on the visual, on the eye and camera, is a hallmark of her work from very early on. In her diary for 1931, just as Rukeyser begins the poems later included in *Theory of Flight,* she writes a suggestion for a story: "Chronicle of the day of my eye—story, expecting man, coarser—sensitivity to visual impressions" (Rukeyser Papers).

15. For a strong discussion of Popular Front policies in general, see Ottanelli, 83–106. Denning provides a thorough discussion of the Popular Front (4–21) and, most interesting, characterizes it as what Raymond Williams calls a "structure of feeling." "To see the Popular Front as a structure of feeling," he writes, "is thus to see it as a political and cultural charter for a generation" (26).

16. For an encyclopedic discussion of the "cultural front" that accompanied the Popular Front (or, according to the book's most compelling argument, preceded and partially enabled it), see Denning.

17. Rukeyser Papers.

18. A copy of the file is in ibid.

19. It should be admitted, such critics as Jane Tompkins observe, that "sentimentality" is often the charge leveled at women who attempt critical cultural work (Tompkins, xi–xix; see also ibid., chap. 5). Indeed, this is the charge leveled at Rukeyser by John Wheelwright in his review of *U.S. 1* and by Philip Rahv and William Phillips in their savage treatment of Rukeyser in the early 1940s. See Matthiessen, 217–18, and Kertesz, 175–77, for discussions of the "Rukeyser imbroglio," which began with the anonymous (though probably written by Delmore Schwartz) "Grandeur and Misery of a Poster Girl." Matthiessen's note to Rukeyser about the *Partisan Review* flap is in the

Rukeyser Papers. See also Daniels. We should, therefore, recall, as Tompkins and Rabinowitz (*They Must Be Represented*) do, the enormous and politically useful affective power of the "sentimental" and the fact that many of the social problems addressed by writers like Harriet Beecher Stowe and photographers like Margaret Bourke-White might go unnoticed without their critical attention and their efforts to draw more politically advantaged readers' attention to them.

20. For comparison, choose almost at random a Caldwell caption: "Snuff is an almighty help when your teeth ache"; "I suppose there is plenty to eat somewhere if you can find it; the cat always does"; "Sometimes I tell my husband we couldn't be worse off if we tried" (Caldwell and Bourke-White, *You Have Seen Their Faces*). A salient difference is that Caldwell tends not to set the "speech" of whites in dialect; the captions for photographs of white tenant farmers typically use standard English. Black "speech," though, is almost always rendered in dialect. Content differs by race as well, with whites expressing stoicism or dignified resignation and blacks setting themselves up as the objects of irony.

21. The African American worker's name, as recorded in the report of the congressional hearings and other documents, was in fact George Robison. Rukeyser gives his name as Robinson in the poem. Since my discussion focuses on the figure in the poem rather than the biographical Robison, I will use Rukeyser's spelling.

22. For an elementary discussion of blues forms and changes wrought on the forms in various venues (vaudeville, records, etc.), see Titon. For strong discussions of blues forms and their broad cultural influence, see Russell and Oakley. On blues as an African American poetic form, see Henderson.

23. Rukeyser Papers.

24. For a discussion of the documentary's inherent voyeurism and its relationship to class-marked subjectivity, see Rabinowitz, *They Must Be Represented,* esp. chap. 3.

25. Rukeyser, *U.S. 1,* 146. The note situates *The Book of the Dead* within a broader project that is "to be a summary poem of the life of the Atlantic coast of this country, nourished by the communications which run down it" (146). It also foregrounds the documentary nature of the sequence when Rukeyser acknowledges the congressional sources on which she drew and the contributions of Congressman Glenn Griswold of Indiana, Nancy Naumberg, and Philippa Allen, "who made the poem possible" (147).

26. Hugh Kenner argues that the "luminous detail" is a key compositional feature for Pound. Luminous details are "the transcendentals in an array of facts" and are "'patterned integrities' which transferred out of their context of origin retain their power to enlighten us" (*Pound Era,* 152, 153). The luminous detail provides "a sudden insight into circumjacent conditions and their causes, their effects, their sequence, and law" (Pound quoted in ibid., 152).

27. See my discussion of Pound's incorporation of historical documents in Chapter 3.

28. Pitts's essay, "Women and Communism," originally appeared in the *New Masses* and Inman's "Manufacturing Femininity" appeared in *People's World*. Both are reprinted in *Writing Red: An Anthology of American Women Writers, 1930–1940,* edited by Charlotte Nekola and Paula Rabinowitz.

29. Recent historical work on the American Left during the 1930s has complicated this picture, discovering or recovering women's groups and institutions inside and outside the Communist Party. Denning surveys some of this work (136–51), concentrating especially on the rearticulation of the discourses of fashion among women on the Left. See also Faue and Gabin. It is increasingly clear that left-wing feminism during the 1930s manifested itself in a variety of sites and styles; what remains unclear is whether Rukeyser participated in any of this. Her work throughout the decade was conducted through and focused on the central, largely male-run and masculinist institutions and aims of the Left, and there is no biographical evidence that she held feminist attitudes or was involved in any of the avenues open to feminism on the Left.

30. Here, Rukeyser follows Naumberg's advice to "stress the relief situation, the inadequacy of it, how far they have to go to get it" (Naumberg to Rukeyser, April 6, [1936/37], Rukeyser Papers).

31. See, for example, the photographs in Caldwell and Bourke-White, *You Have Seen Their Faces,* 56–73, and Dorothea Lange's now-famous photograph of Florence Thompson, "Migrant Mother." See Denning's discussion of that photograph as emblematic of the Popular Front's "gender unconscious" (137–38).

32. Louise Kertesz and M. L. Rosenthal both read these lines in mythic terms as well. Kertesz writes that the interruption of the monologue by the rhythmic lines connects Mrs. Jones's maternal strength "with the universal power of regeneration" (102) and Rosenthal that "the mother's determination to make her youngest child's death count for something, to have him live again in her own work of struggle for a better life, is linked with the rebirth motif of the great religions" (217). Robert Shulman specifies the mythic allusion; he points to Spell 30B in the *Egyptian Book of the Dead,* in which "[t]he heart of the dead man is weighed in the scales of the balance against the feather of righteousness" (205; *Ancient Egyptian Book of the Dead,* 27). Shulman is certainly correct when he finds Rukeyser echoing the Egyptian spells and is especially illuminating when he reads Rukeyser's "*My heart   my mother my heart   my mother*" alongside Spell 30B's "O my heart which I had from my mother!" (27). He overstates the case, however, when he suggests that Rukeyser quotes the Egyptian spells in the sets of italicized lines throughout "Absalom" (206–7). While the lines' incantatory rhythm and repetition formally allude to the Egyptian text (and to numerous other ritual texts, including those of the Judeo-Christian tradition indicated by the poem's title), they do not directly quote the spells toward which Shulman directs

readers in his note. The lines also echo the lament of David at Absalom's death in 2 Samuel 18–19 and many passages in the Psalms.

33. My reading of Eliot's opening as the voice of the buried dead is influenced by Michael Levenson's in *Genealogy of Modernism,* 168–70.

34. Rosenthal, writing in 1953, finds in this figure a pivotal moment in the poem, calling it "one of the strongest images of perverted industrial mastery of nature in American poetry" (218).

35. Rukeyser here seems to share Naumberg's view of the tunnel. In an April 6, [1936/37], letter, Naumberg urges her to "show how the tunnel itself is a splendid thing to look at, but a terrible thing to contemplate" (Rukeyser Papers).

36. This is a mode recognized as important by some of Rukeyser's earliest readers. Isabel Cerney, for example, writes in a 1937 letter to Rukeyser:

> And, oh, after the enforced proletarianitis of poets trying to be people, I have been so grateful for your consistent dialectical fusion of opposites, your awareness of contrasted values, of more than one possibility for everything. There is no bravado in your lines, no posturing, no dogmatic refusal of opposites. You see that as well as tools to the body there must be mind to the bright mind that leaps in necessity. (ibid.)

37. On Gold's *Life of John Brown,* see Maxwell, 104–5. Denning writes that Brown epitomizes the Popular Front's "pan-ethnic Americanism" (131) and adduces not only Gold's book but also W. E. B. Du Bois's 1935 biography and Jacob Lawrence's series of paintings (499).

38. Warren's treatment of Brown is much more historically accurate than any of the other treatments, though its southern authorship and fairly conservative politics are readily apparent throughout. Gold's political use of Brown is also transparent, and he is willing to bend the facts a bit more than Warren (a willingness shared, of course, by Benét's tremendously flexible poetic license). Rukeyser's poem resembles Benét's in various ways. Both open with an invocation that situates their subjects in the history of the nation, both approach a set of events from multiple perspectives and through multiple speakers, both attempt to differentiate speakers through manipulation of poetic meter and other aspects of form, and both use historical documents in the construction of their accounts. Sympathies between Benét's project and poetics and Rukeyser's are suggested by Benét's selection of Rukeyser's *Theory of Flight* for the Yale Younger Poets series and by the introduction he wrote for that volume.

39. *The Soul and Body of John Brown* was published privately as a pamphlet, with etchings by Rudolph C. von Ripper (1940). A manuscript of the poem without the etchings is included in the Rukeyser Papers, and it is from that manuscript that I quote.

40. Richard Gray finds Whitmanic resonances in Rukeyser's earlier poetry but does not mention "The Book of the Dead" (199–202). While the poems of *Theory of Flight* certainly draw on the mysticism Gray attributes to Whit-

man, Rukeyser is more powerfully influenced by the political implications of Whitman's democratic vistas and of his tropes of resurrection and dispersal in "The Book of the Dead."

CONCLUSION

1. David Suchoff draws a similar conclusion: "The use of the death penalty to extract cooperation and information . . . defined the Rosenberg case as a spectacle of defeated revolt, manipulated for coercion to serve the purposes of the state" (158).
2. Perhaps even more than in the case of Sacco and Vanzetti, the historical jury remains out on the guilt or innocence of the Rosenbergs. Information released during the last several years, especially transcriptions of the so-called Venona cables, seems to support the case against Julius Rosenberg. The case against Ethel Rosenberg is much less convincing. That question, though, is not really germane to my discussion. For American writers and others on the Left during the late 1940s and 1950s, the case was as galvanizing and vital as was the Sacco and Vanzetti execution a generation earlier. It is the writers' responses, regardless of the Rosenbergs' guilt or innocence, that I focus on. For sophisticated treatments of the Rosenbergs' cultural significance, see Garber and Walkowitz.
3. Most of these writers published their works in magazines like *Masses and Mainstream,* in which an editorial about Pound's Bollingen Prize appeared in April 1949. The editorial's logic differs dramatically from that of the Bollingen committee or its supporters, like Archibald MacLeish:

> The case of Ezra Pound shows how far advanced is the moral and intellectual rot of capitalism. The $1000 purse for Pound was furnished by the grateful kin of Andrew W. Mellon, the aluminum monopolist, who served as Secretary of the Treasury for Harding, Coolidge, and Hoover. In the bi-partisan spirit, it was a Truman-appointed Librarian of Congress who chose the jury of poets to judge the "highest achievement of American poetry" in 1948. To make sure this slap in the face of the American people should really hurt, the Library of Congress emphasized that this was the first time the government-sponsored award has been made. In St. Elizabeth's Hospital for the mentally ill, Pound must have for the first time suspected his sanity when he was paid off in dollars instead of lire. (Sillen, 3)

4. See Charles Altieri's *Enlarging the Temple,* in which Altieri's focus on formal revolutions and rebellions limits his exploration of "the project of postmodern poets to invent a coherent philosophical poetics able to stand as an alternative to the high modernism of Yeats and Eliot" (16). Altieri presents a revolution solely of the word, a narrative of 1960s poetry whose terms are entirely poetic:

In 1962 it seemed tremendously important to rebel against an aesthetic of impersonality that required poets to use overtly mythical or meditative themes and subjects and to develop these themes in complex linguistic and formal patterns. Then it was revolutionary to present an intensely personal voice dealing with topic and topological materials in forms that approximated direct statement before exploding into moderately surreal images. (15)

More politically attuned readings of postwar poetry include Cary Nelson's *Our Last First Poets,* which sees the turn to open forms by major American poets (Theodore Roethke, Adrienne Rich, W. S. Merwin, Robert Duncan, Galway Kinnell) as itself a *political* turn, a response to the American political scene of the 1960s; Paul Breslin's *Psycho-Political Muse,* which focuses on the representation of political pressures through the fabrication of poetically rendered psychologies; and Robert von Hallberg's *American Poetry and Culture.*

5. I treat the progression of Lowell's poetics through these volumes in "Robert Lowell's Monumental Vision," *American Literary History* 12 (Spring 2000): 79–112. For a sophisticated and persuasive discussion of Lowell's management of his position as Great American Poet vis-à-vis politics, see James Sullivan, *On the Walls,* chap. 3. On Lowell and politics, see von Hallberg and Paul Breslin.

6. McGrath wrote the foreword to Rolfe's posthumously published *Permit Me Refuge.* "De Poetica," a poem McGrath dedicates to Rolfe, makes their commonalities clearer still. McGrath points out the poet's duties, the mission he and Rolfe share, and alludes to Rolfe's own best-known poem, "First Love," to express solidarity and a sense of shared poetics and politics:

[Poets] know that history, a lackwit king,
Blows books past buoys and scatters all the boats,
While drowned in bays of law and literature
A sea-change sinks a sonnet like a stone—
It is that windy beast we must enchain,

Or summoned by the blood of the implacable past
Like ghosts we slake our memory on its fumes.
(111–12)

7. See, for example, Rich's *Will to Change* (1971) and *Dream of a Common Language* (1977); Harper's *Dear John, Dear Coltrane* (1971) and *Debridement* (1973); Howe's *Defenstration of Prague* (1983) and *Articulation of Sound Forms in Time* (1987); and Forché's *Angel of History* (1994).

WORKS CITED

Aaron, Daniel. *Writers on the Left: Episodes in American Literary Communism.* New York: Oxford University Press, 1961.

Agee, James, and Walker Evans. *Let Us Now Praise Famous Men.* 1941. Reprint, Boston: Houghton Mifflin, 1980.

Alpert, Michael. *A New International History of the Spanish Civil War.* London: MacMillan, 1994.

Altieri, Charles. *Enlarging the Temple: New Directions in American Poetry during the 1960s.* Lewisburg, Pa.: Associated University Press, 1979.

The Ancient Egyptian Book of the Dead. Translated by Raymond O. Faulkner; edited by Carol Andrews. Austin: University of Texas Press, 1993.

Anderson, Benedict. *Imagined Communities: Reflections on the Origin and Spread of Nationalism.* London: Verso, 1983.

Auden, W. H. *Collected Poems.* Edited by Edward Mendelson. New York: Vintage, 1976.

Barrett, William. "Comment: A Prize for Ezra Pound." *Partisan Review* 16 (April 1949): 344–47.

Benét, Stephen Vincent. *John Brown's Body.* 1927. Reprint, New York: Holt, Rinehart and Winston, 1968.

Benét, William Rose. Review of *U.S. 1. Saturday Review,* April 30, 1938, 16.

Bernstein, Irving. *The Lean Years.* Boston: Houghton Mifflin, 1960.

Bernstein, Michael. *The Tale of the Tribe: Ezra Pound and the Modern Verse Epic.* Princeton: Princeton University Press, 1980.

Berry, Faith. *Langston Hughes: Before and Beyond Harlem.* 1983. Reprint, New York: Citadel, 1992.

Bérubé, Michael. *The Employment of English: Theory, Jobs, and the Future of Literary Studies.* New York: New York University Press, 1998.

―――. *Marginal Forces/Cultural Centers: Tolson, Pynchon, and the Politics of the Canon.* Ithaca: Cornell University Press, 1992.

Bessie, Alvah, ed. *Heart of Spain.* New York: Veterans of the Abraham Lincoln Brigade, 1952.

Blast. 1914. Reprint, Santa Rosa, Calif.: Black Sparrow, 1992.

Booth, Wayne. *The Company We Keep: An Ethics of Fiction.* Berkeley: University of California Press, 1988.

Bourke-White, Margaret. *Portrait of Myself.* New York: Simon and Schuster, 1963.

Boyle, Kay. *Collected Poems of Kay Boyle.* Port Townsend, Wash.: Copper Canyon Press, 1991.

Brandreth, J. "Epitaph." *Masses and Mainstream* 6 (August 1953): 32–33.

Brenkman, John. *Culture and Domination.* Ithaca: Cornell University Press, 1987.

Breslin, James E. B. *From Modern to Contemporary: American Poetry, 1945–1965.* Chicago: University of Chicago Press, 1984.

Breslin, Paul. *The Psycho-Political Muse: American Poetry since the Fifties.* Chicago: University of Chicago Press, 1987.

Brome, Vincent. *The International Brigades: Spain, 1936–1937.* London: Heinemann, 1965.

Brooks, Cleanth. *Modern Poetry and the Tradition.* Chapel Hill: University of North Carolina Press, 1939.

Buckingham, Peter H. *America Sees Red: Anticommunism in America, 1870s to 1980s: A Guide to Issues and References.* Claremont, Calif.: Regina, 1988.

Buhle, Mari Jo, Paul Buhle, and Dan Georgakas, eds. *The Encyclopedia of the American Left.* Urbana: University of Illinois Press, 1992.

Buni, Andrew. *Robert L. Vann of the "Pittsburgh Courier."* Pittsburgh: University of Pittsburgh Press, 1974.

Bush, Ronald. "Modernism, Fascism, and the Composition of Ezra Pound's *Pisan Cantos.*" *Modernism/Modernity* 2 (September 1995): 69–88.

Buttigieg, Joseph. "The Exemplary Worldliness of Antonio Gramsci's Literary Criticism." *Boundary 2* 11 (Fall-Winter 1982–83): 21–41.

Buttitta, Anthony. "A Note on *Contempo* and Langston Hughes." In *Negro,* edited by Nancy Cunard, 141. London: Cunard, 1934.

Cain, William E. *The Crisis in Criticism: Theory, Literature, and Reform in English Studies.* Baltimore: Johns Hopkins University Press, 1984.

Caldwell, Erskine, and Margaret Bourke-White. *You Have Seen Their Faces.* New York: Modern Age, 1937.

Cannistraro, Philip V., ed. *Historical Dictionary of Fascist Italy.* Westport, Conn.: Greenwood Press, 1982.

Cantrell, Carol H., and Ward Swinson. "Cantos LII–LXXI: Pound's Textbook for Princes." *Paideuma* 18 (Spring and Fall 1989): 67–128.

Carby, Hazel. "It Jus Be's Dat Way Sometime: The Sexual Politics of Women's Blues." In *Unequal Sisters: A Multicultural Reader in U.S. Women's History,* edited by Ellen DuBois and Vicki Ruiz, 8–22. New York: Routledge, 1990.

Carpenter, Humphrey. *A Serious Character: The Life of Ezra Pound.* Boston: Houghton Mifflin, 1988.

———. *W. H. Auden: A Biography.* Boston: Houghton Mifflin, 1981.

Carroll, Peter. *The Odyssey of the Abraham Lincoln Brigade: Americans in the Spanish Civil War.* Palo Alto: Stanford University Press, 1994.

Carter, Dan T. *Scottsboro: A Tragedy of the American South.* Baton Rouge: Louisiana State University Press, 1979.

Carter, John B. "American Reactions to Italian Fascism, 1919–1933." Ph.D. dissertation, Columbia University, 1953.

Casillo, Robert. *The Genealogy of Demons: Anti-Semitism, Fascism, and the Myths of Ezra Pound.* Evanston: Northwestern University Press, 1988.

Caute, David. *The Great Fear: The Anti-Communist Purge under Truman and Eisenhower.* New York: Simon and Schuster, 1978.

Chandler, James K. *Wordsworth's Second Nature: A Study of the Poetry and the Politics.* Chicago: University of Chicago Press, 1984.

Cherniack, Martin. *The Hawk's Nest Incident: America's Worst Industrial Disaster.* New Haven: Yale University Press, 1986.

Cincinnatus [pseud.]. *Veritas Vincit: War! War! War!* N.p., 1940.

Clark, Suzanne. *Sentimental Modernism: Women Writers and the Revolution of the Word.* Bloomington: Indiana University Press, 1991.

Cohn, Norman. *Warrant for Genocide: The Myth of the Jewish World Conspiracy and the Protocols of the Elders of Zion.* New York: Harper and Row, 1967.

Coiner, Constance. *Better Red: The Radical Writing of Tillie Olsen and Meridel LeSueur.* New York: Oxford University Press, 1995.

Collier, Peter. "The Poetry of Protest: Auden, Aragon, and Eluard." In *Visions and Blueprints: Avant-garde Culture and Radical Politics in Early Twentieth-Century Europe,* edited by Edward Timms and Peter Collier, 137–58. New York: Manchester University Press, 1988.

Congressional Record. 74th Congress, 2d sess., vol. 80, pt. 5, April 1–21, 1936.

Coughlin, Charles. *"Am I an Anti-Semite?"* Royal Oak, Mich.: Author, 1939.

Coyle, Michael. "The Implications of Inclusion: Historical Narrative in Pound's Canto LXXXVIII." *English Literary History* 54 (Spring 1987): 215–30.

Cullen, Countee. "Poet on Poet." *Opportunity* 4 (February 1926): 73.

Cunard, Nancy. "Scottsboro and Other Scottsboros." In *Negro,* edited by Nancy Cunard, 245–68. London: Cunard, 1934.

Cunningham, George. "Langston Hughes: A Biographical Study of the Harlem Renaissance Years, 1902–1932." Ph.D. diss., Yale University, 1983.

Dallek, Robert. *Franklin D. Roosevelt and American Foreign Policy, 1932–1945.* New York: Oxford University Press, 1979.

Daniels, Kate. "Muriel Rukeyser and Her Literary Critics." In *Gendered Modernisms: American Women Poets and Their Readers,* edited by Margaret Dickie and Thomas Travisano, 247–63. Philadelphia: University of Pennsylvania Press, 1996.

Dasenbrock, Reed Way. "Jefferson and/or Adams: A Shifting Mirror for Mussolini in the Middle Cantos." *English Literary History* 55 (Summer 1988): 505–26.

D'Attilio, Robert. "The Sacco-Vanzetti Case." In *Encyclopedia of the American Left,* edited by Mari Jo Buhle, Paul Buhle, and Dan Georgakas, 667–70. Urbana: University of Illinois Press, 1992.

Davidson, Michael. *Ghostlier Demarcations: Modern Poetry and the Material Word.* Berkeley: University of California Press, 1997.

Dekker, George. *Sailing after Knowledge: "The Cantos."* London: Routledge, 1963.

Delaney, Robert. *John Brown's Song: A Choral Poem for Mixed Voices and Orchestra*. Boston: Schirmer, 1932.

Denning, Michael. *The Cultural Front: The Laboring of American Culture in the Twentieth Century*. New York: Verso, 1997.

Diggins, John P. *Mussolini and Fascism: The View from America*. Princeton: Princeton University Press, 1972.

Dos Passos, John. *The Major Nonfictional Prose*. Edited by Donald Pizer. Detroit: Wayne State University Press, 1988.

Du Bois, W. E. B. "The Rosenbergs." *Masses and Mainstream* 6 (July 1953): 10–12.

DuPlessis, Rachel Blau. "The Critique of Consciousness and Myth in Levertov, Rich, and Rukeyser." *Feminist Studies* 3 (1975): 199–221.

Eagleton, Terry. *Ideology*. London: Verso, 1991.

———. *The Ideology of the Aesthetic*. Oxford: Blackwell, 1990.

Easthope, Antony. *Poetry as Discourse*. London: Methuen, 1983.

Eastman, Max. "Sacco and Vanzetti: Anarchists and the Revolutionary Science." *New Masses* 3 (October 1927): 4–6.

Eliot, T. S. *Collected Poems, 1909–1962*. New York: Harcourt, 1970.

———. "Tradition and the Individual Talent." In *The Sacred Wood: Essays on Poetry and Criticism*, 47–59. 1920. Reprint, London: Methuen, 1950.

———. *The Waste Land*. New York: Boni and Liveright, 1922.

———. *The Waste Land*. London: Hogarth, 1923.

Emery, Clark. *Ideas into Action: A Study of Pound's "Cantos."* Miami: University of Miami Press, 1958.

Faue, Elizabeth. *Community of Suffering and Struggle: Women, Men, and the Labor Movement in Minneapolis, 1915–1945*. Chapel Hill: University of North Carolina Press, 1991.

Fearing, Kenneth. *Poems*. New York: Dynamo, 1935.

Federal Writers' Project. *These Are Our Lives*. Chapel Hill: University of North Carolina Press, 1939.

———. *U.S. One: Maine to Florida*. New York: Modern Age, 1938.

Fekete, John. *The Critical Twilight: Explorations in the Ideology of Anglo-American Literary Theory from Eliot to McLuhan*. Boston: Routledge and Kegan Paul, 1977.

Flory, Wendy Stallard. *The American Ezra Pound*. New Haven: Yale University Press, 1989.

Flynn, Richard. "'The Buried Life and the Body of Waking': Muriel Rukeyser and the Politics of Literary History." In *Gendered Modernisms: American Women Poets and Their Readers*, edited by Margaret Dickie and Thomas Travisano, 264–79. Philadelphia: University of Pennsylvania Press, 1996.

Ford, Karen Jackson. "Do Right to Write Right: Langston Hughes' Aesthetics of Simplicity." *Twentieth-Century Literature* 38 (Winter 1992): 436–56.

———. "Making Poetry Pay: The Commodification of Langston Hughes." In *Marketing Modernisms: Self-Promotion, Canonization, Rereading*, edited by

Kevin J. H. Dettmar and Stephen Watt, 275–96. Ann Arbor: University of Michigan Press, 1996.

Fowler, Roger. *Literature as Social Discourse.* Bloomington: Indiana University Press, 1981.

Fox, Pamela. *Class Fictions: Shame and Resistance in the British Working-Class Novel, 1890–1945.* Durham: Duke University Press, 1994.

Fraser, Ronald. *Blood of Spain: An Oral History of the Spanish Civil War.* New York: Pantheon, 1979.

Freeman, Joseph. *Daily Worker,* November 20, 1933, 5.

Funaroff, Sol. *Exile from a Future Time.* New York: Dynamo, 1943.

Furey, Hester Leone. "'Raising the Specter': Poems and Songs of the American Radical Left, 1880–1920." Ph.D. diss., University of Illinois, 1992.

Gabin, Nancy F. *Feminism in the Labor Movement: Women and the United Auto Workers, 1935–1975.* Ithaca: Cornell University Press, 1990.

Garber, Marjorie, and Rebecca L. Walkowitz, eds. *Secret Agents: The Rosenberg Case, McCarthyism, and Fifties America.* New York: Routledge, 1995.

Gates, Henry Louis, Jr. *The Signifying Monkey: A Theory of African-American Literary Criticism.* New York: Oxford University Press, 1988.

Gelpi, Albert. *A Coherent Splendor.* New York: Cambridge University Press, 1987.

Gilbert, Roger. *Walks in the World: Representation and Experience in Modern American Poetry.* Princeton: Princeton University Press, 1991.

Gilbert, Sandra, and Susan Gubar. *Sexchanges.* Vol. 2 of *No Man's Land: The Place of the Woman Writer in the Twentieth Century.* New Haven: Yale University Press, 1989.

———. *The War of the Words.* Vol. 1 of *No Man's Land: The Place of the Woman Writer in the Twentieth Century.* New Haven: Yale University Press, 1988.

Ginsberg, Allen. *Collected Poems, 1947–1980.* New York: Harper and Row, 1984.

Gold, Michael. *Daily Worker,* September 30, 1933, 7.

———. *Daily Worker,* December 29, 1933, 5.

———. "Let It Be Really New." *New Masses* 2 (June 1926): 20, 26.

———. *The Life of John Brown.* 1923. Reprint, New York: Roving Eye Press, 1960.

Goldensohn, Barry. "Pound and Antisemitism." *Yale Review* 75 (Spring 1986): 398–421.

Graff, Gerald. *Poetic Statement and Critical Dogma.* Evanston: Northwestern University Press, 1970.

———. *Professing Literature: An Institutional History.* Chicago: University of Chicago Press, 1987.

Graham, Maryemma. "The Practice of a Social Art." In *Langston Hughes: Critical Perspectives Past and Present,* edited by Henry Louis Gates and K. A. Appiah, 213–36. New York: Amistad, 1993.

Gramsci, Antonio. *Selections from the Prison Notebooks.* Translated and edited by Quintin Hoare and Geoffrey Nowell Smith. New York: International, 1971.

"Grandeur and Misery of a Poster Girl." *Partisan Review* 10 (September 1943): 471–73.

Grant, Madison. *Conquest of a Continent.* New York: Scribner's, 1933.

Gray, Richard. *American Poetry of the Twentieth Century.* New York: Longman, 1990.

Grob, Alan. "Wordsworth and the Politics of Consciousness." In *Critical Essays on William Wordsworth,* edited by George H. Gilpin, 339–56. Boston: G. K. Hall, 1990.

Grossberg, Lawrence. *We Gotta Get Out of This Place: Popular Conservatism and Postmodern Culture.* New York: Routledge, 1992.

Guttmann, Allen. "The Brief Embattled Course of Proletarian Poetry." In *Proletarian Writers of the Thirties,* edited by David Madden, 252–69. Carbondale: Southern Illinois University Press, 1968.

Hall, Stuart. "On Postmodernism and Articulation: An Interview with Stuart Hall." Edited by Lawrence Grossberg. *Journal of Communication Inquiry* 10, no. 2 (1986): 45–60.

———. "Signification, Representation, Ideology: Althusser and the Post-Structuralist Debates." *Critical Studies in Mass Communications* 2 (1985): 91–114.

Hall, Stuart, Bob Lumley, and Gregor McLennan. "Politics and Ideology." In *On Ideology,* Working Papers in Cultural Studies, no. 10, 45–76. London: Hutchinson, 1978.

Hamilton, Ian. *Robert Lowell.* New York: Random House, 1982.

Hartman, Stephanie. "All Systems Go: Muriel Rukeyser's 'The Book of the Dead' and the Reinvention of Modernist Poetics." In *"How Shall We Tell Each Other of the Poet?": The Life and Writing of Muriel Rukeyser,* edited by Anne F. Herzog and Janet E. Kaufman, 209–23. New York: St. Martin's Press, 1999.

Heale, M. J. *American Anticommunism: Combating the Enemy Within, 1830–1970.* Baltimore: Johns Hopkins University Press, 1990.

Heaney, Marie. *Over Nine Waves: A Book of Irish Legends.* London: Faber, 1994.

Henderson, Stephen E. "The Blues as Black Poetry." *Callaloo* 5 (October 1982): 22–30.

Hitchcock, Peter. *Dialogics of the Oppressed.* Minneapolis: University of Minnesota Press, 1993.

Homberger, Eric. "Communists and Objectivists." In *The Objectivist Nexus,* edited by Rachel Blau DuPlessis and Peter Middleton, 107–26. Tuscaloosa: University of Alabama Press, 1999.

Hughes, Langston. "Air Raid: Barcelona." *Esquire* 34 (October 1938): 40.

———. *The Big Sea.* 1940. Reprint, New York: Hill and Wang, 1963.

———. "Cowards from the Colleges." *Crisis* 41 (1934): 227.

———. *Good Morning, Revolution: Uncollected Writings of Langston Hughes.* Edited by Faith Berry. New York: Citadel, 1991.

———. "Hughes Bombed in Spain." *Baltimore Afro-American,* October 23, 1937, 1–3.

————. "Hughes Finds Moors Being Used as Pawns by Fascists in Spain." *Baltimore Afro-American,* October 30, 1937, 1–3.

————. *I Wonder as I Wander.* 1956. Reprint, New York: Hill and Wang, 1964.

————. "Laughter in Madrid." *Nation,* January 29, 1938. Reprinted in *Good Morning Revolution: Uncollected Writings of Langston Hughes,* edited by Faith Berry, 119–22. New York: Citadel, 1991.

————. "A Letter from Spain Addressed to Alabama." *Volunteer for Liberty,* November 15, 1937, 3.

————. "Madrid's Flowers Hoist Blooms to Meet Raining Fascist Bombs." *Baltimore Afro-American,* November 27, 1937, 1–3.

————. "My Adventures as a Social Poet." *Phylon* (Fall 1947). Reprinted in *Good Morning, Revolution: Uncollected Writings of Langston Hughes,* edited by Faith Berry, 150–57. New York: Citadel, 1991.

————. "The Negro Artist and the Racial Mountain." *Nation,* June 23, 1926. Reprinted in *The Black Aesthetic,* edited by Addison Gayle, 176–80. New York: Doubleday, 1971.

————. "Negroes in Spain." *Volunteer for Liberty,* September 13, 1937, 4.

————. *A New Song.* New York: International, 1938.

————. "Scottsboro." *Opportunity* 9 (December 1931): 379.

————. "Scottsboro Limited." *New Masses* 7 (November 1931): 18–21.

————. *Scottsboro Limited.* New York: Golden Stair, 1932.

————. "Southern Gentlemen, White Prostitutes, Mill-Owners, and Negroes." *Contempo,* December 1, 1931, 1.

————. "To Negro Writers." In *American Writers' Congress,* edited by Henry Hart, 139–41. New York: International, 1935.

————. "Too Much of Race." *Volunteer for Liberty,* August 23, 1937, 3–4.

Hurley, F. Jack. *Portrait of a Decade: Roy Stryker and the Development of Documentary Photography in the Thirties.* Baton Rouge: Louisiana State University Press, 1972.

Hynes, Samuel. *The Auden Generation: Literature and Politics in England in the 1930s.* Princeton: Princeton University Press, 1972.

I.W.W. Songs. 1923. Reprint, Chicago: Charles H. Kerr, 1989.

Jackson, Gabriel. *The Spanish Republic and the Spanish Civil War, 1931–1939.* Princeton: Princeton University Press, 1965.

Jameson, Fredric. *The Political Unconscious: Narrative as Socially Symbolic Act.* Ithaca: Cornell University Press, 1981.

Juhasz, Suzanne. *Naked and Fiery Forms.* New York: Harper and Row, 1976.

Kadlec, David. "X-Ray Testimonials in Muriel Rukeyser." *Modernism/Modernity* 5 (January 1998): 23–47.

Kalaidjian, Walter. *American Culture between the Wars: Revisionary Modernism and Postmodern Critique.* New York: Columbia University Press, 1993.

————. "Marketing Modern Poetry and the Southern Public Sphere." In *Marketing Modernisms: Self-Promotion, Canonization, Rereading,* edited by Kevin J. H. Dettmar and Stephen Watt, 297–320. Ann Arbor: University of Michigan Press, 1996.

Kelley, Robin D. G. *Race Rebels: Culture, Politics, and the Black Working Class.* New York: Free Press, 1994.

———. "'This Ain't Ethiopia, but It'll Do.'" In *African-Americans in the Spanish Civil War,* edited by Danny Duncan Collum. New York: G. K. Hall, 1992.

Kenner, Hugh. *A Colder Eye: The Modern Irish Writers.* New York: Knopf, 1983.

———. *The Pound Era.* Berkeley: University of California Press, 1971.

Kertesz, Louise. *The Poetic Vision of Muriel Rukeyser.* Baton Rouge: Louisiana State University Press, 1979.

Klare, Karl E. "Arbitrary Convictions?: The Rosenberg Case, the Death Penalty, and Democratic Culture." In *Secret Agents: The Rosenberg Case, McCarthyism, and Fifties America,* edited by Marjorie Garber and Rebecca L. Walkowitz, 275–90. New York: Routledge, 1995.

Klehr, Harvey. *The Heyday of American Communism.* New York: Basic, 1984.

Kraut, Alan M., and Richard D. Breitman. "Anti-Semitism in the State Department, 1933–44: Four Case Studies." In *Anti-Semitism in American History,* edited by David Gerber, 167–200. Urbana: University of Illinois Press, 1987.

Laclau, Ernesto. *Politics and Ideology in Marxist Theory: Capitalism, Fascism, Populism.* London: New Left Books, 1977.

Laclau, Ernesto, and Chantal Mouffe. *Hegemony and Socialist Strategy.* London: Verso, 1985.

Lamb, Richard. *Mussolini and the British.* London: John Murray, 1997.

Landis, Arthur. *The Abraham Lincoln Brigade.* New York: Citadel, 1967.

Lauter, Paul. *Canons and Contexts.* New York: Oxford University Press, 1991.

Lentricchia, Frank. *Modernist Quartet.* Cambridge: Cambridge University Press, 1994.

Levenson, Michael. *A Genealogy of Modernism: A Study of English Literary Doctrine, 1908–1922.* Cambridge: Cambridge University Press, 1984.

Levi, Jan Heller, ed. *A Muriel Rukeyser Reader.* New York: Norton, 1994.

Levinson, Marjorie. *Wordsworth's Great Period Poems.* Cambridge: Cambridge University Press, 1986.

Locke, Alain. Review of *The Weary Blues. Palms* 1 (1926–27): 25–26.

Longenbach, James. *Modern Poetry after Modernism.* New York: Oxford University Press, 1997.

Lowell, Robert. *Life Studies.* New York: Farrar, Straus and Giroux, 1959.

Lowney, John. "Truths of Outrage, Truths of Possibility: Muriel Rukeyser's 'The Book of the Dead.'" In *"How Shall We Tell Each Other of the Poet?": The Life and Writing of Muriel Rukeyser,* edited by Anne F. Herzog and Janet E. Kaufman, 195–208. New York: St. Martin's Press, 1999.

Maas, Willard. "Lost between Wars." *Poetry* 51 (May 1938): 101–4.

McGann, Jerome. *The Romantic Ideology: A Critical Investigation.* Chicago: University of Chicago Press, 1984.

———. *The Textual Condition.* Princeton: Princeton University Press, 1991.

McGrath, Thomas. *The Movie at the End of the World: Collected Poems.* Chicago: Swallow, 1972.

MacLeish, Archibald. *Poetry and Opinion.* Urbana: University of Illinois Press, 1950.

McWilliams, Carey. *Witch Hunt: The Revival of Heresy.* Boston: Little Brown, 1950.

Magil, A. B. "Elegy for Two Forever Living." *Masses and Mainstream* 6 (August 1953): 33–35.

Maidment, Brian, ed. *The Poorhouse Fugitives: Self-Taught Poets and Poetry in Victorian Britain.* Manchester: Carcanet, 1987.

Marcantonio, Vito. "Dusty Death." *New Republic,* March 4, 1936, 105–6.

Marcus, Sheldon. *Father Coughlin: The Tumultuous Life of the Priest of the Little Flower.* Boston: Little Brown, 1973.

Marek, Jayne E. *Women Editing Modernism: "Little" Magazines and Literary History.* Lexington: University Press of Kentucky, 1995.

Mariani, Paul. *Lost Puritan: A Life of Robert Lowell.* New York: Norton, 1994.

Marx, Karl. "The Eighteenth Brumaire of Louis Napoleon." In *Karl Marx on Revolution,* translated and edited by Saul K. Padover, 243–328. New York: McGraw-Hill, 1971.

Matthiessen, F. O. Letter to editors. *Partisan Review* 11 (Spring 1944): 217.

Maxwell, William J. *New Negro, Old Left: African-American Writing and Communism between the Wars.* New York: Columbia University Press, 1999.

Millett, Martha. "In Memoriam." *Masses and Mainstream* 6 (August 1953): 28–32.

Montefiore, Jan. *Feminism and Poetry: Language, Experience, Identity in Women's Writing.* London: Routledge, 1987.

Morgan, Philip. *Italian Fascism, 1919–1945.* London: MacMillan, 1995.

Mukarovsky, Jan. *Aesthetic Function, Norm, and Value as Social Facts.* Translated by Mark E. Suino. Michigan Slavic Contributions. Ann Arbor: Department of Slavic Languages and Literature, University of Michigan, 1970.

Murphy, James F. *The Proletarian Moment: The Controversy over Leftism in Literature.* Urbana: University of Illinois Press, 1991.

Nelson, Cary. "Lyric Politics: The Poetry of Edwin Rolfe." In Edwin Rolfe, *Collected Poems,* edited by Cary Nelson and Jefferson Hendricks, 1–55. Urbana: University of Illinois Press, 1993.

———. *Our Last First Poets: Vision and History in Contemporary American Poetry.* Urbana: University of Illinois Press, 1981.

———. "Politics and Labor in Poetry of the Fin-de-Siècle and Beyond: Fragments of an Unwritable History." In *Modernism, Inc.: Body, Memory, Capital,* edited by Jani Scandura and Michael Thurston, 268–88. New York: New York University Press, 2001.

———. *Repression and Recovery: Modern American Poetry and the Politics of Cultural Memory, 1910–1945.* Madison: University of Wisconsin Press, 1989.

Nelson, Cary, and Jefferson Hendricks. *Edwin Rolfe: A Biographical Essay and Guide to the Rolfe Archive at the University of Illinois at Urbana-Champaign.* Urbana: University of Illinois Press, 1990.

———, eds. *Madrid, 1937: Letters of the Abraham Lincoln Brigade and the Spanish Civil War.* New York: Routledge, 1996.

Nicholls, Peter. *Ezra Pound: Politics, Economics, and Writing: A Study of "The Cantos."* London: MacMillan, 1984.

North, Michael. *The Political Aesthetic of Yeats, Pound, and Eliot.* New York: Cambridge University Press, 1993.

Nourie, Barbara, and Alan Nourie, eds. *American Mass-Market Magazines.* Westport, Conn.: Greenwood Press, 1990.

Nye, Russell. *The Unembarrassed Muse: The Popular Arts in America.* New York: Dial, 1970.

Oakley, Giles. *The Devil's Music: A History of the Blues.* 2d ed. New York: DaCapo, 1997.

O'Reilly, Kenneth. *Hoover and the Un-Americans: The FBI, HUAC, and the Red Menace.* Philadelphia: Temple University Press, 1983.

Orwell, George. *Homage to Catalonia.* 1952. Reprint, New York: Harcourt Brace, 1980.

Ottanelli, Fraser M. *The Communist Party of the United States: From the Depression to World War II.* New Brunswick, N.J.: Rutgers University Press, 1991.

Ottley, Roi. *The Lonely Warrior: The Life and Times of Robert S. Abbott.* Chicago: Henry Regnery, 1955.

Pearlman, Daniel. *The Barb of Time: On the Unity of Pound's "Cantos."* New York: Oxford University Press, 1969.

Perkins, David. *A History of Modern Poetry.* 2 vols. Cambridge: Harvard University Press, 1987.

Perloff, Marjorie. *Dance of the Intellect: Studies in the Poetry of the Pound Tradition.* New York: Cambridge University Press, 1985.

———. *Poetry on and off the Page: Essays for Emergent Occasions.* Evanston: Northwestern University Press, 1998.

Phillips, William, and Philip Rahv. "Literature in a Political Decade." In *New Letters in America,* edited by Horace Gregory, 170–80. New York: Norton, 1937.

Pike, Frederick B. "Introduction: The Background to the Civil War in Spain and the U.S. Response to the War." In *The Spanish Civil War, 1936–1939: American Hemispheric Responses,* edited by Mark Falcoff and Frederick Pike, 1–49. Lincoln: University of Nebraska Press, 1982.

Pitts, Rebecca. "The Rukeyser Imbroglio." *Partisan Review* 11 (Winter 1944): 125–27.

Pound, Ezra. *The Cantos.* New York: New Directions, 1986.

———. *"Ezra Pound Speaking": Radio Speeches of World War II.* Edited by Leonard W. Doob. Westport, Conn.: Greenwood Press, 1978.

———. *Ezra Pound's Poetry and Prose Contributions to Periodicals.* 10 vols. Edited by Lea Baechler, A. Walton Litz, and James Longenbach. New York: Garland, 1991.

———. *Jefferson and/or Mussolini.* New York: Liveright, 1935.

———. *The Letters of Ezra Pound, 1907–1941.* Edited by D. D. Paige. New York: Harcourt, Brace, 1950.

———. "Little Review Calendar." *Little Review* 8 (Spring 1922): 2.

———. "Note to the Calendar." *Little Review* 8 (Spring 1922): 40.

———. *Personae: The Shorter Poems.* Rev. ed. Edited by Lea Baechler and A. Walton Litz. 1926. Reprint, New York: New Directions, 1990.

———. *Selected Letters, 1907–1941.* Edited by D. D. Paige. New York: New Directions, 1950.

———. *Selected Prose, 1909–1965.* Edited by William Cookson. London: Faber, 1973.

Rabinowitz, Paula. *Labor and Desire: Women's Revolutionary Fiction in Depression America.* Chapel Hill: University of North Carolina Press, 1991.

———. *They Must Be Represented: The Politics of Documentary.* London: Verso, 1994.

Rahv, Philip. "Twilight of the Thirties." *Partisan Review* 6 (Summer 1939): 11–16.

Rainey, Lawrence. "'All I Want You to Do Is to Follow the Orders': History, Faith, and Fascism in the Early Cantos." In *A Poem Containing History: Textual Studies in "The Cantos,"* edited by Lawrence Rainey, 63–116. Ann Arbor: University of Michigan Press, 1997.

———. *Ezra Pound and the Monument of Culture: Text, History, and the Malatesta Cantos.* Chicago: University of Chicago Press, 1991.

———. "The Price of Modernism: Publishing *The Waste Land.*" In *T. S. Eliot: The Modernist in History,* edited by Ronald Bush, 91–133. Cambridge: Cambridge University Press, 1991.

Rampersad, Arnold. "Langston Hughes and His Critics on the Left." *Langston Hughes Review* 5 (1986): 34–41.

———. *1902–1941: I, Too, Sing America.* Vol. 1 of *The Life of Langston Hughes.* New York: Oxford University Press, 1986.

Read, Forrest. *'76, One World, and "The Cantos" of Ezra Pound.* Chapel Hill: University of North Carolina Press, 1981.

Redman, Tim. "An Epic Is a Hypertext Containing Poetry: Eleven New Cantos (31–41) by Ezra Pound." In *A Poem Containing History: Textual Studies in "The Cantos,"* edited by Lawrence Rainey, 117–50. Ann Arbor: University of Michigan Press, 1997.

———. *Ezra Pound and Italian Fascism.* New York: Cambridge University Press, 1991.

Rella, Ettore. "To the Rosenbergs." *Masses and Mainstream* 6 (March 1953): 2–4.

Ribuffo, Leo. *The Old Christian Right: The Protestant Far Right from the Great Depression to the Cold War.* Philadelphia: Temple University Press, 1983.

Rice, Philip Blair. Review of *U.S. 1. Nation,* March 19, 1938, 335.

Rich, Adrienne. "Beginners." *Kenyon Review* 15 (1993): 16.

Rolfe, Edwin. *Collected Poems.* Edited by Cary Nelson and Jefferson Hendricks. Urbana: University of Illinois Press, 1993.

————. *Daily Worker,* October 13, 1933, 5.

————. *First Love and Other Poems.* Los Angeles: Larry Edmunds Bookstore, 1951.

————. Holograph manuscript, n.d. Edwin Rolfe Archive, University of Illinois at Urbana-Champaign.

————. *The Lincoln Battalion: The Story of the Americans Who Fought in Spain in the International Brigades.* New York: Veterans of the Abraham Lincoln Brigade, 1939.

————. "Poetry." *Partisan Review* 2 (April–May 1935): 32–42.

————. *To My Contemporaries.* New York: Dynamo Press, 1936.

————. Unpublished manuscript, September 1947. Edwin Rolfe Archive, University of Illinois at Urbana-Champaign.

————. Unpublished manuscript, December 1947. Edwin Rolfe Archive, University of Illinois at Urbana-Champaign.

————. Unpublished manuscript, 1951. Edwin Rolfe Archive, University of Illinois at Urbana-Champaign.

————. Unpublished manuscript, n.d. Edwin Rolfe Archive, University of Illinois at Urbana-Champaign.

Rolfe, Edwin, Herman Spector, Joseph Kalar, and Sol Funaroff. *We Gather Strength.* New York: Liberal Press, 1933.

Roosevelt, Franklin D. *F.D.R.: His Personal Letters.* Edited by Elliot Roosevelt. New York: Duell, Sloan and Pearce, 1950.

Rosenberg, Ethel. "If We Die." Cover of *Masses and Mainstream* 6 (July 1953).

Rosenstone, Robert A. *Crusade of the Left: The Lincoln Battalion in the Spanish Civil War.* New York: Pegasus, 1969.

Rosenthal, M. L. "Muriel Rukeyser: The Longer Poems." In *New Directions in Poetry and Prose,* edited by James Laughlin, 202–29. New York: New Directions, 1953.

Rudd, Margaret Thomas. *The Lone Heretic: A Biography of Miguel de Unamuno y Jugo.* Austin: University of Texas Press, 1963.

Rukeyser, Muriel. *Collected Poems.* New York: McGraw-Hill, 1978.

————. *The Life of Poetry.* New York: Current Books, 1949.

————. Muriel Rukeyser Papers, Library of Congress, Washington, D.C.

————. *Out of Silence: Selected Poems.* Edited by Kate Daniels. Evanston: Triquarterly, 1992.

————. *A Turning Wind.* New York: Covici and Friede, 1939.

————. *U.S. 1.* New York: Covici and Friede, 1938.

————. "With Leftward Glances." *New Masses* 12 (July 1934): 28.

Russell, Tony. *The Blues: From Robert Johnson to Robert Cray.* New York: Schirmer, 1997.

Sanders, Frederick. *John Adams Speaking: Pound's Sources for the Adams Cantos.* Orono: University of Maine Press, 1975.

Scheckner, Peter, ed. *An Anthology of Chartist Poetry: Poetry of the British*

Working Class, 1830s–1850s. Rutherford, N.J.: Fairleigh Dickinson University Press, 1989.

Scholes, Robert. *Textual Power: Literary Theory and the Teaching of English.* New Haven: Yale University Press, 1985.

Schrecker, Ellen. *Many Are the Crimes: McCarthyism in America.* Boston: Little, Brown, 1998.

Scott, William R. "Black Nationalism and the Italo-Ethiopian Conflict, 1934–1936." *Journal of Negro History* 63, no. 2 (1978): 118–34.

Seldes, George. *Lords of the Press.* New York: Julian Messner, 1938.

Seltzer, Mark. *Henry James and the Art of Power.* Ithaca: Cornell University Press, 1984.

Sharpe, Tony. "W. H. Auden and the Rules of Disengagement." *Critical Survey* 6, no. 3 (1994): 336–42.

Showalter, Elaine, ed. *Feminist Criticism: Women, Literature, and Theory.* New York: Pantheon, 1985.

Shulman, Robert. *The Power of Political Art: The 1930s Literary Left Reconsidered.* Chapel Hill: University of North Carolina Press, 2000.

"Silicosis." *Time,* January 6, 1936, 58.

"Silicosis." *Newsweek,* January 25, 1936, 33–34.

"Silicosis: Gauley Bridge Affair." *Time,* February 3, 1936, 54.

"Silicosis Village." *Nation,* February 5, 1936, 162.

Sillen, Samuel. "A Prize for Ezra Pound." *Masses and Mainstream* 2 (April 1949): 3–6.

Singerman, Robert. "The Jew as Racial Alien: The Genetic Component of American Anti-Semitism." In *Anti-Semitism in American History,* edited by David Gerber, 103–28. Urbana: University of Illinois Press, 1987.

———, ed. *Antisemitic Propaganda: An Annotated Bibliography and Research Guide.* New York: Garland, 1982.

Singh, Amaranjit. "Beyond the Mountain: Langston Hughes on Race/Class and Art." *Langston Hughes Review* 6 (1987): 37–43.

Slack, Jennifer Daryl. "The Theory and Method of Articulation in Cultural Studies." In *Stuart Hall: Critical Dialogues in Cultural Studies,* edited by David Morley and Kuan-Hsing Chen, 112–30. London: Blackwell, 1996.

Smethurst, James. *The New Red Negro: African American Writing and Communism.* New York: Oxford University Press, 1999.

Spender, Stephen. *The Thirties and After.* Glasgow: Collins, 1978.

Steffens, Lincoln. "Lynching by Law or by Lustful Mob North and South: Red and Black." *Contempo,* December 1, 1931, 1.

Steinberg, Peter L. *The Great "Red Menace": United States Prosecution of American Communists, 1947–1952.* London: Greenwood Press, 1984.

Stevenson, Burton Egbert, ed. *The Home Book of Verse, American and English, 1580–1920.* 5th ed. New York: Holt, 1922.

Stott, William. *Documentary Expression and Thirties America.* Chicago: University of Chicago Press, 1986.

Subcommittee of the Committee of Labor. *An Investigation Relating to Health*

Conditions of Workers Employed in the Construction and Maintenance of Public Utilities. Washington, D.C.: Government Printing Office, 1936.

Suchoff, David. "The Rosenberg Case and the New York Intellectuals." In *Secret Agents: The Rosenberg Case, McCarthyism, and Fifties America,* edited by Marjorie Garber and Rebecca L. Walkowitz, 155–70. New York: Routledge, 1995.

Sullivan, James D. *On the Walls and in the Streets: American Poetry Broadsides from the 1960s.* Urbana: University of Illinois Press, 1997.

Sullivan, Robert. "History and Desire: Auden's 'Spain' and Caudwell's *Illusion and Reality.*" In *Rewriting the Good Fight: Critical Essays on the Literature of the Spanish Civil War,* edited by Frieda S. Brown, Malcolm Alan Compitello, Victor M. Howard, and Robert A. Martin, 229–42. East Lansing: Michigan State University Press, 1989.

Synnott, Marcia Graham. "Anti-Semitism and American Universities: Did Quotas Follow the Jews?" In *Anti-Semitism in American History,* edited by David Gerber, 233–74. Urbana: University of Illinois Press, 1987.

Taggard, Genevieve. *The Long View.* New York: Harper, 1943.

Terrell, Carroll F. *The Companion to "The Cantos."* 2 vols. Berkeley: University of California Press, 1982.

Thomas, Hugh. *The Spanish Civil War.* New York: Harper and Row, 1977.

Thompson, E. P. *The Making of the English Working Class.* Rev. ed. Harmondsworth: Penguin, 1978.

Titon, Jeff Todd. *Early Downhome Blues: A Musical and Cultural Analysis.* Urbana: University of Illinois Press, 1977.

Todd, Janet. "Jane Austen, Politics, and Sensibility." In *Feminist Criticism: Theory and Practice,* edited by Susan Sellers, Linda Hutcheon, and Paul Perron, 71–87. Toronto: University of Toronto Press, 1991.

Tomkins, Calvin. *Duchamp: A Biography.* New York: Holt, 1996.

Tompkins, Jane. *Sensational Designs: The Cultural Work of American Fiction, 1790–1860.* New York: Oxford University Press, 1985.

Trent, Lucia, and Ralph Cheyney, eds. *America Arraigned!* New York: Dean, 1928.

Unamuno, Miguel de. *The Tragic Sense of Life.* Translated by J. E. Crawford Flitch. 1921. Reprint, New York: Dover, 1954.

Untermeyer, Louis. Review of *U.S. 1. Yale Review,* 2d ser., 27 (Spring 1938): 608.

"*U.S. 1.*" *Time,* March 28, 1938, 63.

Van Wienen, Mark. *Partisans and Poets: The Political Work of American Poetry in the Great War.* Cambridge: Cambridge University Press, 1997.

von Hallberg, Robert. *American Poetry and Culture, 1945–1980.* Cambridge: Harvard University Press, 1985.

Wald, Alan. *The Revolutionary Imagination: The Poetry and Politics of John Wheelwright and Sherry Mangan.* Chapel Hill: University of North Carolina Press, 1983.

———. "Revolutionary Intellectuals: *Partisan Review* in the 1930s." In

Literature at the Barricades: The American Writer in the 1930s, edited by
Ralph F. Bogardus and Fred Hobson, 187–203. Tuscaloosa: University of
Alabama Press, 1982.

Walton, Eda Lou. Review of *U.S. 1. New York Times Book Review,* March 27,
1938, 19.

Ware, Michele S. "Opening 'The Gates': Muriel Rukeyser and the Poetry of
Witness." *Women's Studies* 22 (1993): 297–308.

Warren, Robert Penn. *John Brown: The Making of a Martyr.* New York: Payson
and Clark, 1927.

Washburn, Patrick S. *A Question of Sedition: The Federal Government's
Investigation of the Black Press during World War II.* New York: Oxford
University Press, 1986.

Wechsler, Shoshana. "A Ma(t)ter of Fact and Vision: The Objectivity
Question and 'The Book of the Dead.'" In *"How Shall We Tell Each Other of
the Poet?": The Life and Writing of Muriel Rukeyser,* edited by Anne F.
Herzog and Janet E. Kaufman, 226–40. New York: St. Martin's Press, 1999.

Weiss, Jeffrey S. *The Popular Culture of Modern Art: Picasso, Duchamp, and
Avant-Gardism, 1909–1917.* New Haven: Yale University Press, 1994.

Wheelwright, John. Review of *U.S. 1. Partisan Review* 4 (March 1938): 54–56.

Williams, Raymond. *Culture.* London: Fontana, 1981.

———. *Marxism and Literature.* New York: Oxford University Press, 1977.

———. *The Sociology of Culture.* New York: Schocken, 1981.

Williams, William Carlos. Review of *U.S. 1. New Republic,* March 9, 1938,
141–42.

Wolff, David. "Document and Poetry." *New Masses* 14 (February 1938): 23–24.

Wordsworth, William. *Selected Poems and Prefaces.* Edited by Jack Stillinger.
Boston: Houghton-Mifflin, 1965.

Yeats, William Butler. *Selected Poems and Plays of W. B. Yeats.* Edited by M. L.
Rosenthal. New York: Macmillan, 1962.

Zabel, Morton Dauwen. "Two Years of Poetry, 1937–39." *Southern Review* 5
(1939–40): 568–608.

INDEX

68 passim, 221; biography of, 2; compared to Rukeyser, 41, 174, 188–89; as political poet, 132–33; political aims of, 136, 142; incorporation of historical documents by, 136–38; works of, described, 147–48; reception of works of, 148, 238 (nn. 9, 10); and anti-Semitism, 156–68; radio speeches by, 163, 165, 167; anti-Semitic conspiracy theories of, 165, 167; Bollingen Prize awarded to, 215, 246 (n. 3); in 1950s, 219

—Works: Adams Cantos, 40–41, 136, 139, 149–56, 168; "Are Universities Valid," 147; *The Cantos,* 132, 137, 147, 188; Canto 1, 14, 150; Canto 2, 150; Canto 8, 138, 188; Canto 13, 150; Canto 14, 160, 161; Canto 15, 160, 161; Canto 31, 148–49; Canto 35, 160; Canto 42, 153; Canto 43, 153; Canto 45, 159, 161; Canto 51, 159, 161; Canto 52, 157–59, 161; Canto 62, 149–50, 155–56; Canto 65, 150–56, 161, 162, 168; *A Draft of XVI Cantos,* 13–14, 21; "Hugh Selwyn Mauberley," 13; "Infamy of Taxes," 162; "Introductory Text Book," 146–47; *Jefferson and/or Mussolini,* 146, 152; *Pisan Cantos,* 215; "A Place for English Writers," 162; "Reorganize Your Dead Universities," 144; "Salutation the Third," 161

Price, Victoria, 95, 172
Proletarian theater, 109
Protocols of the Elders of Zion, 163, 164, 165
Publication: as influence on poem's cultural work, 66, 108, 114; as signifying practice, 78, 100, 106, 113, 128

Rabinowitz, Paula, 170, 178–79, 196
Race: and international Left, 116;

and Spanish Civil War, 116, 236 (n. 36); in *Book of the Dead,* 182–85
Radial reading, 137–38
Rahv, Philip, 8–9, 43
Rampersad, Arnold, 87, 116, 128, 134; on Hughes's "Letter from Spain," 130
Ransom, John Crowe, 10
Reid, Arnold, 67–69, 75, 132, 213
Repetition, 111
Rich, Adrienne, 214, 221
Robeson, Paul, 93, 122
Rolfe, Edwin, 16, 32–33, 35–36, 40, 42–85 passim, 132, 171, 177, 179, 213, 214, 217, 218, 221; biography of, 2–3; goals as political poet, 44; against polemic, 45; and romanticism, 47, 51; joins International Brigades, 56; illustrations described, 57–61; structure of works of, 61–63; and Hughes, 116–17, 132; in 1950s, 219

—Works: "Asbestos," 50; "Ballad of the Noble Intentions," 81–82; "Brickyards at Beacon," 51; "City of Anguish," 63–65; "Definition," 48; "Elegia," 70–71; "Entry," 63; "Epitaph," 67–69, 75, 132, 213; "First Love," 74–77, 84–85; *First Love and Other Poems,* 48, 56; "In Praise Of," 33, 48–50; "Kentucky—1932," 39; "Madrid" (excerpt from "City of Anguish"), 66; "No Man Knows War" (excerpt from "City of Anguish"), 66; "Pastoral (2)," 58; *Permit Me Refuge,* 48, 78, 81; "Poetry," 44, 84; "Portrait of a Death," 31–32; "Song for a Birthday in Exile," 71–73; "These Men Are Revolution," 53–54, 59, 179; *To My Contemporaries,* 47, 56, 63
Roosevelt, Franklin D., 139, 141, 143, 145, 177
Rosenberg, Ethel, 211, 212, 214, 219